AYODHYA

Umesh Raghuvanshi, a distinguished journalist, serves as senior associate editor at the *Hindustan Times* in Lucknow, India. He previously worked at *The Pioneer* in the same city. He has reported extensively on the twists and turns that changed India and its politics, including the Ram Janmabhoomi movement.

Raghuvanshi has an impressive academic background, having been a visiting scholar at the Graduate School of Journalism, University of California, Berkeley, USA, and a Metcalf Fellow at the Metcalf Institute of Marine and Environmental Reporting, University of Rhode Island, USA.

His accolades include the KC Kulish International Merit Award for excellence in journalism, received in New Delhi in 2017. He is also the winner of a competition organized by the United Nations Environment Programme DTIE OzonAction Programme in 2009 that assessed coverage of the interlinkages between ozone and climate change. He was awarded at Beijing, China, in 2010.

Raghuvanshi is a science graduate from DBS College, Dehradun, and holds an MA in Political Science from DAV (PG) College, Dehradun.

The author can be reached on:

Facebook: https://www.facebook.com/umesh.raghuvanshi.90
X: @Uraghuvanshi
Email: uraghuvanshi@gmail.com

AYODHYA
—— THE GODS ARE LIBERATED ——

UMESH RAGHUVANSHI

RUPA

Published by
Rupa Publications India Pvt. Ltd 2024
7/16, Ansari Road, Daryaganj
New Delhi 110002

Sales centres:
Bengaluru Chennai
Hyderabad Jaipur Kathmandu
Kolkata Mumbai Prayagraj

Copyright © Umesh Raghuvanshi 2024

The views and opinions expressed in this book are the author's own and the facts are as reported by him which have been verified to the extent possible, and the publishers are not in any way liable for the same.

All rights reserved.
No part of this publication may be reproduced, transmitted, or stored in a retrieval system, in any form or by any means, electronic, mechanical, photocopying, recording or otherwise, without the prior permission of the publisher.

P-ISBN: 978-93-6156-132-0
E-ISBN: 978-93-6156-949-4

First impression 2024

10 9 8 7 6 5 4 3 2 1

The moral right of the author has been asserted.

This book is sold subject to the condition that it shall not, by way of trade or otherwise, be lent, resold, hired out, or otherwise circulated, without the publisher's prior consent, in any form of binding or cover other than that in which it is published.

To my parents
(Late) Mrs Prem Lata Raghuvanshi
Ranvir Singh Raghuvanshi

Contents

Preface	*ix*
1. Traditional History	1
2. The Dispute Begins	27
3. Pent-Up Emotions	51
4. The Congress Role	81
5. Saffron Surge	104
6. Mandal vs Kamandal Politics	127
7. The Build-Up to the Demolition, Rising Pitches	149
8. The Demolition	179
9. The Dispute Continues: Who Demolished the Mosque?	203
10. A Grand Ram Temple	229
11. A New Beginning	252
Acknowledgements	266

Preface

My grandmother was a great storyteller. She used to narrate tales of generational rivalry between the great-grandfather of Rama and the great-grandfather of the demon king Ravana. I also grew up hearing stories about Mahatma Gandhi's reverence for Rama and how he visualized the concept of Ram Rajya in contemporary India. Since then, I have read books on traditional Indian history that examined the Vedas, the Vedic literature, the epics, the Puranas and other ancient literature, to get a complete sense of Lord Rama and Ayodhya.

I watched Ayodhya turn from a non-issue to a major issue in the mid-1980s. This developed an urge in me to delve deep into history and know more about Ayodhya. I always felt that there should be one book that provides complete information about Ayodhya in ancient and contemporary India. I also felt the need to know more about the kings who ruled ancient Ayodhya. So when my friend Dev Chatterjee, a senior journalist covering business and finance, authored a book about economic meltdowns, the idea of writing a book on Ayodhya occurred to me. I visualized this book in consultation with him and began writing in early 2020.

Our view of ancient India is mostly based on the knowledge provided to us in the Vedic literature, the epics Mahabharata and the Ramayana, the Puranas, and other ancient accounts. This knowledge comes mainly in the form of religious compositions that lack a sense of historical perspective.

As prehistoric archaeology has not been able to get the desired attention and no other accounts about the dynasties of, and occurrences in, ancient India are available, the history of ancient India continues to remain a weak spot. It has been constructed from literature passed on from generation to generation, orally or through other traditional mediums. These accounts give an idea about the period, and help place when and where some of the major events took place. The chronology of these accounts of major events is, however, different in style and order from the ones widely accepted in the West. This chronology speaks about Manu cycles and the cycle of the four ages: Satya Yuga, Treta Yuga, Dwapara Yuga and Kali Yuga, the last being the present age. These four ages are also described as golden age, silver age, copper age and iron age. These accounts also give information about genealogies and achievements of kings from several dynasties who ruled in various regions in different periods.

∽

Under the prevailing circumstances, venturing into writing on an issue like Ayodhya was bound to catch unnecessary attention and be fraught with dangers of being pushed close to one or the other side of the political divide. Hence, adequate precaution has been taken to maintain political neutrality while navigating through various important issues in this book.

I worked on this book with an open mind, with no prejudices in terms of religious belief. This book is a sincere attempt to provide a complete traditional account of the kings of Ayodhya, with the most credible references and a balanced version of all the most important events that unfolded in Ayodhya over the years.

Various references from leading news magazines and newspapers have also been incorporated. This book is a journalistic work providing a glimpse of tradition along with being a progressive account of the unfolding events traced from the ancient period to the origin of the dispute that began with the construction of the Babri Masjid. It also speaks about the impact that these events have had on the political horizons of India for the past four decades and more. It summarizes the turn of events relating to the dispute, including the rising communal tension over the issue in British India. This book gives an account of placing of the idols inside the central dome of the Babri mosque after India gained independence, the rising passions following the placing of the idol, the opening of locks of gates, and the demolition of the disputed structure. It incorporates an account of the trial of the accused and questions their acquittal.

As efforts have been made to encapsulate the big events spanning years, centuries and ages into a few pages, there are bound to be certain omissions, and there may be only a brief mention of some big events. This book touches the most relevant aspects, giving accounts of the antediluvian period, India's tale of the Great Flood with reference to the Matsya Avatar (Fish Incarnation), the appearance of the first of 10 incarnations of Vishnu, and the survival of Manu Vaivasvata (3100 BCE), whose eldest son Ikshvaku, the progenitor of the solar race (Suryavanshis), became the first king of Ayodhya.

Ayodhya was the capital city of the kings of the solar race. Its glory finds mention in ancient literature. It is believed to be one of the seven cities that liberates one from the cycle of life and death. This book provides information, citing credible references, about genealogy of most of the kings of the solar race, beginning from Ikshvaku to legendary kings like Harishchandra (thirty-third in line from Manu), Mandhatri (2750 BCE), Bhagiratha (forty-fifth in line from Manu) and Rama (sixty-fifth in line from Manu), the hero of the Ramayana and *Ramcharitmanas*, who is worshipped as the seventh incarnation of Vishnu. Rama (1950 BCE), his brothers Bharat, Laxmana and Shatrughana, two sons Luv and Kusa, and their successors have been covered in some detail.

Although credible references have been given for all the kings and their genealogy, the information collected is based on analysis of the traditional accounts and may not be conclusive. It should be noted that there are kings mentioned in the Ramayana and Mahabharata who may have really existed and ruled in ancient India. Yet, there is a need for further research. Various seats of learning in leading universities should be set up in India and abroad for further research to separate myths from facts, and question the former with reason. Accounts of ancient Indian literature, the Supreme Court's 1,045-page judgement dated 9 November 2019 (plus the addenda), and the observations made by experts following the excavations carried out by the Archaeological Survey of India (ASI), along with the beliefs of the people, provide sufficient material to ponder over the Ayodhya issue afresh.

Ayodhya has seen a transformation over the years. It continues to change. It has also changed the politics in India. With the new Ram Temple, Ayodhya is seeing an influx of tourists. It is being developed as a solar city. An all-round development of the city has been undertaken to make it globally appealing. An international airport named after Maharshi Valmiki, who composed the Ramayana, has come up there. A modern Ayodhya, using technology to its optimum, will portray and showcase its glorious past to visitors in the coming years.

An amalgamation of tradition and development is being carried out. This may blur the difference between tradition and modernity. An eye for reason is going to be the need of the hour in the new Ayodhya. And this book is a sincere attempt to take up this role in the time to come.

1

Traditional History

At the dawn of the history of the universe, the Great Flood submerged the whole earth. Various myths attached to the devastation following the Great Flood speak volumes about the creation of the universe.

Till now, modern science has failed to expound any universally acknowledged theory for the creation of the world or the one about the end. How humans or other living beings appear on the blue ball that is earth has always remained a point to ponder. People belonging to different regions and religions understand the creation and the end differently.

Many Hindus believe there is no beginning or end, and cycles of creation, existence and death are repeated in an eternal universe. This also reflects their belief in reincarnation. The debate over creation, survival, scientific evidence and the theory of evolution, as propounded by Charles Robert Darwin, has thrown the myth and the traditional tales into backwaters.

Darwin, who set off from England in 1831 on a five-year voyage, visited the Galapagos Island, a part of the country of Ecuador in South America. He noted that unique creatures like finches, though similar from island to island, adapted to the local environment over time, leading to variation in their beaks, which made them well-equipped to acquire a variety of food from different sources.

The Great Flood too has numerous myths attached to it, and the stories may have evolved adapting to local variations from region to region.

The Sumerian Flood History, also known as Eridu Genesis, the Flood Story, Sumerian Creation Myth, Sumerian Deluge Myth—is the oldest Mesopotamian text relating the tale of the Great Flood... The tale is also—most famously—told as the story of Noah and his ark from the biblical Book of Genesis (earliest possible date c. 1450 BCE, latest, c. 800–600 BCE). The story is dated to c. 1600 BCE in its written form, but is thought to be much older, preserved by oral tradition until committed to writing.[1]

The story of Noah's Ark speaks of faith, hope and survival in the Great Flood.

Amid a large mix of myth and legends, there is a long list of dynasties that ruled in the pre- and post-diluvian periods in different parts of the world. Some sources of traditional history indicate that the Great Flood in Mesopotamia may have occurred in about 3100 BCE—nearly the same time when it hit India, in 3102 BCE.[2] India or Bharat of the ancient period broadly comprised of large part of the present Indian subcontinent that included not only modern India but also Pakistan, Bangladesh and beyond.

Indian traditions, naturally beginning with mythology, give different accounts of the Supreme God who performs three distinct functions through the trinity of Brahma (Creator), Vishnu (Preserver) and Mahesh (Destroyer). The acronym 'GOD' stands for three attributes: the Generator, the Operator and the Destroyer.

The India Flood Tale

The Shatpatha Brahmana,[3] a recension of the Shukla Yajurveda, gives

---

[1] Mark, Joshua J., 'Eridu Genesis', *World History Encyclopedia*, 7 May 2020, https://tinyurl.com/5fuppauc Accessed on 20 June 2024.
[2] Pusalker, A.D., 'Traditional History from the Earliest Times to the Accession of Parikshit', *The History and Culture of the Indian People: The Vedic Age*, Volume 1, R.C. Majumdar (ed.), Bharatiya Vidya Bhawan, Mumbai, 2021, p. 273.
[3] Weber, Albrecht (ed.), 'Brahmin 1', *Shukla Yajurvediya Shatpath Brahmana*

an account of the legend of the Great Flood in India. There are other accounts of the story, including one mentioned in the Puranas.

Manu, believed to be the first human on earth, is said to have survived the flood. The earliest account of this traditional tale begins with a morning when Manu was washing his hands in a river and a small fish swam into his cupped hands. The fish sought protection from Manu, saying, 'Rear me, I will protect you.' It feared being devoured by larger fish in the river. This illustrates an ancient version of the term 'survival of the fittest' popularized by Charles Darwin. The small fish asked for protection to grow by being kept in a vessel, later shifted to a pond and subsequently to the sea when it grew. Manu did so. When the flood was about to strike, the fish warned Manu—it told him to prepare a boat and board it when the flood came. He entered the boat when the flood struck and the water level rose. He tied the boat to the fish's horn by a rope and was thus steered swiftly towards the northern mountains. There, Manu fastened the boat to a tree and climbed the mountain. He was thus saved from the flood that swept away all others. Once the flood was over, he gradually descended the northern mountains, and the slope has since been called Manoravataranam—Manu's descent.[4]

Some reports have suggested that the flood, widely believed to be a mythological phenomenon, was real, and that the mythical river Saraswati actually existed.[5] B.B. Lal, former director general of the Archaeological Survey of India (ASI), had presented a research paper on the Great Flood at a seminar organized by the Indian Council of Historical Research in 2017. He observed: 'Archaeologically, the deluge of the Saraswati took place around 2000–1900 BCE, or broadly in the

---

Madhyandini Shakha, Swami Satyaprakash Saraswati (ed.), Gangaprasad Upadhyay (trans.), Vijaykumar Govindram Hasanand, Delhi, 2019, p. 151.
[4]Pusalker, A.D., 'Traditional History from the Earliest Times to the Accession of Parikshit', *The History and Culture of the Indian People: The Vedic Age*, Volume 1, R.C. Majumdar (ed.), Bharatiya Vidya Bhawan, Mumbai, 2021, p. 275.
[5]Pandey, Neelam, 'Manu's Flood Was Real, Saraswati Nurtured Harappan Settlements: Indian Experts', *Hindustan Times*, 27 March 2017, https://tinyurl.com/yvwxs3b2. Accessed on 20 June 2024.

first quarter of second millennium BCE. This was exactly the time of Manu's flood, which occurred after the Rigveda, but before the beginning of the second millennium BCE. Should we still call Manu's flood a myth.'[6]

Vishnu's First Incarnation

There are several tales providing a divine perspective on the flood by pointing out that God decided to flood the earth to begin the process of creating a new world, as the people on earth had become dishonest or irreligious. The story attributed to the Mahabharata describes the *matsya* (fish) as Brahma. The Matsya, according to Puranas, is an incarnation of the deity Vishnu. It is the first of his *dashavtara*s. Vishnu is believed to take 10 avatars to end the evil and re-establish dharma on earth. It is said that Vishnu will take the tenth avatar at the end of Kali Yuga. Some other sources also speak about 22 or 24 avatars of Vishnu.[7]

Vishnu is believed to come to earth to maintain righteousness and balance the scales of good against evil. He incarnated as the small fish to save Manu from the deluge that submerged the earth. He descended from the northern mountain, as described in the flood tale, to a place in present-day Manali, Himachal Pradesh.[8] A temple called Manu Temple exists in (old) Manali, about 1,200 km northwest of Ayodhya. This temple is situated at a walking distance of about 3 km from Manali town. It is believed to be the place where Manu sat in meditation after being saved by the Matsya avatar of Vishnu from the Great Flood.[9]

---

[6]Ibid.
[7]Raghavan, Kishan, '22 Avatars of Lord Vishnu', *Speakingtree.in*, 21 December 2016, https://tinyurl.com/36v2ehvn. Accessed on 20 June 2024; Chopra, Pooja, 'The 24 Avatars of Lord Vishnu', Speakingtree.in, 2 August 2019, https://tinyurl.com/bdd2b4tb. Accessed on 20 June 2024.
[8]'History', *Kullu, Government of Himachal Pradesh*, https://tinyurl.com/yc3j5vxv. Accessed on 22 August 2024.
[9]Neeraj, D., 'Manu Temple: Progenitor of Mankind', *Mysterious Himachal: Land of Faith & God*, https://tinyurl.com/mt7rzvbh. Accessed on 22 August 2024; 'Manu Temple in

The Manu Temple is a fine stone-and-wood monument roofed with slate tiles. A Manu temple is rare in the country, and Manali derives its name from Manu Alya (home of Manu), sanctified in the temple.[10]

The name 'Manu' has many meanings. He is called the progenitor of the human race. He is also believed to have codified the Manusmriti. Doniger and Smith state:

> *Manu* means 'the wise one', and Manu is also the name of a king (an interesting attribution, given the priestly bias of Manu's text), who is the mythological ancestor of the human race, the Indian Adam. Thus, *manava* ('descended from Manu') is a common word for 'human' (which in terms of the lexical meaning of Manu as 'wise', might also be the Sanskrit equivalent of homo sapiens). The title therefore conceals a pun: manava, 'of Manu', also means 'of the human race'.[11]

The Pre-Flood Traditional History

The traditional lists of Indian dynasties of the pre-diluvian period have a blend of myths and legends. The traditional accounts begin with the king Manu Svayambhuva (self-created), born of Brahma and also known as Viraj.[12] He was the first Manu in the series of 14 Manus.[13] The Brahma Purana declares: 'To continue with Creation, Brahma gave form to a Man and a Woman. The man was Manu Svayambhuva and the woman was named Shatrupa. Humans descended from Manu,

---

Manali', Manalionline.in, https://tinyurl.com/3fade4ca. Accessed on 22 August 2024.
[10]'Manali', *Himachal Tourism*, https://tinyurl.com/3t3afxnd. Accessed on 22 August 2024.
[11]Doniger, Wendy and Brain K. Smith (trans), *The Laws of Manu*, Penguin Random House, India, 1991, p. xviii.
[12]Pusalker, A.D., 'Traditional History from the Earliest Times to the Accession of Parikshit', *The History and Culture of the Indian People: The Vedic Age*, Volume 1, R.C. Majumdar (ed.), Bharatiya Vidya Bhawan, Mumbai, 2021, p. 274.
[13]Ibid; Rapson, Edward James, 'The Puranas', *The Cambridge History of India, Volume 1: Ancient India*, Edward James Rapson (ed.), Cambridge University Press, 1922, p. 303.

that is the reason they are known as Manavas.'[14] Shatrupa is also said to be the female half of Manu Svayambhuva's body.[15] Another view is that Adi Para Shakti, the great Cosmic Mother, manifested the entire *vishwa* (world) and 'heeding the command of Devi, Sage Kashyapa and Aditi manifested on Earth as Swayambhu Manu and his consort, Satyarupa.'[16]

As no historical work about the pre-diluvian period is available, it is important to study the traditional accounts about the ruling dynasties of the time. These accounts give fair knowledge about the kings and their successors, and thus assume significance. The genealogies provide possibly the best chronological order, though this chronology has to meet the test of history.

Various traditional accounts that are relied upon to construct ancient history are the Vedas, epics and Puranas. The epics Mahabharata and Ramayana give a detailed description of the ruling dynasties, the royal houses, and the battles fought during that period. The sociological aspects reflect on the moral rules being followed, though tricks were sometimes justified. This was much before the coining of the phrase 'The rules of fair play do not apply in love and war' by John Lyly in *Euphues: The Anatomy of Wit*, published in 1578. But putting the inputs from traditional history to the test of modern history may not be justifiable.

Manu Svayambhuva has been described as the paramount king having his capital on the banks of Saraswati River, which finds a mention in Vedic literature.[17] A reference to Saraswati River has been

---

[14]Boddupalli, Phani, 'Manu—The First Man', *Speakingtree.in*, 14 June 2013, https://tinyurl.com/ebvpkrd6. Accessed on 20 June 2024.
[15]Pusalker, A.D., 'Traditional History from the Earliest Times to the Accession of Parikshit', *The History and Culture of the Indian People: The Vedic Age*, Volume 1, R.C. Majumdar (ed.), Bharatiya Vidya Bhawan, Mumbai, 2021, p. 274.
[16]Nimishananda, 'Beginning of Human Race', *The New Indian Express*, 25 March 2017, https://tinyurl.com/428yhcvb. Accessed on 25 August 2024.
[17]Pusalker, A.D., 'Traditional History from the Earliest Times to the Accession of Parikshit', *The History and Culture of the Indian People: The Vedic Age*, Volume 1, R.C. Majumdar (ed.), Bharatiya Vidya Bhawan, Mumbai, 2021, p. 274.

made earlier in this chapter. The confluence of three rivers—Ganga, Yamuna and the now-mythical Saraswati—in Prayagraj district of Uttar Pradesh, a northern state in India, is called Triveni Sangam.

The Vayu Purana mentions Ananda as a Brahma (supreme ruler), who was a predecessor of Manu Svayambhuva, and he is said to have established the varnas or the castes (given their duties) and set up the institution of marriage. These fell into abeyance for a short time and were revived by Manu Svayambhuva.[18]

Besides Manu Svayambhuva (1), the names of six other Manus are: (2) Swaarochish, (3) Uttama, (4) Tamasa, (5) Raivata and (6) Chakshusha. These Manus have passed. Presently, Manu Vaivasvata (7) is ruling. The Manus (8) Ark Saavarni, (9) Brahm Saavarni, (10) Rudra Saavarni, (11) Dharm Saavarni, (12) Daksh Saavarni, (13) Rauchya and (14) Bhautya will rule in the future.[19]

Manu Svayambhuva had two sons, Priyavrata and Uttanpada, and three daughters, Akuti, Devahuti and Prasuti.[20] They are connected with legends, linking them to gods, sages, sacrifices, etc.

> Manu Svarochisa, the second Manu, was the son of Svayambhuva's daughter Akuti. Priyavrata, the eldest son of Manu Svayambhuva, is said to be the first of Kshatriyas. Three of his sons renounced the world in childhood in order to perform penance and became Manus in the next Manvantaras. These were Uttama, Tamasa and Raivata, the third, fourth and fifth Manus, respectively.[21]

Manu Svayambhuva's second son Uttanpada had two wives, Suniti and Suruchi. Suniti was the elder one, but King Uttanpada loved his younger wife Suruchi more. Suniti bore him a son, Dhruva. Dhruva, a devotee

---

[18]Ibid.
[19]Agrawal, Pravin, 'Names of 14 Manu, 14 Indra etc', *Speakingtree.in*, https://tinyurl.com/yyx7su97. Accessed on 20 June 2024.
[20]Pusalker, A.D., 'Traditional History from the Earliest Times to the Accession of Parikshit', *The History and Culture of the Indian People: The Vedic Age*, Volume 1, R.C. Majumdar (ed.), Bharatiya Vidya Bhawan, Mumbai, 2021, p. 274.
[21]Ibid. 274–5.

of Vishnu, was a child ascetic. He is believed to have left the world for penance on account of being insulted by his stepmother, the favourite queen of Uttanpada. There are stories that Dhruva became the pole star as an outcome of Vishnu's blessings.[22] Dhruva had a mighty son named Shlishta,[23] and others in this line included Chakshusha, who was the sixth Manu. Vena in this line was an atheist and was killed by sages.[24] His son was Prithu. The earth (*prithvi* in Hindi) derives its name from Prithu, and he has been referred to as the first consecrated king of the same line.[25] Fifth in line from Prithu was Daksha, whose daughter's grandson Manu Vaivasvata (3110 BCE) is believed to be the one who survived and saved mankind from the deluge.[26]

There is also a story about King Satyavrata surviving in the flood and later taking birth as Manu Vaivasvata. Manu Vaivasvata has been called Satyavrata in some stories. He is also referred as Shradhadeva Manu.[27]

The Solar Race

Manu Vaivasvata has also been described as the son of Vivasvanta (the Sun God). According to F.E. Pargiter, ICS (Indian Civil Service) and former judge of Calcutta High Court, the myths have linked the royal dynasties that ruled in ancient India to Manu Vaivasvata.[28] All the royal

---

[22]Inner Voice and Swami Tapasyananda, 'The Story of Dhruva', *Hindustan Times*, 24 January 2007, https://tinyurl.com/yc6jy699. Accessed on 24 August 2024.
[23]'The Dhruva Dynasty', *Wisdom Library*, 16 February 2018, https://tinyurl.com/592xeew7. Accessed on 24 August 2024.
[24]'The Kings Vena and Prithu', *Wisdom Library*, 16 February 2018, https://tinyurl.com/45p9b7xk. Accessed on 24 August 2024.
[25]Pusalker, A.D., 'Traditional History from the Earliest Times to the Accession of Parikshit', *The History and Culture of the Indian People: The Vedic Age*, Volume 1, R.C. Majumdar (ed.), Bharatiya Vidya Bhawan, Mumbai, 2021, p. 274.
[26]Ibid.
[27]Deepti Ns, 'Manu and Matsya Katha', *Speakingtree.in*, 14 November 2019, https://tinyurl.com/2fswzdre. Accessed on 24 August 2024.
[28]Pargiter, F.E., *Ancient Indian Historical Tradition*, Motilal Banarsidass Publishers, 1997, Delhi, p. 253.

lineages can be traced back to Manu Vaivasvata, who was the father of nine valiant sons and a daughter Ila (or an eldest son Ila who was turned into a woman). There are divergent views about the names of Manu's nine sons. The compiled texts, however, list them as Ikshvaku, Nabhaga, Dhrishta, Saryati, Narishyanta, Pramsu, Nabhagodishta (or Nabhanedishtha), Karusha and Prishadhra.[29]

Ayodhya's First King

Ikshvaku was the eldest son of Manu Vaivasvata and became the first king of Ayodhya, a city situated on the banks of Saryu River in the state of Uttar Pradesh in northern India. He may have ruled Ayodhya around 3110 BCE. Ikshvaku got Madhyadesh (literally 'middle country') from his father. Ikshvaku is also the progenitor of the Suryavanshis. Manu Vaivasvata's descent has been traced down to the reign of Rama, hero of the Ramayana (sixty-fifth in the line of descent),[30] and followed up to 113 generations, with some unexplained omissions or inclusions in the genealogical order. This obviously includes the lineage after Rama, starting with his sons Kusa and Luv. Rama, the seventh incarnation of Vishnu, is worshipped as a popular deity. Some other sources have put Rama as sixty-fourth in line of descent from Manu.[31] Rama is also revered as the Maryada Purushottam for upholding honour and righteousness. He is seen as the embodiment of the rule of dharma. His governance of Ayodhya evolved the concept of the Ramarajya (a system where a society is run by the principles practised by Rama), as visualized in the Ramayana in ancient India and *Ramcharitmanas* in medieval India. Mahatma Gandhi's concept of Ramarajya in contemporary India was a vision to bring about just rule and social harmony in a democratic system.

---

[29]Ibid. 84, 255.
[30]'Appendix II : Genealogical Tables', *The History and Culture of the Indian People: The Vedic Age*, Volume 1, R.C. Majumdar (ed.), Bharatiya Vidya Bhawan, Mumbai, 2021.
[31]Bala, Saroj, 'Scientific Dating of Ancient Events from 7000 BC to 2000 BC', *Vivekananda International Foundation*, 3 July 2012, https://tinyurl.com/ms4p426. Accessed on 24 August 2024.

Mahatma Gandhi has observed:

By Ramarajya I do not mean Hindu Raj. I mean by Ramarajya Divine Raj, the Kingdom of God. For me Rama and Rahim are one and the same deity. I acknowledge no other God but the one God of truth and righteousness.

Whether Rama of my imagination ever lived or not on this earth, the ancient ideal of Ramarajya is undoubtedly one of true democracy in which the meanest citizen could be sure of swift justice without an elaborate and costly procedure. Even the dog is described by the poet to have received justice under Ramarajya.[32]

The Genealogy

The genealogy of Manu discussed above has been often questioned on account of being a mix of religious lore and etymology, though this line of kings has been given great importance in ancient literature. The genealogies are corroborated by the testimony of support that the same work may find in other ancient scriptures or composition. The Puranas and the two epics have given different versions of this genealogy. Kalidasa, who composed *Raghuvamsam*, has specified names of kings after Rama in his work. The genealogies are mostly legendary and trace the descent of families of Rajput princes from the Suryavanshis (solar race) and the Chandravanshis (lunar race).

The Cambridge History of India has pointed out that such pedigrees have been placed together from fragments of religious lore or from fancied etymologies on to which old-world traditions and speculations have been engrafted. Ila, the daughter of Manu, from whom the Lunar family is derived, personifies the sacrificial offering made by Manu in the legend of the flood: when the flood receded, Manu performed puja and yajna and made offerings of milk, curd and buttermilk to the

---

[32]'Ramrajya', *Mahatma Gandhi*, https://tinyurl.com/yb3anw7v. Accessed on 26 August 2024.

water. A year later, a woman appeared from waters and announced herself to be the daughter of Manu.

> Such legendary characters are everywhere the result of man's early speculation on the origin of the world. The first glimpses of authentic history appear only when tribal names are inserted in the genealogies under the disguise of eponymous ancestors. These too are outcomes of hypothesis, but hypothesis founded on facts. All the members of a tribe are presumably descended from a common ancestor, and related tribes are descended from related ancestors. On these supposed individuals the names of the tribes are conferred; and they supply a sort of genealogical framework which continues to be filled in by tradition until the age of records. Once fashioned in this way such genealogies are accepted without question until the period when critical scholarship arises and undertakes its first duty, which is to discriminate between legend and fact in the story of past ages.[33]

The Cambridge History of India has also pointed out that the Puranas have names of kingdoms mentioned in the Vedic literature. A family of the princes of the solar dynasty having the Ikshvaku name finds mention there. So, it is quite possible that the solar dynasty of Kosala, and other kingdoms to the east of the Madhyadesh, may be descendants of this family in the Vedic period. 'If so,' Rapson states, 'the Ikshvaku of the genealogical tree must be regarded as an eponymous ancestor; and his superhuman origin had to be explained, a myth found on a far fetched etymology of his name was invented. Ikshvaku was so called because he was born from the sneeze (Kshava) of Manu.'[34]

---

[33]Rapson, Edward James, 'The Puranas', *The Cambridge History of India, Volume 1: Ancient India*, Edward James Rapson (ed.), Cambridge University Press, 1922, p. 305.
[34]Ibid.

Solar Race Descent

There are two versions about the descent of the line of Ikshvaku. One of them mentioned in some of the Puranas says that Ikshvaku was blessed with 100 sons.[35] Half of them, it is said, ruled in northern India, while the remaining ones established their rule in southern India. Three of Ikshvaku's sons, Vikukshi (or Sasada), Nimi and Danda, are the most famous of the lot. Vikukshi succeeded his father as the king of Ayodhya and founded the solar line. From Nimi began the Videha line. Dandakaranya forest is named after Danda, whose kingdom was between the mountains of Vindhya and Himalaya.[36]

The Puranas have mentioned that Vikukshi violated some rules of the regime set by Ikshvaku and thus incurred his father's wrath. The former, however, ascended the throne after the death of his father and ruled in accordance with the law of the time. The next king in line after Vikukshi was his son Paranjaya. The *deva*s (deities) sought Paranjaya's help, as they were being harassed by the *asura*s (demons). It is said that the king laid down a condition that he would aid the devas if he was allowed to mount the shoulders of Indra. The latter took the form of a bull and Paranjaya destroyed the asuras sitting on the *kukud* (hump) of the bull. The king thus got the name Kakutstha. Sixth in line from Kakutstha was King Sravasta, the founder of the city of Sravasti (Shravasti), which later became the capital of northern Kosala.[37] Shravasti, now a district with headquarters at Bhinga in eastern Uttar Pradesh, is situated at a distance of about 110 km north of Ayodhya.

Ayodhya's Glory

Ayodhya has remained a city of great culture and religious importance that treasures the ancient history of India. The city is now becoming

---

[35]Pargiter, F.E., *Ancient Indian Historical Tradition*, Motilal Banarsidass Publishers, 1997, p. 257.
[36]'Glossary', *Valmiki Ramayana*, https://tinyurl.com/34vmass7. Accessed on 24 August 2024.
[37]Law, Bimala Churn, *Tribes in Ancient India*, Oriental Research Institute, Pune, 1973 p. 121.

a symbol of the advent of modern India. It finds a mention as Kosala or Saket in the ancient scriptures.

The solar line of kings, descendants of Ikshvaku, produced a large number of sovereigns. They held the glory of the family line very high.

However, there is a difference in the lists of kings of Ayodhya that the 13 Puranas and the Ramayana have given, going up to Rama from the time of Manu. Most authorities have corroborated the lists of the Puranas. The kings who brought glory to the family of the solar race include Sagar, Bhagiratha and Raghu, occupying the highest positions among the kings of ancient India.[38] Mandhatri, son of Yuvanasva and twenty-first in line, was also one such king. He brought glory to the family. He is believed to have ruled on a geographical area so large that the sun never set on his empire. Mandhatri was considered the fifth incarnation[39] of the dashavtara of Lord Vishnu. Other sources, however, say Vamana (the dwarf avatar) was the fifth avatar of Vishnu.

Mandhatri, also known as Mandhatra, married Bindumati, the daughter of Sasabindu of the Yadavas, and had three sons, Purukutsa, Ambrisha and Muchukunda.[40] Purukutsa, who finds a mention in the Rigveda, had defeated the Gandharvas. He married a Naga princess, and his grandson (or great grandson) Anaranya was killed in a battle fought at Raunahi, about 22 km southwest of Ayodhya. It is believed that Mandhatri conquered the whole earth in one day, and he or his sons carried their arms south to the river Narmada. It has been said that Narmada was the wife of Purukutsa and mother of Trasadasyu.[41]

Muchukunda was also a famous king. It is believed that it was he who built and fortified a town on the rocky banks of the Narmada on the foot of both the Vindhya and Raksa (Satpura), at a place where the two ranges approach the river. It was called Mahishmati, the modern

---

[38]Ibid. 120.
[39]Pusalker, A.D., 'Traditional History from the Earliest Times to the Accession of Parikshit', *The History and Culture of the Indian People: The Vedic Age*, Volume 1, R.C. Majumdar (ed.), Bharatiya Vidya Bhawan, Mumbai, 2021, p. 281.
[40]Ibid.
[41]Pargiter, F.E., *Ancient Indian Historical Tradition*, Motilal Banarsidass Publishers, 1997, p. 69.

Mandhata, and was located on an island in Narmada River.[42] It is said that the Haiya king Mahishmat conquered the town and named it Mahishmati. Mahishmati was an ancient town in ancient India and the capital of the Avanti kingdom. Omkareshwar, a Hindu temple dedicated to Shiva, is situated on the banks of the Narmada in Mandhata, a rocky island in Khandwa district, Madhya Pradesh, at a distance of about 1,000 km southwest of Ayodhya.

Indian cine director S.S. Rajamouli's blockbuster *Bahubali* was shot in a fictional Mahishmati empire, but the empire may have existed in ancient India.

Harishchandra's Truthfulness

As discussed above, the kingdom of Ayodhya gained glory during the period of Mandhatri, Purukutsa and Trasadasyu. Names of other important kings heard after him are Satyavrata, Trishanku and Harishchandra. The thirty-third king of this lineage, Hairshchandra, who ruled Ayodhya, is also called *satyavadi* (truth-speaking) for his truthfulness and honesty. One of the many stories regarding Harishchandra begins with the gods deciding to put the king to a test with the help of Sage Vishwamitra. According to one version, Harishchandra, while hunting in the woods, heard a woman crying. This was an illusion. So, he entered the 'ashram' of Vishwamitra, who was meditating and got angry for being disturbed. Harishchandra donated his kingdom to the sage to pacify him. Vishwamitra also demanded *dakshina* (payment to a priest for services) as was the tradition to be followed when kings met a sage.

Vishwamitra had already accepted the kingdom as donation and so Harishchandra was left with no money to give dakshina to the sage. He sought a month's time to pay the dakshina and left his kingdom. He took his wife Shaivya and son Rohitashwa (also known as Rohita) along with him and reached Kashi. (His wife has been named Taramati

---
[42]Ibid. 262.

in some stories.) Harishchandra could not earn anything in Kashi, and the granted period of one month was about to come to an end. Shaivya suggested her husband sell her as a slave and use the money to pay dakshina to the sage as promised. Harishchandra did so. When the brahmin who had bought Shaivya was about to leave, Rohitashwa did not let his mother go and started crying. So, Harishchandra requested the brahmin to buy his son as well. The king still did not have enough money to pay the dakshina to Vishwamitra. He then sold himself to a *chandal* (one who works at a cremation ground to dispose of corpses).

One day, Rohitashwa died due to a snake bite. Shaivya took Rohitashwa's body to the same cremation ground to perform his last rites. Harishchandra recognized his wife and was shocked to see his son's body. He was filled with grief. He asked Shaivya to pay tax for performing the last rites at the cremation ground, as he was duty-bound to ask her to do so. Neither Shaivya nor Harishchandra had money to pay the tax. Shaivya agreed to give half of her sari as tax and Harishchandra agreed to it. Both of them decided to end their lives on the funeral pyre of their son. As Shaivya was about to tear her sari, God appeared and blessed the family. The chandal, who turned out to be Yama, the God of Death, brought Rohitashwa back to life. Harishchandra, along with his family, passed the test with virtue and righteousness. The gods were pleased and blessed Harishchandra.

Another legend around the king is as follows: Indra announced that he would take Harishchandra to heaven with him. But the king refused to go without his subjects who, he felt, were suffering. He urged Indra to take his subjects along to heaven. Indra told him that one went to heaven only on the basis of one's good deeds. Harishchandra said he would give all his good deeds to his subjects. The gods were pleased again and thus agreed. Vishnu took the subjects along with the king to heaven. Vishwamitra made Rohitashwa the new king of Ayodhya.[43]

---

[43]'Story of Harishchandra in English for Kids', *Vedantu*, https://tinyurl.com/yc3hammv. Accessed on 21 June 2024.

Sagar's Sons Dig Deep

Sagar, forty-first in line, is believed to be another great king of the solar dynasty in Ayodhya. He wanted to perform the Ashvamedha Yajna, a ritual performed by the kings in ancient India to declare imperial sovereignty. This ritual involved a horse followed by warriors of the king being released to move freely for a year. If the horse entered other kingdoms, it would be seen as a challenge to their kings, who would then fight wars or accept the sovereignty of the master of the horse. Sagar, in order to assert his supremacy, sent out the horse, as was the custom, to see if anybody would challenge the king's authority.

Sagar's move made Indra jittery, so the latter decided to take the horse to the ashram of Sage Kapila in Patal Lok (the nether world). When the horse did not return, King Sagar sent out his 60,000 sons who dug the earth deep to search for the horse in Patal Lok. They found it in the ashram of Sage Kapila who was immersed in penance. They mistook the sage for a thief and attacked him. The moment the sage opened his eyes, they were turned into ashes. Sagar then deputed his grandson Amsumanth, who took the same route. However, unlike the others, the grandson recognized the sage and his greatness. He praised the latter and sought permission to enable his grandfather to complete the Ashvamedha Yajna. Sage Kapila allowed the horse to be taken back and the Ashvamedha Yajna could be performed. Sage Kapila said Amsumanth's predecessors could be resurrected if Ganga flowed over them. Sagar tried to get Ganga on earth and so did his grandson, but both of them failed. Sagar's great-grandson Bhagiratha was able to succeed through his penance, and the large pit thus dug was filled with water forming the *sagar* or the sea.[44]

---

[44]Yayavaram, Krishnamurthy, 'The Story of King Sagara', *Speakingtree.in*, 23 November 2016, https://tinyurl.com/yw6m58t5. Accessed on 21 June 2024.

Bhagiratha Brings Ganga to Earth

One of the more known stories about Bhagiratha is where he brought Ganga to earth when he came to know about his duty to rescue his ancestors from their evil fate. He left his vast empire in the care of his ministers to perform the severest penance to bring the divine river down from the Himalayas. He succeeded in this endeavour, and the holy stream thus brought down by him came to be known as Bhagirathi.[45] Bhagiratha's grandson Ambarisha, forty-eighth in line from Manu, was a devotee of Vishnu. It was during his tenure as the king that Ayodhya rose to prominence again. Ambarisha's grandson Rituparna is stated to be a contemporary of Vidarbha monarch Nala. Rituparna's grandson was Sudasa, who is understood to be the one mentioned in the Vedic period for winning the Dasarajna War (Battle of Ten Kings). Dilipa was in line after some generations.

The Great Raghu

Dilipa was the sixtieth king in line from Manu. The Ramayana names only one Dilipa as the king, while the Puranas have mentioned two. King Dilipa's son was the great Raghu who is believed to have conquered the whole earth, and his lineage is called Raghuvansha. Kalidasa, who traces the great lineage of Rama in his literary magnum opus *Raghuvamsam*, introduced King Dilipa using the following words: 'There was a scion of the Sun, a Manu named Vaivasvata. Respected by the sages, he was the first of this earth's rulers, like the sacred syllable Om is of all the Vedic hymns. Born in his noble family was Dilipa, purest of the pure, one radiant midst the kings, arisen like, from the sea of milk, the moon.'[46]

---

[45]Law, Bimala Churn, *Tribes in Ancient India*, Oriental Research Institute, Pune, 1973, p. 123. Bhagirathi, a source stream of the Ganga, originates from Gangotri glacier in Gaumukh, Uttarakhand. Other small streams that form the Ganga include Alaknanda, Dhauliganga, Pindar, Mandakini and Bhilangana. Alaknanda and Bhagirathi join at Devprayag, Uttarakhand, and the joint stream get the name Ganga there.
[46]Kalidasa, *Raghuvamsam: The Line of Raghu*, A.N.D. Haksar (trans.), Penguin Random

Raghu became the king after Dilipa, and Kalidasa has thus observed in his *Raghuvamsam*:

> As the fuming hearts of other rulers flamed like fire at the news that he was duly established after Dilipa as the king, the people and their progeny, their eyes raised up, were overjoyed to behold this new elevation, like that of Indra's flag celestial. For this royal elephant-rider had taken into full control both his father's throne as well as a whole circle of enemies. The goddess of prosperity, Padma, though unseen, with divine glow, herself served this new crowned king, and Saraswati, of speech the goddess, stood with bards to sing his praise in paeans which were meaningful.[47]

His son Aja was married to the Vidarbha princess Indumati, the mother of Dashratha, whose eldest son Rama was sixty-fifth in line from Manu. The *Valmiki Ramayana*, in Balkand (18.8–10), refers to the planetary situation at the time of Rama's birth and observes that it was indeed Vishnu who took birth as the son of Kaushalya. Rama's birth is described as a delight for the Ikshvaku dynasty, and it is mentioned that he was born with divine characteristics.

Ancient scriptures have provided the planetary positions and the time period of different kings of the solar dynasty in ancient India. Questions about the trustworthiness of the genealogical lists that the epics and other ancient literature may provide remain unanswered. There are also questions regarding synchronization of these lists.

Age of Rama

As mentioned above, questions are also raised about the period of the kings of the solar dynasty with special focus on Rama, hero of the Ramayana. The traditional history divides time into four *yuga*s (ages):

House, India, 2016, p. 5.
[47]Ibid. 59.

the Satya Yuga, the Treta Yuga, the Dwapara Yuga and the Kali Yuga.[48] Taking the complete list of kings of the solar dynasty as his guide, Pargiter found that a period of 1,400 years intervened between the first king Ikshvaku (son of Manu) and the Great War of Kurukshetra. Rama existed five centuries before the Great War. Traditional history counts Treta Yuga as the age of Rama's appearance on earth as the seventh incarnation of Vishnu. These figures help arrive at a rough estimation of the time of Rama's reign in Ayodhya. The genealogical list given in the *History and Culture of the Indian People: Vedic Age* places Rama in 1950 BCE.

Kosala Country's Boundaries

An understanding about the geographical extent of the Kosala country in the times of the Mahabharata and Ramayana may be derived from the story of Rama's exile. The young princes Rama and Laxmana, along with Sita, are said to have proceeded on a chariot after leaving Ayodhya (then capital of Kosala), situated on the banks of river Saryu.

> Evidently, then, there were good roads, in the Kosala country, as we may also get from the Jataka stories, where we read that the merchants loading as many as 500 wagons with their merchandise went from Magadha and the Lichhvi countries through Kosala up to the western and north-western frontiers of India. Ram made his first halt at the river Tamasa (the modern Tons)... After proceeding a long distance, he crossed the Gomti and the Syandika. Having crossed Syandika, Ram pointed to Sita the wide plane given by Manu to Ikshvaku.[49]

---

[48]Pargiter, F.E., *Ancient Indian Historical Tradition*, Motilal Banarsidass Publishers, 1997, p. 175.
[49]Law, Bimala Churn, *Tribes in Ancient India*, Oriental Research Institute, Pune, 1973, p. 119.

After Rama

Rama's brother Bharata worked as regent, keeping his elder brother's *khadau* (ancient form of wooden footwear) on the throne during the period of Rama's exile. The latter became the king after his return to Ayodhya and reigned for many years. After him, the Kosala kingdom was divided among his three brothers—Bharata, Laxmana and Shatrughana—and his two sons—Kusa and Luv. Kusa, the elder son of Rama, became the king of Ayodhya, while the younger son Luv became the king of the northern part of the region, with headquarters at Shravasti, which was founded by King Sravasta. Kusa soon founded Kusasthali in the Vindhya range and shifted the capital of his kingdom there. He appears to have extended Aryan culture in the Vindhya region. A story about Kusa's marriage to a Naga princess gives indications about the spread of Vedic culture among the aborigines.[50]

Bharata, known for his love for his elder brother Rama, got his mother's Kekaya kingdom, and is said to have founded Srinagar in the Garhwal region of Uttarakhand (a hill state carved out of Uttar Pradesh on 9 November 2000). A.H. Bingley, a scholar of the history and origin of Rajputs, has pointed out in his book that all solar races that adopted 'Surajbansi' as their title claim their descent from Rama's brother Bharata, while all other solar races claim descent from Luv and Kusa.

> All the Solar tribes except the *Surajbansi* claim descent from Lava and Kusha, the sons of Ram. The latter, however, claim Bharat, the brother of Ram, as their ancestor and state that he left Ajudhya to assist his uncle, the ruler of an Aryan principality in the Himalayas or Kashmir, in repelling an invasion of barbarians from China and Tibet. Bharat never returned, and is credited with having founded Srinagar in Garhwal (Uttarakhand).[51]

---

[50]Pusalker, A.D., 'Traditional History from the Earliest Times to the Accession of Parikshit', *The History and Culture of the Indian People: The Vedic Age*, Volume 1, R.C. Majumdar (ed.), Bharatiya Vidya Bhawan, Mumbai, 2021, p. 304.

[51]Bingley, A.H., *Hand-Book on Rajputs: History and Origin, Geographical Distribution*,

No wonder Srinagar is considered sacred, being the land of penance of various sages, and Uttarakhand is called Devbhoomi, the land of the gods. Bharata's two sons Taksha and Pushkar are said to have founded Takshashila and Pushkaravati (both sites in Pakistan now) after conquering the Gandharvas.

Rama gifted the territory of Lucknow, situated at a distance of nearly 136 km west of Ayodhya, to his brother Laxmana after conquering Lanka (the kingdom of Ravana) and completing his *vanvas* (exile) in the jungle. It is also said that the original name of Lucknow was Lakshmanpur, also known as Lakhanpur or Lachmanpur.[52] Laxmana's sons Angada and Chandraketu were given separate kingdoms near the Himalayas. Rama's brother Shatrughana became the king of Mathura after killing a demon there. The ASI plaque at the Mathura Museum says Mathura is mentioned in the Ramayana. In the oldest epic, the Ikshvaku prince Shatrughana slays a demon called Lavanasura and claims the land there. Afterwards, the place came to be known as Madhuvan, as it was thickly wooded. Later, the name changed to Madhupura and then Mathura.[53] Kusa continued his efforts to bring back the glorious status of Ayodhya. Hiranyabha Kausalya, seventeenth in line from Kusa, was a great king and a disciple of Sage Jaimini. He was the eighty-first king in line from Ikshvaku. Brihadbala was the last famous king of Ikshvaku dynasty (ninety-third generation from Ikshvaku, ninety-fourth from Manu). He was thirtieth in line from Rama and was killed by Abhimanyu in the Battle of Kurukshetra while leading the Ayodhya forces against the Pandavas.[54]

A king named Divakar ruled Ayodhya after five generations.[55]

Religion, Custom and Festivals, Asian Educational Services, New Delhi, 2011, p. 131.
[52]'History', *Lucknow, Government of Uttar Pradesh*, https://tinyurl.com/45j7wpne. Accessed on 21 June 2024.
[53]'History', *District Mathura, Government of Uttar Pradesh*, https://tinyurl.com/35n9629b. Accessed on 21 June 2024.
[54]Pusalker, A.D., 'Traditional History from the Earliest Times to the Accession of Parikshit', *The History and Culture of the Indian People: The Vedic Age*, Volume 1, R.C. Majumdar (ed.), Bharatiya Vidya Bhawan, Mumbai, 2021, p. 304.
[55]Joshi, Esha Basanti (ed.), *Uttar Pradesh District Gazetteers*, Faizabad, 1960, p. 30.

Ayodhya's last king known in the solar line was Sumitra.⁵⁶ Following the fall of Raja Sumitra, the 113th monarch, the last king in line, Ayodhya's royal family dispersed.⁵⁷

Ayodhya in Age of Mahavira and the Buddha

The Jain traditions indicate that five Tirthankaras, including Adinatha or Rishabhdeva who was the first, were born in Ayodhya.⁵⁸ The town also finds a mention in the age of Tirthankara Mahavira and Gautam Buddha. Pali Buddhist literature mentions Kosala as one of the 16 great countries (*mahajanapadas*) of Jambudipa or India.⁵⁹ Kosala has also been described as one of the most important kingdoms of North India during the lifetime of the Buddha.⁶⁰ Panini, a Sanskrit grammarian and a revered scholar, has mentioned Kosala among the important 'janpadas' in ancient India.

Chandragupta I was the founder of the kingdom that extended up to Saket or Awadh and Prayag, now called Prayagraj. If a spurious copper-plate inscription in Gaya is to be believed, the son and successor of Chandragupta I, the great conqueror Samudragupta, had a *jayskandhavara* (camp of victory) in Ayodhya. The Vayu Purana mentions that Saket was included in the domain of the Guptas.⁶¹ The Hindu traditions give credit for the restoration of Ayodhya to King Vikramaditya of Ujjain. He is also identified as Chandragupta II (CE 379–413), the son and successor of Samudragupta. There is reason to

---

⁵⁶Pargiter, F.E., *The Purana Text of the Dynasties of the Kali Age*, Oxford University Press, 1913, p. 67.
⁵⁷The Imperial Gazetteer of India Vol. V, Abazai to Arcot, published under the authority of his Majesty's Secretary of State for India in Council, Oxford, Clarendon Press, 1908; cited in Singh, Devi Prasad, *Ramrajya Adhunik Parivesh Mein*, Kitabwale, New Delhi, 2020, p. 46.
⁵⁸Joshi, Esha Basanti (ed.), *Uttar Pradesh District Gazetteers*, Faizabad, 1960, p. 28.
⁵⁹Law, Bimala Churn, *Tribes in Ancient India*, Oriental Research Institute, Pune, 1973, p. 117.
⁶⁰Rhys Davids, T.W., 'The Early History of the Buddhists', *The Cambridge History of India, Volume 1: Ancient India*, Edward James Rapson (ed.), Cambridge University Press, 1922, p. 178.
⁶¹Joshi, Esha Basanti (ed.), *Uttar Pradesh District Gazetteers*, Faizabad, 1960, p. 34.

believe that in the fifth century, Ayodhya, rather than Patliputra, was the premier city of the Gupta empire. It is also possible that Kalidasa wrote his *Raghuvamsam* during his stay in Ayodhya during this period.[62]

Vikramaditya II Restored the Temples of Ayodhya

King Chandragupta II, Vikramaditya, is said to have worked for the restoration of important temples of Ayodhya, an important city for the Gupta empire. Fa-Hien, the Chinese traveller who was in India for more than 10 years (CE 400–11), travelled through Awadh and Sanchi during the reign of Chandragupta II and saw a *stupa* (shrine) where four previous Buddhas had walked and sat.[63]

Ayodhya had reached its culmination during the reign of Rama. Valmiki's *Ramayana* and the Mahabharata have described the city as one of *punyalakshana* (city with auspicious signs), and other subsequent ancient texts like Goswami Tulsidas's *Ramcharitmanas* have immortalized this epoch. In *Ramcharitmanas*, Rama, while speaking to Sugreeva and Vibhishana, says, '*Jadyapi sab baikunthbakhana, Bed purana bidit sab jana. Awadhpuri, Ram priyanahin sou, yeh prasangjanaikou, kou* (Although all have extolled Vaikuntha [My divine abode], which is familiar to the Vedas and the Puranas and known throughout the world, it is not so dear to Me as the city of Ayodhya: only some rare soul knows this secret).'[64]

Guru Nanak Dev's Visit to Ayodhya

Guru Nanak Dev, founder of Sikhism, visited Ayodhya for *darshan* (divine sight) of the Ram Janmabhoomi temple in 1510–11.[65] This visit

---

[62]Ibid. 35.
[63]Ibid.
[64]*Sri Ramacharitamanasa: With Hindi Text and English Translation (A Romanized Edition)*, Gita Press, Gorakhpur, n.d., p. 973, https://tinyurl.com/5dn4zjj2. Accessed on 27 September 2024.
[65]*M Siddiq (D) Thr Lrs vs Mahant Suresh Das & Ors*, (2019), CA 10866-10867/2010, https://tinyurl.com/bdfjzf3k. Accessed on 25 August 2024.

clearly shows that the Ram temple existed at the birthplace of Rama before the invasion of Babur in India.

The Uttar Pradesh Sunni Central Waqf and other Muslim residents of Ayodhya, in a suit instituted in 1961, contended that Babri Masjid was built on the instructions of Emperor Babur by Mir Baqi, who was commander of his forces. This was done following Babur's conquest of the subcontinent. Muslims denied that the mosque was constructed on the site of a destroyed temple. As Rama's *janmabhoomi* (birthplace) has been of prime importance for Hindus, the mosque at the janmabhoomi remained a cause of concern and led to dispute between Hindus and Muslims for centuries.

The dispute has been talked about by various British officials who worked in or visited India. In *A Historical Sketch of Faizabad*, P. Carnegy, the officiating commissioner and settlement officer in India, referred to three religious sites in Ayodhya, including the *janmasthan* (place of birth).

> Ajudhia—Ajudhia, which is to the Hindu what Macca is to the Mohammedan, Jerusalem to the Jews, has the traditions of the orthodox, a highly mythical origin, being founded for additional security not on the earth for the transitory, but on the chariot wheel of the Great creator himself which will endure forever.[66]

Surgeon General Edward Balfour, who wrote the *Cyclopedia of India and of Eastern and Southern Asia*, said, '[Ayodhya] has now a population of 7,518 of Hindus and Mohammedans but in ancient time it was capital of the kingdom of Kosala, the Modern Oudh, ruled over by the great King Dashrath of the Solar Line and father of Ram Chandra.'[67]

As mentioned earlier in this chapter, Rama is sixty-fifth in the line of descendants in genealogical order from Manu and may have lived during 1950 BCE.[68]

---

[66]Ibid.
[67]Ibid.
[68]'Appendix II: Genealogical Tables', *The History and Culture of the Indian People: The Vedic Age*, Volume 1, R.C. Majumdar (ed.), Bharatiya Vidya Bhawan, Mumbai, 2021.

Traditional History

Other kings who ruled Ayodhya before Rama include: Manu (1), Ikshvaku (2), Vikukshi (3), Kakustha (4) Kuvalasava (12), Yuvanasva II (20), Mandhatri (21), Purukutsa (22), Trasadasyu (23), Trayyaruna (30), Trishanku (32), Harishchandra (33), Rohita (34), Bahu (39), Sagar (41), Brahadaratha (45), Ambarisha (48), Rituparna (51), Sudasa (53), Kalmashapadu (54), Asmaka (55), Mulaka (56), Dilipa (60), Raghu (62), Aja (63) and Dashratha (64).[69]

The Missing Dots

The Institute of Scientific Research on Vedas worked on a research project for scientific determination of dates of major events based on planetary references given in ancient Sanskrit manuscripts, using planetarium software.[70] Valmiki's *Ramayana* has astronomical references, and these details were used to determine dates of important events beginning with birth of Rama to his return to Ayodhya after spending 14 years in exile. This study gives 10 January 5114 BCE as the date of Rama's birth.[71]

Analyses of traditional sources of history have indicated that Rama may have ruled Ayodhya around 1950 BCE. This points towards a huge gap of nearly 3,000 years in determination of the era of Rama, of the time when the Great Flood may have occurred in India and Mesopotamia. Today, some sources of history have indicated that the Great Flood in India occurred around 3102 BCE.[72] An archaeological study, as discussed earlier in this chapter, indicates that the deluge of the Saraswati took place around 2000–1900 BCE, or broadly in the first quarter of the second millennium BCE.[73]

---

[69] Ibid.
[70] Bala, Saroj, 'Scientific Dating of Ancient Events from 7000 BC to 2000 BC', *Vivekananda International Foundation*, 3 July 2012, https://tinyurl.com/yp2dxjzt. Accessed on 25 August 2024.
[71] Bhatnagar, Pushkar, *Dating the Era of Lord Ram*, Rupa Publications, New Delhi, 2023, p. 31.
[72] Keay, John, 'The Harappan World', *India: A History*, William Collins 2022, p. 2.
[73] Pandey, Neelam, 'Manu's Flood Was Real, Saraswati Nurtured Harappan Settlements:

The Great Flood that Manu survived may be an important event to ascertain the period of Ikshvaku and other kings of the solar race leading to Rama. So, it is important to conduct further research to know about the flood and its connection with the deluge that may have hit the rest of the world. William Ryan and Walter Pittman, senior scientists at Columbia University's Lamont-Doherty Earth Observatory, in their research have found evidence of a catastrophic event that changed history, a gigantic flood which took place in the Black Sea.[74] A *Time* magazine report mentioned that the Sumerian epic, *Gilgamesh*, dates back nearly 5,000 years and indicated that various archaeologists have suggested timing of the historical deluge between 5,000 and 7,000 years ago.[75]

There are striking similarities between the flood tales of India and Mesopotamia, despite the many differences. It is important to mention that such events should not be read without the help of historiography. It is, however, time to rework the traditional accounts and connect the missing dots to know more about the era of Rama or the Treta Yuga, and establish that India was the cradle of civilization, which may have once flourished during the rule of the hero of the Ramayana in Ayodhya, in ancient years.

Indian Experts', *Hindustan Times*, 27 March 2017, https://tinyurl.com/yvwxs3b2. Accessed on 20 June 2024.
[74]Fairfield, Hannah, 'Noah's Flood: Evidence of Ancient Disaster Is Linked to Biblical Legend', *Columbia University Record*, Vol. 24, Issue 12, https://tinyurl.com/n37kwdrn. Accessed on 25 August 2024.
[75]Tharoor, Ishaan, 'Before Noah: Myths of the Flood Are Far Older than the Bible', *Time*, https://tinyurl.com/2bk7dsne. Accessed on 25 August 2024.

2

The Dispute Begins

Ayodhya changed the course of history of ancient India, and its history changed the course of politics in present-day India. Ayodhya's history will remain incomplete without understanding the dispute over the Babri Masjid built in the name of Zahir-ud-din Muhammad Babur or Zahir al-Din Muhammad Babur (CE 1483–1530).

When Babur undertook the journey in 1488 from his home in Fergana Valley of modern Uzbekistan, to Samarkand, one of the oldest cities in Central Asia, he was only a child.[1]

The Fergana Valley, a picturesque region in Uzbekistan, is situated at a distance of about 2,000 km northwest of Ayodhya in India. It is a part of the larger Mawarannahr region, also known as Transoxiana, the 'land beyond the river'. Amu Darya marks the border between Uzbekistan and Afghanistan.

A young prince of Turco-Mongol descent, Babur travelled about 500 km to begin this journey in 1488. About four decades later, he travelled a distance of nearly 1,000 km, crossing the Pamir, the Hindu Kush ranges, and the Khyber Pass to reach Panipat, a historic city of India, situated 90 km north of New Delhi (now in Haryana), near which three important battles were fought in 1526, 1556 and 1761.

Babur defeated Ibrahim Lodi, the last Delhi Sultan of the Lodi dynasty, in the first battle of Panipat in 1526. Ibrahim Lodi had become Delhi's ruler on 21 November 1517 following the death of his father

---

[1] Dale, Stephen F., *Babur: Timurid Prince and Mughal Emperor (1483–1530)*, Cambridge University Press, 2018, p. 23.

Sikandar Lodi. Babur's victory in Panipat created the foundation of the Mughal Empire in India. This battle proved to be a turning point in the history of India, and so did the demolition of the controversial mosque constructed in his name—the Babri mosque—in Ayodhya.

The Golden Bird

Babur undertook his journey from Fergana Valley to Samarkand (the city was earlier the capital of Temur, the Turco-Mongol conqueror [1336–1405] also known as Timur-i-lang or Tamerlane) to be betrothed to the young daughter of his paternal uncle and Samarkand's ruler Ahmad Mirza, Aiysha Sultan Begum.[2] He eventually got married to her in 1500. Babur had become a ruler at the age of 12 following the death of his father in June 1494. A large army of soldiers, clerks and servants accompanied him as he undertook what he himself called the *safar* (expedition) to India. He was lured by the lucre, obviously hearing stories of India being called the *sone ki chidiya* (golden bird) for its immense gold, vast agriculture lands, beautiful mountain ranges and rivers, and abundant natural resources.

A number of Muslim invaders had led such expeditions much before Babur's invasion of India. These invaders too were attracted towards India for its wealth. Despite inheriting his family's wealth, Babur was keen to get more. He also wanted to demonstrate his valour to the world. Niccolao Manucci, a Venetian traveller in his travel account of Mughal India, has given a faithful and vivid description of mediaeval India from 1656 to 1680: 'Although, Sultan Babar had inherited so much wealth from his father, Sultan Mahmud, he was not thereby induced to be content with the countries conquered by his predecessors. But instigated by their victories, he, too, was anxious to give ... proof of his valour.'[3]

Babur was very clear about what he valued India for. Stephen

---

[2]Ibid. 23.
[3]Manucci, Niccolao, *Mogul India or Storia Do Mogor*, William Irvine (trans.), Atlantic Publishers and Distributors, New Delhi, 2022, p. 108.

Fredric Dale, professor emeritus of South Asian and Islamic History at Ohio State University, USA, has quoted the seventeenth-century Safavid poet Ashraf Mazandarani to make his point about Babur's appreciation of India's wealth. Dale notes that Babur's appreciation for India's wealth echoes the understanding of previous invaders and is nicely expressed in the words of Ashraf Mazandarani as: 'Whoever comes to Hindustan from Iran imagines, that in India gold is scattered like stars in the evening sky.'[4]

Dale quotes Babur himself writing in his autobiography that he valued five things about Hindustan: '[I]ts numerous craftsmen, its refreshing air following monsoon rains, the system of calculation and categories of measures and the fact that it was a large country awash in gold and silver coins'.[5]

Babur would not have been in as much focus as he was, unlike many other rulers, had he not been the founder of the Mughal Empire, and had his name not been linked to the now demolished mosque Babri Masjid, which was named after him. He believed in efficacy of prayers and his belief in them was immense. This has been demonstrated in the manner in which he offered to sacrifice himself to save his son's (Humayun) life.[6]

The Kohinoor

Besides wealth, Dale also refers to the 'Mountain of Light', possibly the Kohinoor diamond, that Babur gave to Humayun and others. Dale writes:

> Its wealth, he (Babur) pointedly mentions, was arithmetically reflected in its numbering system, which included such high values as lacs (100,000), crores (10,000,000) and even greater

---

[4]Dale, Stephen F., *Babur: Timurid Prince and Mughal Emperor (1483–1530)*, Cambridge University Press, 2018, p. 139.
[5]Ibid.
[6]Prasad, Ishwari, *A Short History of Muslim Rule in India*, Surjit Publications, 2016, p. 208.

amounts that were needed to calculate the monetary value of the country's agriculture and commercial economy. His knowledge of India's wealth, which contrasted with Kabul's relative poverty, was fully documented when he distributed the coin of Laudi's Agra treasury. He gave Humayun 70 lacs (7,000,000 coins) or approximately 56,000 or 57,000 pound sterling, in nineteenth-century values along with a separate uncounted treasure house and the extraordinary 'Mountain of Light' diamond. This stone was apparently the kuh-I nur Humayun took from the family of the former Rajput ruler of Gwalior, Bikramjit Rajah, who had been killed fighting as a tributary of Ibrahim Lodi.[7]

The *BBC* has called the Koh-i-Noor one of the world's most controversial diamonds. In an article on the Koh-i-Noor titled 'Six Myths about a Priceless Diamond', it observed that the Koh-i-Noor has been the subject of conquest and intrigue for centuries, passing through the hands of Mughal princes, Iranian warriors, Afghan rulers and Punjabi Maharajas.

> The 105-carat gemstone came into British hands in the mid-19th century, and forms part of the Crown Jewels on display at the Tower of London. Ownership of the gem is an emotional issue for many Indians, who believe it was stolen from them by the British.[8]

There are stories about Muslim invaders who invaded Awadh, which derives its name from Ayodhya, the capital of the Kosala kingdom in ancient India. Ayodhya, a city situated on the banks of Saryu River, is also the name of a district and a division earlier known as Faizabad. Muslim invaders took control of Awadh, which now comprises a part of central and eastern Uttar Pradesh, a state in northern India. Awadh was a province of Delhi Sultanate and a part of the Mughal Empire.

---

[7]Dale, Stephen F., *Babur: Timurid Prince and Mughal Emperor (1483–1530)*, Cambridge University Press, 2018, p. 139.

[8]'Koh-i-Noor: Six Myths about a Priceless Diamond', *BBC News*, 9 December 2016, https://tinyurl.com/d2ub2y73. Accessed on 22 June 2024.

Masud Ghazi, also known as Salar Masud and Ghazi Mian, is said to be among the first who invaded Awadh. There are tales about the battle fought between Salar Masud and Raja Suheldev, the king of Shravasti, at Bahraich, a district in eastern Uttar Pradesh situated near Ayodhya. According to the *Mirat-i-Masudi*, a Persian-language historical romance by Abdur Rahman Chishti (who died in 1683), Ghazi Mian occupied Awadh sometime in about 1030. The story of Salar Masud and Suheldev is a mix of history and myth. Ghazi Mian is believed to have acquired popularity as a warrior in the twelfth century. He was the nephew of the eleventh-century Turkish invader Mahmud of Ghazni, whose invasion of India is known as the moment when Islam entered large parts of the subcontinent. Interestingly, his tomb at Bahraich in Uttar Pradesh stands as a place of pilgrimage for a large number of Muslims as well as Hindus. The Uttar Pradesh government celebrated Raja Suheldev's birth anniversary on 16 February 2021, and released an official note, which stated that Raja Suheldev fought, defeated and killed the Ghaznavid commander Ghazi Sayyid Salar Masood on the banks of Chittaura Lake in Bahraich in a famous battle in 1034.[9]

Ayodhya was under the rule of the Gahadavala dynasty before 1194. The dynasty ruled from two capital cities: Kanyakubja (Kannauj) and Varanasi. The Gahadavala king Chandradev, who conquered Kannauj, visited Ayodhya and bathed in the Saryu on the occasion of a solar eclipse on 23 October 1093.[10] Muiz-ud-din Mohammad bin Sam (commonly known as Shihad-ud-din Ghori), one of the founders of Muslim rule in India, is said to have occupied Ayodhya himself or through one of his lieutenants in 1194.[11]

It cannot be categorically said when Ayodhya became a Muslim province of Delhi's rulers. It gradually became the headquarters of

---

[9]'Maharaja Suheldev a Legendary King', *Bahraich, Government of Uttar Pradesh*, https://tinyurl.com/yb4eh4cr. Accessed on 9 August 2024.
[10]Thomas, F.W. (ed.), *Epigraphia Indica and Record of Archaeological Survey of India*, Vol. XIV 1917–18, p. 193, https://tinyurl.com/k2eekp5a. Accessed on 13 August 2024.
[11]Joshi, Esha Basanti (ed.), *Uttar Pradesh District Gazetteers*, Government of Uttar Pradesh, Revenue Department, 1960, p. 41.

an Awadh Muslim province in the kingdom of Delhi. Many of those appointed as governors of the province rebelled against their rulers. Minhaj-us-Siraj, a contemporary of the early Turkish sultans of Delhi, has given accounts of the governors of Awadh appointed between 1206 and 1260.[12] Some of them have been discussed in this chapter. His accounts indicate that during the initial years of Turkish rule, Awadh remained a stronghold of local Hindu kings. Some of the governors used Awadh as the centre for expansion of their territory and became more powerful. This made their respective kings apprehensive, and such governors were transferred frequently from Ayodhya.[13]

Qutub-ud-din Aibak assigned Awadh to one of his lieutenants, Malik Husam-ud-din Ughulbak,[14] transferring him from another territory which had been given to him in CE 1193. Muhammad Bakhtiyar Khalji joined Ughulbak from Badaun and, with the latter's aid, extended the Muslim rule to Bihar and Bengal.

Nasir-ud-Din Mahmud, the eldest son of Sultan Shams-ud-Din Iltutmish, was made the governor of Awadh in 1226. He crushed the local Bhar chieftains who rose in rebellion and killed a large number of Muslims. In 1242, Qamar-I'd-din Kairan, one of the patrons of Minhaj-us-Siraj, the author of *Tabaqat-i-Nasiri*, was put in charge of the province. Malik Nusrat-ud-Din Taisi was the governor of Awadh during the regime of Razia, who became the first woman ruler of Delhi and ruled from 1236 to 1240. Awadh was given to Qutlugh Khan, husband of Malika-i-Jahan, in 1255. She was the widow of Iltutmish and mother of Sultan Nasir-ud-din.[15] Ayodhya's command was passed on to Malik Taj-ud-Din Irsalan Khan, who rebelled in 1259 and shifted from Ayodhya. His successor Malik Amir Khan Altagin had control over Ayodhya for 20 years. He was hanged at the gate of Ayodhya following his defeat when sent to quell a rebellion by Tughril Beg of Lakhnauti.[16]

---

[12]Ibid. 42.
[13]Ibid.
[14]Ibid.
[15]Ibid. 43.
[16]Nevill, H.R., *Fyzabad: A Gazetteer, Volume XLIII of the District Gazetteers of the United Provinces of Agra and Oudh*, Allahabad, Superintendent Government Press, 1905,

The Dispute Begins

In 1321, Malik Tigin ruled Awadh. He was murdered after joining the revolt against Muhammad Tughlaq.[17] In 1376, Awadh was placed under the charge of Malik Hisam-ud-din Nawa. In 1394, Malik-ush-Sharq Khwaja-i-Jahan took possession of Awadh and the area between Bihar and Kannauj. He also assumed control over the royal state of Jaunpur and founded the independent Sharqi dynasty of Jaunpur.[18] The Jaunpur kingdom was conquered by Bahlul Lodi (founder of Lodi dynasty), who gave Awadh to Muhammad Farmuli (Kala Pahar). Farmuli ruled the province while Ibrahim Lodi ruled India when Babur invaded.[19] Bayazid Farmuli controlled Awadh when Ibrahim Lodi died in the Battle of Panipat in 1526.[20]

Babur had conducted a number of preliminary raids in India before his final invasion in 1526. He was well aware of the prevailing situation in the country before his invasion. He had identified seven 'respected and independent' rulers of India at the time of invasion. In his autobiography, he named the seven rulers; these included five Muslim and two Hindu rulers. Ibrahim Lodi (1517–26) was one of them.[21]

At the Saryu

Bayazid Farmuli, along with a number of other Afghan chiefs, switched loyalties and joined the victorious forces led by Babur following Ibrahim Lodi's death in the Battle of Panipat in 1526. However, Farmuli soon rebelled. Babur proceeded towards Awadh in February 1528, ordering Chin Timur Sultan to crush the rebels. He is said to have

---

pp. 149–53, https://tinyurl.com/2u6dcdw2. Accessed on 26 August 2024.
[17]Ibid.
[18]Joshi, Esha Basanti (ed.), *Uttar Pradesh District Gazetteers*, Government of Uttar Pradesh, Revenue Department, 1960, pp. 45–6.
[19]Nevill, H.R., *Fyzabad: A Gazetteer, Volume XLIII of the District Gazetteers of the United Provinces of Agra and Oudh*, Allahabad, Superintendent Government Press, 1905, pp. 149–53, https://tinyurl.com/2u6dcdw2. Accessed on 26 August 2024.
[20]Joshi, Esha Basanti (ed.), *Uttar Pradesh District Gazetteers*, Government of Uttar Pradesh, Revenue Department, 1960, pp. 41–6.
[21]Dale, Stephen F., *Babur: Timurid Prince and Mughal Emperor (1483–1530)*, Cambridge University Press, 2018, p. 17.

stayed there for a few days. Babur appointed Baqi Tashqandi as the governor of Awadh for quelling the rebellion.[22] Did he order Baqi Tashquandi for the demolition of the Ram temple or the construction of Babri Masjid? *Babur-Nama*, the memoirs of Zahir-ud-Din Muhammad Babur Padshah Ghazi, the founder of the Mughal Empire, does not make a mention of him doing so. *Babur-Nama*, however, makes a mention of the invader Babur reaching 'Gagar', on the banks of which Ayodhya is situated. 'March 28th (1528): On Saturday the 7th of Rajab we dismounted 2 or 3 kurohs from Aud above the junction of the Gagar (Gogra) and Sird,' reads the translation of *Babur-Nama*.[23]

Annette Susannah Beveridge has countered the observation that the Gagar or Gogra mentioned in *Babur-Nama* is the Saryu. Explaining in one of the footnotes of the translation, she observes, 'I take this to be the Kali-Sarda-Chauka affluent of the Gogra and not its Sarju or Saru one. To so take it seems warranted by the context; there could be no need for the fords on the Sarju to be examined, and its position is not suitable.'[24]

Babur-Nama next mentions: '(April 2nd) On Thursday the 12th of month, I rode out intending to hunt.'[25] Beveridge, in a footnote, further observes: 'Unfortunately no record of the hunting expedition survives.'[26] There is a break in the contents in Babur's memoirs from 2 April to 18 September 1528 in the *Babur-Nama*. This may be a result of missing pages in the autobiography.

Did Babur reach the banks of the Gagar? This question remains unanswered, though some writers have narrated stories about his Ayodhya adventure.

---

[22]Joshi, Esha Basanti (ed.), *Uttar Pradesh District Gazetteers*, Government of Uttar Pradesh, Revenue Department, 1960, p. 47.
[23]Ghazi, Zahiru-d-din Muhammad Babur Padshah, *Babur-Nama (Memoirs of Babur)*, Annette Susannah Beveridge (trans.), Oriental Books Reprint Corporation, New Delhi, 1970.
[24]Ibid.
[25]Ibid.
[26]Ibid.

The Dispute Begins

> On a day, he (Babur) came to meet Faqir Fazal Abbas Qalandar of Ayodhya. Babur's commander Mir Baqi Tashqandi accompanied him. Babur offered expensive gifts of clothes and gemstones. But Faqir refused to accept them. When he reached his camp he saw the offerings made to the Faqir were already there. Babur then began meeting the Faqir daily and on one day the Faqir asked Babur to demolish the temple and get a mosque constructed for him… Babur was compelled to fulfill the wish of Faqir and he ordered Mir Baqi to do so.[27]

The Gagar or Ghaghra, having its source in Tibet, probably derives its name from the Sanskrit word *gharghara* meaning 'rattling' or 'laughter'. It is called Karnali or Kauriala in Nepal and Saryu in Ayodhya. The Uttar Pradesh government recently approved the proposal to rename the entire stretch of the Ghaghra as Saryu, believed to be the daughter of Sage Vashishtha, and some people call the river Vashishtha-ki-Kanya. It is also called Vashishtha Ganga. Sage Vashishtha is believed to have brought this river to Ayodhya from Mansarovar Lake, where Brahma had deposited the tears of joy shed by Vishnu. For this reason, the river is considered sacred by Hindus.[28]

The Saryu has been witness to the various twists and turns in Ayodhya from ancient times. The Uttar Pradesh tourism department describes the river as one of the most prominent waterways in Uttar Pradesh: '[T]he river finds mention in ancient Hindu scriptures such as the Ved and Ramayan. Literally translating to "that which is streaming", it flows through Ayodhya, and as is believed, rejuvenates it and washes away impurities off this religious town.'[29]

---

[27]Sitaram, Rai Bahadur Lala, *Ayodhya Ka Itihas*, Vishwavidyalya Prakashan, Varanasi, 2022, p. 150; translated from Hindi.
[28]Joshi, Esha Basanti (ed.), *Uttar Pradesh District Gazetteers*, Government of Uttar Pradesh, Revenue Department, 1960, p. 9.
[29]'Saryu River', *Uttar Pradesh Tourism, Government of Uttar Pradesh*, https://tinyurl.com/yr59evc7. Accessed on 24 June 2024.

Babri Mosques

Amid questions over the destruction of the Ram temple in Ayodhya, where Babri Masjid existed till 6 December 1992, there are important observations about Babur's connection with the mosque in Ayodhya.

H.R. Nevill, a British officer, ICS, and author of *Fyzabad: A Gazetteer*, has observed:

> After the defeat of Ibrahim (Lodi) at Panipat, the Afghan nobles assembled at Jaunpur and thither Babar sent Kamran with Amir Quli Beg in pursuit. The Afghans retired before him to Patna, and thus Oudh fell into the hands of the Mughal invaders... The country was retained by Babar and Humayun till the defeat of the latter by Sher Shah and his Afghans (in the Battle of Chausa). In 1528 Babar built the mosque at Ajodhya on the traditional spot where Rama was born.[30]

Nevill has observed further:

> The Janamasthan was in Ramkot (Ayodhya) and marked the birthplace of Rama. In 1528 A.D. Babar came to Ajodhya and halted here for a week. He destroyed the ancient temple and on its site built a mosque, still known as Babar's mosque ... no record of the visit to Ajodhya is to be found in the Musalman historians. It must have occurred about the time of his expedition to Bihar.[31]

This idea that Babur reached Ayodhya and halted there for a week is countered in the absence of any incontrovertible evidence. *Fyzabad: A Gazetteer* has mentioned that Babri Masjid was built using the material from the old structure of the Ram temple. Many of the columns made of close-grained black stone, called *kasauti* by the locals, were used. Nevill noted that the mosque had two inscriptions, one on the outside

---

[30]Nevill, H.R., *Fyzabad: A Gazetteer*, Volume XLIII of the District Gazetteers of The United Provinces of Agra and Oudh, Allahabad, Superintendent Government Press, 1905, p. 153, https://tinyurl.com/2u6dcdw2. Accessed on 26 August 2024.
[31]Ibid. 173-4.

The Dispute Begins

and the other on the pulpit; the inscriptions were in Persian and bear the date 935 Hijri (Islamic calendar). 'Of the authenticity of the inscriptions there can be no doubt,'[32] observed Nevill.

The authenticity and genuineness of the inscriptions, however, has been questioned. A. Fuhrer in his book *The Sharqi Architecture of Jaunpur* gave details about three inscriptions and concluded that Babri Masjid was constructed in CE 1523 on the very spot where the old temple of 'Janmasthanam of Ramchandra was standing'.[33] It may be noted here that the date of construction given by Fuhrer is prior to the invasion of Babur and defeat of Ibrahim Lodi in the battle of Panipat in CE 1526.

Beveridge referred to two inscriptions: one inside and another outside the mosque. The inscription inside the mosque, as quoted by Beveridge, read:

> 1) By the command of the Emperor Babur whose justice is an edifice reaching up to the very height of the heavens. (2) The good-hearted Mir Baqi built this alighting place of angels. (3) It will remain an everlasting bounty, and (hence) the date of its erection became manifest from my words. It will remain an everlasting bounty.[34]

The inscription outside the mosque read:

> (1) In the name of One who is Great (and) Wise (and) who is Creator of the whole world and is free from the bondage of space. (2) After His praise, peace and blessings be on Prophet Muhammad, who is the head of all the Prophets in both the worlds. (3) In the world, it is widely talked about Qalandar Babur that he is a successful emperor.[35]

---

[32] Ibid. 174.
[33] Fuhrer, A. Sharqi, 'Ayodhya, Bhuia Tal and Sahet Mahet', *The Sharqi Architecture of Jaunpur*, Archaeological Survey of India, Calcutta, 1889, p. 67, https://tinyurl.com/4setjhbj. Accessed on 26 August 2024.
[34] *M Siddiq (D) Thr Lrs vs Mahant Suresh Das & Ors*, (2019), CA 10866-10867/2010, https://tinyurl.com/bdfjzf3k. Accessed on 25 August 2024.
[35] Ibid. 88–9.

Beveridge observed that the second inscription outside the mosque was incomplete.

The Epigraphia Indica-Arabic-Persian Supplement also carries a reference about the inscriptions, with text attributed to Maulvi M. Ashraf Husain and edited by Z.A. Desai.[36]

This text has reference to the construction of Babri Masjid. It reads:

> The Babri Masjid, which commands a picturesque view from the riverside, was constructed according to A. Fuhrer in AH 930 (CE 1523–1524) but his chronology based upon incorrect readings of inscriptions supplied to him, is erroneous. Babur defeated Ibrahim Lodi only in AH 933 (CE 1526), and moreover, the year of construction, recorded in two of the three inscriptions is clearly AH 935 (CE 1528–1529). Again, it was not built by Mir Khan as stated by him (Fuhrer). The order for building the mosque seems to have been issued during Babur's stay at Ayodhya in AH 934 (CE 1527–28), but no mention of its completion is made in the Babur Nama. However, it may be remembered that his diary for the year AH 934 (CE 1527–28) breaks off abruptly, and throws the reader into the dark in regard to the account of Oudh (Awadh).[37]

Ashraf Hussain noted that the mosque had several inscriptions and, out of them, two epigraphs had disappeared. 'They (two epigraphs) were reportedly destroyed in the communal vandalism in 1934... the present inscription restored by the Muslim community, is not only in inlaid Nasta'liq characters, but is also slightly different from the original, owing perhaps to the incompetence of the restorers in deciphering it properly.'[38]

Beveridge had also not seen the inscriptions herself and got the purported text of the inscriptions through her spouse, an ICS officer, the deputy commissioner of Faizabad. 'She had neither read the

---

[36]Ibid. 89.
[37]Ibid. 89–90.
[38]Ibid. 90.

original nor is there anything to indicate that she was in a position to translate it. Beveridge states that she made "a few changes in the term of expression". What changes were made by Beveridge has not been explained. According to her, the text of two inscriptions was incomplete and was not legible.[39]

Another version of the inscriptions came from a report of a court-appointed commissioner following directives of the Faizabad court issued on 26 March 1946 in *Shia Central Waqf Board vs Sunnis Central Board of Waqf*. This report reproduced in the judgement dated 30 March 1946 mentioned that 'by the order of Shah Babar, Amir Mir Baki built the resting place of angels in 923 AH i.e. CE 1516–17.'[40] There is a reference to Mir Baki of Isphahan in 935 AH, i.e., CE 1528–29 in respect to the second inscription.[41]

The authenticity of the inscriptions on Babri Masjid has already come into question.[42] So, the reference made about Babur ordering his commanders to construct Babri Masjid in Ayodhya also lacks irrefutable evidence. Mir Baqi may have been one of Babur's commanders referred to as Baqi Tashqandi. Some writers have referred to Mir Baqi as Mir Baqi Tashqandi. A question mark also hangs over the identity of Baqi Ishphahan who has been referred to as Mir Baqi of Ishphan.

Did Babur order the construction of any other mosque in India? No such mention has been made in the *Babur-Nama*. There are two other mosques built in his name in Sambhal and Panipat. Sambhal is a district near Moradabad in western Uttar Pradesh. The district's official website acknowledges the construction of the mosque:

> Babar, the first Mughal ruler constructed the first Babri Masjid in Sambhal which is to date considered to be a historic monument. He later on made his son Humayun the governor of Sambhal and Humayun in turn passed on the reigns to his son Akbar.

---

[39]Ibid. 92.
[40]Ibid. 95.
[41]Ibid.
[42]*M Siddiq (D) Thr Lrs vs Mahant Suresh Das & Ors*, (2019), CA 10866-10867/2010, pp. 93–5. https://tinyurl.com/bdfjzf3k. Accessed on 25 August 2024.

Sambhal is said to have flourished under the Akbar rule but subsequently deteriorated in popularity when Akbar's son Shah Jahan was made the in-charge of the city.[43]

Panipat is a city in Haryana, a north Indian state that shares its borders with Uttar Pradesh and India's capital New Delhi. Haryana Tourism's website gives the following description about this mosque:

> The story of original Babri Masjid is very interesting and lesser known to people. History says that when Babur came to India in 1526, he had to fight a battle against Ibrahim Lodi. When he won the battle, he built a mosque at the site of Panipat as a mark of gratitude. This masjid is original Babri Masjid. This mosque is in the middle of a small garden called Kabuli Bagh and is under protection of the Archaeological Survey of India… The inscription on the mosque states 1528–29, as period of its completion.[44]

Absence of any direct mention of Babur's visit to Ayodhya or construction of any mosque in India in his memoirs has strengthened the arguments that Babur never visited Ayodhya. Some writers have strongly contested the claims about Babur's possible visit to Ayodhya and Mir Baqi getting Babri Masjid constructed.

On the other hand, Dilip Hiro, who has come out with an abridged and edited version of *Babur-Nama* (translated by Annette Susannah Beveridge), has observed:

> Coinciding with AH 934–AH 935, during his return journey to Agra after a successful expedition to eastern India, Babur rested a while in Ayodhya on the banks of the Saryu River, and ordered Mir Baqi to construct a mosque in the town. Known as the Babri Masjid, it would become a controversial monument in the late

---

[43]'About District', *District Sambhal*, https://tinyurl.com/4e6tuptd. Accessed on 24 June 2024.
[44]'The Original Babri Masjid', *Haryana Tourism*, https://tinyurl.com/3ak3a83f. Accessed on 9 August 2024.

1980s when claims were made that it had been built on the site of an earlier temple devoted to Lord Rama.[45]

Ram of Treta Yuga in *Ain-i-Akbari*

A reference to Ayodhya has been made by Akbar's courtier and historian Abu'l Fazl in *Ain-i-Akbari*. He observed:

> Awadh (Ajodhya) is one of the largest cities in India. It is situated in longitude 118°, 6', and latitude 26°, 22'. In ancient times its populous site covered an extent of 148 kos (a unit of distance) in length and 36 in breadth, and it is esteemed one of the holiest places of antiquity. Around the environs of the city, they sift the earth and gold is obtained. It was the residence of Ramchandra who in the Treta age combined in his own person both the spiritual supremacy and kingly office.[46]

Abu'l Fazl, however, did not mention any temple existing there or the spot where Ram was born.

Babur Stories

There are tales galore going around in the villages of Ayodhya claiming that Babur, who is believed to have stayed in the outskirts of Ayodhya, had sent his soldiers to the temple town. These soldiers came across a faqir living on a mound in the Ramkot area of Ayodhya. 'A group of two to three horse mounted soldiers reached the "faqir" who was lying near the "tila" (mound) in Ramkot area of Ayodhya,' said elderly Mohammad Iliyas, a resident of Sahanva village of Ayodhya, in a personal interview.

"'We are the soldiers of Emperor Babur's army," said one of them,' Iliyas said while narrating the tale.

---

[45]Hiro, Dilip (ed.), *Babur Nama, Journal of Emperor Babur*, Penguin Random House, India, 2017, pp. xix–xx.
[46]Abu'l Fazl, *Ain-i-Akbari*, Colonel H.S. Jarret (trans.), Asiatic Society of Bengal, 1891, https://tinyurl.com/bdek7kem. Accessed on 24 June 2024.

'How come you are here?' asked Faqir.

'We are on a round trip to this area. We are soldiers of Emperor Babur. This is our area. We want our emperor to prosper and succeed in all his endeavours.'

Faqir asked the soldiers to tell the Mughal emperor to get a mosque constructed as the place was very sacred. If the emperor constructed the mosque, he would prosper and be successful in all his endeavours. Soldiers went back to Babur and informed him about what the faqir had told them. Babur asked Mir Baqi to construct a mosque at the spot suggested by the faqir.

Iliyas added that Mir Baqi got the mosque constructed on orders of Babur. He, however, contested the claims that any temple was demolished for the construction of the mosque that was once situated at a distance of about 10–15 km from his village.[47]

Another tale points to almost a similar story mentioned earlier. According to it, Babur, during his stay on the outskirts of Ayodhya, met a faqir there. Babur offered some gifts to the faqir who refused to accept them. The latter asked Babur to construct a mosque for him to offer namaz. Babur initially did not agree to the demand, but when the faqir insisted, he asked Mir Baqi to demolish the Ram temple there.[48]

Such tales came to fore after the agitation for the construction of the Ram temple intensified in the mid-eighties. There are tales about the demolition of temples by Mahmud Ghaznavi, including temples in Mathura and the famous Somnath Temple in Gujarat. Mohammad Gori destroyed a number of temples in Varanasi, including the Kashi Vishwanath Temple. Aurangzeb, who is often described as the 'last effective Mughal emperor' is also associated with the demolition of temples in India.[49] He is said to have demolished the Ram temple in Ayodhya.

---

[47]Personal interview with Mohammad Iliyas of Sahanwa village in Ayodhya.
[48]Ibid.
[49]Pandey, Geeta, 'Why Is a Mughal Emperor Who Died 300 Years Ago Being Debated on Social Media?', *BBC*, 21 May 2022, https://tinyurl.com/3kvcupu8. Accessed on 24 June 2024.

There are many evidences which prove that the Svargadvara temple (Ayodhya) was demolished by the order of Aurangzeb. From the *Ayodhya Mahatmya* it appears that this was the most magnificent temple. It does not appear probable that any group of marauders which came to Ayodhya for the demolition of one temple could have another equally important temple at a short distance. Therefore, all the three temples Janamsthan, Svargadvara and Treta ka Thakur were demolished by the same group of iconoclasts. Since there are positive evidences of Tieffenthaler, Mentelle and many Muslim authors that Svargadvara temple was demolished by Aurangzeb, it is but natural to presume that the Janmasthan temple, too, was demolished by him only.[50]

Tales of Resistance

There are tales of resistance against Muslim invaders or how sections of society vowed to protest the demolition of the Ram temple and construction of the Babri Mosque in Ayodhya. Raja Suheldev, the legendary king of Shravasti, had resisted the invasion and killed a Ghaznavid general in a battle in the Bahraich region close to Ayodhya. A tale about the Kshatriyas of Ayodhya region not wearing a *pagri* (headgear worn by Kshatriyas with pride) was also a talking point in some villages of Ayodhya. A report published in the Hindi daily *Dainik Bhaskar* after the Supreme Court pronounced its verdict on the Ram temple issue said that a pagri-distribution programme was organized in some of the villages close to Ayodhya. The report in Hindi was titled 'Kshatriyas of 105 Villages Will Now Wear Pagri and Leather Shoes, Did Not Cover Head for 500 Years to Protest the Attack on Ram Temple'. It pointed out that Suryavanshi Kshatriyas of 105 villages in the region had resolved not to tie a pagri till the decks were cleared for construction of a Ram temple. The Kshatriyas of these 105 villages of Pura Bazar block of Ayodhya, who consider

---

[50]Kishore, Kunal, *Ayodhya Revisited*, Ocean Books, 2016, p. 275.

themselves to be descendants of Lord Rama, had also decided to refrain from using an umbrella to cover their head and wear khadau instead of leather shoes. The Kshatriyas did not cover their heads by wearing a pagri and instead opted for *mori* (a headgear worn around the head without covering the top) while attending wedding ceremonies. Later, the khadau was replaced with non-leather shoes. The report quoted Justice (Retd) D.P. Singh of Allahabad High Court saying that his ancestors had fought to save the temple from attacks of Mughals under the leadership of Thakur Gaj Singh (who was defeated in the fight).[51]

First Indications about Dispute

Such stories indicate that the local people must have been resisting the Ram temple's demolition in one form or the other. The Babri Masjid must have obviously remained a point of discord between the Hindus and Muslims ever since the debate that it may have been constructed by Babur or any of his successors following the demolition of the Ram temple. The first recorded indications of a dispute may be traced back only to the mid-1850s, during the tenure of Nawab Wazid Ali Shah, the last ruler of Awadh. The incident apparently took place in 1853. The British East India Company annexed Awadh on 11 February 1956, deposing Wazid Ali Shah who was exiled to Calcutta (now Kolkata).

> The cause of the occurrence was one of the numerous disputes that have sprung up from time to time between Hindu priests and Musalmans of Ajodhya with regard to the ground on which formerly stood the Janmasthan temple, which was destroyed by Babur and replaced by a mosque. Other mosques had been built there by Aurangzeb and others and some of them had fallen into

---

[51]Upadhyay, Vijay, '105 Gaon ke Kshatriya Ab Pagdi aur Chamreke Jute Pehenenge, Mandir par Hamle ke Virodh mein 500 Saal se Nange Sir Pair Ghoom Rahe The', *Dainik Bhaskar*, https://tinyurl.com/489y5phc. Accessed on 25 June 2024.

decay. The ground, being peculiarly sacred to the Hindus, was at once seized by the *Vairagis* (Hindu ascetics) and others, thus affording a fertile source of friction.[52]

There is another reference about the confrontation between the Vairagis and Muslims in the mid-1850s.

> A serious conflict broke out between the Vairagis and the Muslims at the site of Hanumangarhi in Ayodhya, both claiming it to be a place of worship connected with their respective religions. King Wazid Ali Shah is said to have appointed a committee to investigate this which held a public meeting in Gulab Bari. It appears that among those assembled no one testified to the existence of the mosque. Therefore, the committee unanimously decided the issue in favour of Vairagis.[53]

The report caused concern among the Muslims in Lucknow. A council of action led by Maulvi Amir Ali of Amethi (district Lucknow) was formed, and he was able to mobilize a large crowd. When the Vairagis came to know about this, they began making arrangements to defend the Hanumangarhi site. Wazid Ali Shah consequently ordered for security there. On 7 November 1855, Maulvi Amir Ali started for Rudauli with his followers.

Discordant Notes

P. Carnegy, who was posted as officiating commissioner and settlement officer in Faizabad (now Ayodhya), wrote *Historical Sketch of Tahsil Faizabad and Zillah Fyzabad* in 1870. He has referred to the dispute between Hindus and Muslims in Hanumangarhi and Ram Janmabhoomi area in Ayodhya in 1855. He has observed:

---

[52]*M Siddiq (D) Thr Lrs vs Mahant Suresh Das & Ors*, (2019), CA 10866-10867/2010, p. 1022, https://tinyurl.com/bdfjzf3k. Accessed on 25 August 2024.
[53]Joshi, Esha Basanti (ed.), *Uttar Pradesh District Gazetteers, Government of Uttar Pradesh*, Revenue Department, 1960, pp. 63–4.

The Mohammadans on that occasion actually charged up the steps of Hanumangarhi, but were driven back with considerable loss. The Hindus then followed up this success, and at the third attempt took the Janmasthan at the gate of which 75 Muhammadans are buried in the martyr's grave (*ganj-i-shahid*). Several of the King's regiments were looking on all the time, but their orders were not to interfere. It is said that up to that time the Hindus and Mohammedans alike used to worship in the mosque-temple. Since British rule, a railing has been put up to prevent the disputes, within which in the mosque, the Mohammedans pray, while outside the fence the Hindus have raised a platform on which they make their offering.[54]

Indian Rebellion

This was the time when widespread dissension was growing against the British, who had established their rule in India through the East India Company. The Indian Rebellion of 1857, also called India's First War of Independence was a major uprising that gave signals of prevailing dissent among the masses, and eventually led to transfer of power from the Company to the British crown. The riots that took place around Hanumangarhi and the Ram Janmabhoomi–Babri Mosque area in Ayodhya led to the setting up of a railing made of a grill-brick wall outside the mosque to maintain peace. This bifurcation of the inner courtyard (having the structure of the mosque) and the rest of the area (in the outer courtyard) of the disputed complex has its origin from this dispute. This railing subsequently led to the construction of a *chabutra* (platform) by the Hindus. This platform was called Ram Chabutra and became a place of worship for the Hindus.

A Nihang Sikh (Nihang Singh Faqir Khalsa, resident of Punjab) performed *hawan* (ritual performed by fire) and puja of Guru Gobind Singh inside the mosque and erected a religious symbol there on

---

[54] *M Siddiq (D) Thr Lrs vs Mahant Suresh Das & Ors*, (2019), CA 10866-10867/2010, pp. 688–9, https://tinyurl.com/bdfjzf3k. Accessed on 25 August 2024.

28 November 1858. About 25 Sikhs provided security at the time the rituals were performed.⁵⁵

Nihang Faqir Evicted

On 28 November 1858, the *thanedar* (police station officer) of Oudh, Sheetal Dubey, filed an application accusing Nihang Singh Khalsa of organizing hawan and puja and requested action. A report in *India Today* quoted Dubey's report and said Baba Fakir Singh barged inside the mosque, raising slogans in the glory of the tenth Sikh guru, Guru Gobind Singh, and erected a symbol of 'Sri Bhagwan' (Lord Rama). He also wrote 'Ram Ram' on the walls of the mosque.⁵⁶ On 30 November 1858, Syed Mohammad Khateeb, *muezzin* (official who issues the call to Muslims for prayers) of the mosque, informed that 'Mahant Nihang Singh Faqir' was creating a situation of riot at the Janam Sthan Masjid (mosque at the place of birth). A chabutra had been put up inside the mosque and an idol was placed there. Nihang Singh Faqir was residing within the Masjid Janam Sthan and in spite of being admonished, he continued to insist that 'every place belonged to Nirankar'. Tension continued to rise between both communities. A demand for removal of the platform and restraining the Hindus from causing any interference in offering of prayers in the mosque was subsequently made. There was counter reaction from the Hindus by blowing of conch shells when azaan was recited to summon the Muslim community members for prayers. On 10 December 1858, an order was passed recording that Nihang Singh had been ousted from the site.⁵⁷

On 5 November 1860, the deputy commissioner was requested for removal of the chabutra that had been constructed 'within Babri Masjid

---

⁵⁵Ibid. 64.
⁵⁶Sharma, Rishabh, 'Ram Mandir Consecration: How Nihang Sikhs Started the Temple Movement 165 Years Ago', *India Today*, https://tinyurl.com/42zvyzrk. Accessed on 28 July 2024.
⁵⁷*M Siddiq (D) Thr Lrs vs Mahant Suresh Das & Ors*, (2019), CA 10866-10867/2010, p. 801, https://tinyurl.com/bdfjzf3k. Accessed on 25 August 2024.

Oudh', with the argument that '[b]esides, when the Muezzin recites Azaan, the opposite party begins to blow conch (*shankh/naqoos*). This has never happened before.'[58]

In about 1877, local administration allowed construction of another door for visitors to the outer courtyard in the northern side, in addition to the existing door in the east. The deputy commissioner refused to entertain a complaint against the door opening made in the wall of the Janmasthan, saying that it was necessary. He observed, 'This opening was necessarily to give a separate route on fair days to visitors to the Janmasthan... I marked out the spot for the opening myself so there is no need to depute any Europe officer. This petition is merely an attempt to annoy the Hindu (community) by making it dependent on the pleasure of the mosque people to open or close the 2nd door in which the Mohammedans can have no interest.'[59]

Mahant Raghubar Das Files Suit

The commissioner dismissed an appeal against this order on 13 December 1877. He observed, 'As this door in question has been opened in the interests of public safety, I decline to interfere. Appeal dismissed.'[60] The Muslim parties were apparently not satisfied. The *mutwalli* of the mosque, Mohammad Asghar, instituted a suit number 374/943 of 1882 against Mahant Raghubar Das of Nirmohi Akhara claiming rent for use of the chabutra and *takht* (wooden bench) near the door of Babri Masjid and also for organizing the Kartik Mela, or on the occasion of Ram Navami. This suit was dismissed on 18 June 1883. Mahant Raghubar Das later instituted a suit in the court of the Munsif, Faizabad, on 29 January 1885 calling himself 'Mahant Janmasthan at Ayodhya', and urged the court to restrain the administration from causing any obstruction in the way of construction of a temple over the chabutra measuring 17 × 21 feet. Das said that a *charan paduka* was

---
[58]Ibid. 66.
[59]Ibid. 67.
[60]Ibid.

affixed on the chabutra and a small temple built next to it was being worshipped. He also said that the deputy commissioner of Faizabad obstructed the construction of a temple there following objections from Muslims in April 1883.

Mohammad Asghar, as mutawalli of the mosque who was impleaded as the second defendant, filed a statement on 22 December 1885, saying that Babur had created a *waqf* (an Islamic endowment of property in a trust used for religious and charitable purposes) by constructing a masjid, and the word 'Allah' was inscribed above the door. Babur was also said to have declared a grant for its maintenance. This suit was dismissed on 24 December 1885. Mahant Raghubar Das filed an appeal against the decision of the trial court. Mohammad Asghar filed cross-objections. In a judgement in March 1886, the district judge dismissed the appeal observing it was 'most unfortunate' that the mosque was built on land held especially sacred by the Hindus. The district judge further observed that since the construction had been made 358 years ago, it was too late in the day to reverse the process. The judicial commissioner of Oudh on 1 November 1886 dismissed another (second) appeal, observing that it was inappropriate to disturb the status quo, especially when a mosque had been in existence for over 350 years.[61]

Time for Action

Another communal incident in 1934 caused damage to the mosque, following which the administration sanctioned repair work and renovation of the damaged structure. Arrangements were made for commencement of namaz after the completion of repair work. A fine was imposed on 'the Hindus' for the damage caused to the mosque. This did not work as a deterrent, and the situation did not go back to normal in the coming years in Ayodhya. After the riots of 1934, Mahant Ramcharan Das instituted a suit against Raghunath Das and others pertaining to the properties claimed by Nirmohi Akhara,

---
[61]Ibid. 68–71.

describing Ram Chabutra as the Janmabhoomi mandir. Nirmohi Akhara is a prominent Hindu religious order of the Vaishnavite sect. This suit, a dispute between the Nirmohis (Nirmohi Akhara), was disposed of by a compromise on 4 June 1942.[62] Another important development took place with a litigation between Shias and Sunnis over ownership of Babri Masjid. This litigation was decided on 30 March 1946 with a trial court declaring Babri Masjid as Sunni Waqf Board's property. The grievance of the Shias, as stated in their notice dated 11 April 1945, was that the commissioner of waqfs included Babri Masjid in the list of Sunni mosques. The suit was dismissed by holding that the mosque was indeed a Sunni mosque.[63]

A series of events took place in Ayodhya in 1949. A deed was executed by the Nirmohi Akhara to reduce, in writing, its customs on 19 March 1949, and it claimed that the management of the Ram temple was vested in the Nirmohi Akhara. The deed document read:

> Temple of Janam Bhoomi is situated in Mohalla Ram Ghat of City, Ayodhya which is under the 'Baithak' (seat) of this Akhara and its whole management is trust upon to this Akhara. It stands in name of Mahant of Akhara as Mahant and Manager. This is the best well reputed, moorty of worship temple of Ayodhya. Being the birthplace of Lord Rama, it is the main temple of Ayodhya. The deity of Shri Ram Lalaji is installed there and there are other deities also.[64]

The dispute continued with the passage of time. It was time for action. The Hindu parties began working on formulating a new strategy to bring about a complete change at Rama's birthplace in Ayodhya. India's partition and Mahatma Gandhi's assassination widened the gulf between the Hindus and Muslims.

---

[62] Ibid. 814.
[63] Ibid. 815.
[64] Ibid. 73.

3

Pent-Up Emotions

India gained independence on 15 August 1947. Its partition into two independent dominions, India and Pakistan, led to large-scale communal violence. The communal divide caused displacement of a population of 10–20 million people, and left between 200,000 and 1 million people dead (including those who died of ailments) in the refugee camps.[1] Both parts suffered deep scars.

The sharp division existing between Hindus and Muslims widened further. Ayodhya was no exception to this yawning gulf. Hindus there began looking for opportunities to get control over Ram Janmabhoomi, the birthplace of Lord Rama in Ayodhya, where Babri Masjid had been erected in the name of the Mughal dynasty's founder Zahir al-Din Muhammad Babur.

Passions Run High

Hindus demanded that Ram Janmabhoomi be handed over to them. Muslims, apprehending trouble, consistently exerted pressure on the authorities to ensure that the status quo was maintained. Passions ran high on both sides.

The premier of the United Provinces (now Uttar Pradesh), Pt Govind Ballabh Pant (the premier's post was renamed as chief minister [CM] later in 1950) was well aware of the ground situation in Ayodhya and Uttar Pradesh at large. Pant gave out conflicting signals. He assured

---

[1] 'Partition: Why Was British India Divided 75 Years Ago?', *BBC*, 15 August 2022, https://tinyurl.com/4fjmunp6. Accessed on 24 June 2024.

Muslims that the state government would not disturb the status quo in Ayodhya. At the same time, he appeared sympathetic towards the demand of Hindus. Pant's acts of omission and commission hinted that he may have been truly sympathetic to the Hindu side. Harold A. Gould, an author and American anthropologist, observed:

> Pant rejected the attempts of several deputations of local Muslims to win assurances that the United Provinces government would not disturb the prevailing religious status quo. Simultaneously, he intimated that his sympathies really lay with the Hindu side of the dispute, in part by supporting the authority and continued presence in Faizabad (now Ayodhya) of its current deputy commissioner K.K. Nayar, who was notoriously pro-Hindu, a member of the Rashtriya Swayamsevak Sangh (RSS), and busily engaged in helping to lay the foundation for the rise of the Bharatiya Jana Sangh (BJS) in both the district (of Ayodhya) and the province.[2]

An impression that Pant was being gentle towards Hindus can be drawn from his inaction, which becomes clear in the exchange of letters quoted later in this chapter.

The Hindu Card

The Congress played the Hindu card to the optimum to defeat socialist leader Acharya Narendra Dev in the by-election to Faizabad (including Ayodhya city) for the seat of the United Provinces legislative assembly in June 1948. Acharya had resigned from the Congress in 1948 after his long association with the party since 1916. Also known as the doyen of Indian socialism, he was considered to be close to India's first PM, Jawaharlal Nehru. The Congress chose to appoint Gopal Narain Saxena to oversee the campaign against Dev. Saxena was a Congress leader from Sitapur, about 220 km northwest of Ayodhya. He knew

---

[2]Gould, Harold A., *Grass Roots Politics in India: A Century of Political Evolution in Faizabad District*, Oxford and IBH Publishing Company, 1994, p. 181.

the Congress leaders of Faizabad well. The Congress initially decided to field Siddheshwari Prasad as its candidate from the seat; the party, however, changed its mind later.

The CM of the United Provinces, Congress' Govind Ballabh Pant, a masterful tactician and a known sympathizer of the communal Hindu Mahasabha, changed the official candidate at the last minute in the June 1948 by-election for the Faizabad seat. This had become necessary to defeat the socialist leader Acharya Narendra Dev, Pant's rival and someone who enjoyed Nehru's confidence more than Pant.[3]

The Congress's choice fell on Raghavendra Sheshappa, alias Baba Raghav Das, a saintly politician from Deoria district in eastern Uttar Pradesh who led an ascetic life.[4] Das, who originally was from Maharashtra, joined the Congress in 1920. His knowledge of Hinduism and Buddhism brought him a following among the masses in the area.

The Congress's move to field Das was a major shift in the party's way of politics. Gould wrote: 'This was a critical turning point in the evolution of Congress politics, not because the ethnic variable had never been employed for political purposes before but because this was an explicit decision to do so in the context of electoral politics made by party leaders who had heretofore loudly condemned any resort to "casteism and communalism" as morally reprehensible.'[5]

Tulsi, the Sacred Connect in the By-Election

The Congress leaders thought a shift in the ways of the party's politics was necessary. Pant apparently did not approve of Acharya Narendra

---

[3]Singh, Valay, *Ayodhya: City of Faith, City of Discord*, Aleph Book Company, New Delhi, 2018, p. 185.
[4]*Selected Works of Jawaharlal Nehru: 15 November 1949–8 April 1950*, Series 2, Vol. 14, Part 1, Jawaharlal Nehru Memorial Fund, p. 445, https://tinyurl.com/4p47k6mp. Accessed on 28 June 2024.
[5]Gould, Harold A., *Grass Roots Politics in India: A Century of Political Evolution in Faizabad District*, Oxford and IBH Publishing Company, 1994, p. 179.

Dev's proximity to Nehru. He wanted to make sure that Dev was defeated in the polls. A strategy was worked out to defeat him. Pant extensively campaigned for Baba Raghav Das, made several visits to Faizabad, and made pointed references indicating that Dev did not follow Hindu customs. The Congress candidate used distribution of tulsi leaves, considered sacred by the Hindus, to connect with the Hindu saints and masses in Ayodhya. Gould wrote further about Pant:

> Pandit Pant made several visits to Faizabad during which he pointedly catered to the prejudices and political whims of the religious communities in Ayodhya. In his speeches, Pant repeatedly declared that Narendra Dev does not believe in lord Ram Chandra and does not wear the 'chhot', or tuft of hair, worn by all devout Hindus... On his part, once Baba Raghava Das commenced campaigning in the city, he distributed 'tulsi' leaves. No opportunity was lost to point out the fact that both the Baba and Pandit Nehru were devout Brahmans.[6]

The Congress's by-poll strategy worked perfectly in Ayodhya. Das won the by-election and defeated Acharya.

The Ayodhya Strategy

Unfolding developments, amid rising communal tension, provided an apt environment and opportunity to Hindu leaders to execute a well-planned strategy to reclaim Ram Janmabhoomi in Ayodhya. A series of events preceded the execution of the strategy that the Hindu Mahasabha leaders, along with some local saints, had worked out to achieve their objective. The Hindu Mahasabha realized what more could be achieved there:

> On 14 August 1949, two-and-a-half months after it resumed its political activities, the United Provincial Hindu Mahasabha passed a resolution reminding the Congress of the double

---

[6]Ibid. 181.

standards of the government regarding the Somnath temple on the one hand and the temples in Ayodhya, Mathura and Kashi on the other... As the atmosphere started heating up, the Hindu Mahasabha opted for the back seat and the All India Ramayan Mahasabha (AIRM), a cultural organization formed and controlled by the local Hindu Mahasabha leaders of Ayodhya, took over its activities. While Ramchandra Paramhans was the general secretary of the AIRM, Gopal Singh Visharad was its joint secretary and Abhiram Das the organization secretary.[7]

Baba Abhiram Das, a Vairagi from Bihar's Darbhanga district, was the one who took the idol of Ram Lalla beneath the central dome of Babri Mosque on the intervening night of 22–23 December 1949.[8] This was one of the major turning points in the movement supporting the Ram temple. A nine-day *Akhand Path* (uninterrupted recitation) of the Ramcharitamanas, a popular version of the Ramayana, had been organized ahead of the placement of the idol of Ram Lalla (Rama in child form) on the intervening night of 22–23 December.

> The Ramayan Mahasabha stepped up its mobilization of the naga Vairagis residing in Hanumangarhi and announced a nine-day recitation of the *Ramcharitmanas*, a popular version of the Ramayan, starting on 20 October 1949, the day of Hanuman Janmotsava ... there was nothing unusual about it, except that in 1949 it was organized on a much larger scale ... Only on the concluding day of the *navahpaath* (nine-day recitation)—on 28 October 1949—did something unusual happen. In the evening of that day, the Ramayan Mahasabha organized a public meeting in Hanumangarhi...Not many in the audience could have realized then that the Hindu Mahasabhaites present in the meeting had rolled out a blue print for capturing the Babri Masjid ...

---

[7]Jha, Krishna, and Dhirendra K. Jha, *Ayodhya: The Dark Night-The Secret History of Rama's Appearance in Babri Masjid*, HarperCollins Publishers, Uttar Pradesh, 2016, p. 47.
[8]Ibid. 69–75.

Significantly, it was none other than Congress leader Baba Raghav Das who moved the proposal to organize a massive navahpaath in Ram Chabutra on the auspicious day of Ram Vivah (falling on 24 November 1949).[9]

Baba Raghav Das, Swami Karpatri Maharaj and the Hindu Mahasabha leader Mahant Digvijay Nath were three prominent leaders who worked to organize the recitation under the aegis of the Akhil Bharatiya Ramayana Mahasabha. Baba Raghav Das's pro-Hindu stance was already established in the region after the Faizabad by-election. Karpatri Maharaj, in 1948, founded the Akhil Bhartiya Ram Rajya Parishad Party, which was associated with the movement of the construction of the Ram temple. Mahant Digvijay Nath, the chief priest of Gorakhnath Math—a temple of Nath monastic tradition situated in Gorakhpur about 137 km east of Ayodhya—had joined the freedom struggle and mobilized the people against the British government in 1920. He worked for the cause of the Ram temple in Ayodhya and was a leading force of the movement. The *Hindustan Times* in a report observed that the Gorakhnath Math played a big role in keeping the Ram temple movement alive.

> Digvijay Nath, who became mahant in 1935 not only made the math a centre of right-wing political activities, but also became a leading light of the temple movement. After joining the Hindu Mahasabha in 1937, he started mobilizing the Hindu community for the Ram temple in Ayodhya. He led a team of volunteers to Ayodhya in 1949, held a meeting with then Raja (Maharaj) of Balrampur, Pateshwari Prasad Singh and Swami Karpatri Maharaj, a prominent seer.[10]

Mahant Digvijay Nath's successors Mahant Avaidyanath and now Mahant Adityanath (CM of Uttar Pradesh) have played a pivotal role in

---

[9]Ibid. 47–9.
[10]Singh, Rajesh Kumar, 'Tracing the Role of Yogi Adityanath and Gorakhnath Math in Ram Temple Movement', *Hindustan Times*, 3 August 2020, https://tinyurl.com/4cmca66b. Accessed on 25 June 2024.

pushing the cause of the Ram temple. Others who pushed the agenda of the Ram temple forward and executed well-worked-out plans there included two officers of Faizabad: K.K. Nayar and Guru Dutt Singh. Nayar, an ICS officer, was a native of Alappuzha district of the southern state of Kerala. He was posted as deputy commissioner-cum-district magistrate (DM), Faizabad. Singh, an officer of the Provincial Civil Service, was posted as Faizabad city magistrate at the same time. Singh was a graduate from Allahabad University.[11]

Grand Ram Temple Proposed

K.K. Nayar came in close contact with the Maharaj when he was posted as the DM, Gonda, in northwest of Ayodhya, in 1946; he played tennis with the latter. He, along with Mahant Digvijay Nath and Karpatri Maharaj, attended a yajna organized by the Maharaj in early 1947. He was briefed about the efforts being made by the Hindus to take back Ram Janmabhoomi where Babri Masjid stood. A preliminary discussion was held about the next course of action in Ayodhya. This was the time efforts were being made to construct a Ram temple at the Ram Chabutra, which was in possession of Hindus.

Nayar was sent to Faizabad as the new DM on 1 June 1949. *The Wall Street Journal* in an article titled 'Ayodhya, the Battle for India's Soul: The Complete Story' has quoted Guru Dutt Singh's son Guru Basant Singh saying a meeting was held at his residence and attended by Nayar and Abhiram Das in mid-1949.

> The Singhs (Guru Dutt Singh and family) moved into Lorpur House, a yellow, British-era mansion. Starting in mid-1949, Mr Singh, Mr Nayar, Abhiram Das and other local officials met there to plan how to install Ram in the Babri Masjid, according to Mr Singh's son (Guru Basant Singh).

---

[11]Pokharel, Krishna, and Paul Beckett, 'Ayodhya, the Battle for India's Soul: The Complete Story', *The Wall Street Journal*, 10 December 2012, https://tinyurl.com/3ys863ss. Accessed on 2 August 2024.

As the family's only child, Guru Basant Singh was then about 15 years old. He said he was in charge of serving tea and water at the meetings and at times hid behind the door to listen in on the planning.

The meetings were held in secret after sunset, he said. A Hindu servant was posted at the door with instructions to tell any visitors that his father was resting.

His version of events is confirmed by Mahant Satyendra Das, one of Abhiram Das's surviving disciples, who is now the government-appointed head priest at the site of the mosque.[12]

Changes Noticed

Hectic activity was witnessed in Ayodhya for a few weeks ahead of the move to place the idol. A representation was made to the then government of United Provinces requesting construction of the Ram temple on Ram Chabutra. Kehar Singh, deputy secretary to Uttar Pradesh government, sought a report from Nayar on the issue on 20 July 1949.[13]

Nayar asked Guru Dutt Singh to visit the spot and submit a report. Singh submitted his report to the former on 10 October 1949, observing that the mosque and temple were situated side by side and permission could be given for the construction of a Ram temple.[14]

Some senior district officials were watching the developments. When Kripal Singh, superintendent of police, Faizabad, went to the spot of the Babri Masjid and Ram Janmabhoomi, he noticed some changes in the area that included construction of some *hawan kund*s (sacred fire pits). He wrote a letter to Nayar on 29 November 1949, referring to his visit to the spot of the Babri Masjid and Ram Janmabhoomi, and said that there was a move to construct a large

---

[12]Ibid.
[13]Jha, Krishna, 'Ayodhya: The Villain Nobody Knows', *Open*, 6 December 2012, https://tinyurl.com/ycx88b86. Accessed on 2 August 2024.
[14]Ibid.

hawan kund where *kirtan* (devotional singing) and yajna were to be held on Puranmashi (full moon marking division of two lunar fortnights in a month). This was apparently yet another step to achieve the main objective. He said several thousand Hindus, Vairagis and sadhus from outside would participate and the chanting may continue till Puranmashi. 'The plan appears to be to surround the mosque in such a way that entry for the Muslims will be very difficult and ultimately, they might be forced to abandon the mosque. There is a strong rumour that on Puranmashi the Hindus will try to force entry into the mosque with the object of installing a deity,' said Kripal Singh.[15]

Threat to Mosque

Waqf inspector Mohd Ibrahim, in a report to the secretary of the Masjid on 10 December 1949, said that there was apprehension of danger to the mosque, as Muslims were being prevented from offering Isha (the namaz at night) at the mosque due to fear of Hindus and Sikhs.[16] Nayar also wrote a letter to Uttar Pradesh Home Secretary Govind Narayan on 16 December 1949, stating that a 'magnificent temple' at the site, constructed by Vikramaditya, had been demolished by Babur for the construction of the mosque known as Babri Masjid.[17] He pointed out that the building material of the temple had been used to construct the mosque, and added that a long time had elapsed before Hindus were again allowed the possession of a site therein, 'at the corner of two walls'.[18] He said that a police picket was deployed there on 12 November 1949 and added that Vairagis resented association of Muslims with the shrine, and that some grave mounds were partially destroyed by them in October–November 1949.

---

[15]*M Siddiq (D) Thr Lrs vs Mahant Suresh Das & Ors*, (2019), CA 10866-10867/2010, p. 74, https://tinyurl.com/bdfjzf3k. Accessed on 25 August 2024.
[16]Ibid.
[17]Ibid. 74–5.
[18]Ibid.

Muslims, mostly of Faizabad, have been exaggerating these happenings and giving currency to the report that graves are being demolished systematically on a large scale. This is entirely a canard inspired apparently by a desire to prevent Hindus from securing in this area possession or rights of a larger character than have so far been enjoyed. Muslim anxiety on this score was heightened by the recent Navami Ramayan Path, a devotional reading of Ramayan by thousands of Hindus for nine days in a stretch. This period covered a Friday on which Muslims who went to say their prayers at the mosque were escorted to and from safely by the Police. As far as I have been able to understand the situation the Muslims of Ayodhya proper are far from agitated over this issue with the exception of one Anisur Rahman who frequently sends frantic messages giving the impression that the Babri Masjid and graves are in imminent danger of demolition.[19]

Ram Lalla's Idol Is Placed

Nayar's communication to Govind Narayan apparently was an assurance about there being no threat to the mosque. This was indicative of Nayar's obvious plans that appeared to be a prelude to the events scheduled for the night of 22–23 December 1949.

Mahant Digvijay Nath was present in Ayodhya for the Akhand Path well before the intervening night of 22–23 December 1949, when the idol of Ram Lalla was placed inside the central dome of Babri Masjid, called the sanctum sanctorum. Baba Raghav Das was also present for the ceremony.

The Wall Street Journal quoted in its story that Abhiram Das told Satyendra Das in 1958 that some of the top district officials, including Nayar and Singh, were working with the ascetic on how the idol might be placed inside Babri Masjid, which was locked and guarded.

---

[19]Ibid. 75.

One guard, a Hindu, took the afternoon and evening shift. Another guard, a Muslim, took night watch, Mr (Satyendra) Das said he was told.

The Hindu guard agreed to let Abhiram Das and a small group of sadhus sneak into the mosque with an idol of Rama during his watch, Abhiram Das told his disciple, adding: 'We took the Hindu guard into confidence by telling him about the virtues he will earn by being part of this extremely holy work.'

The Hindu guard would then hand over the keys to the Muslim guard at midnight, as usual, Mr Das said the sadhu told him.

On the other hand, the Muslim guard was 'briefed' by Guru Dutt Singh and K.K. [Nayar] 'what he had to do', according to Guru Dutt Singh's son. He was threatened with his life if he did not cooperate, Mr Singh's son said.[20]

It was about midnight of 22–23 December 1949. Abhiram Das, along with some others, entered the Babri Masjid with an idol of Ram Lalla.

In the chill of the north Indian winter, the Hindu guard ended his shift that night. But before he left, as planned, Abhiram Das and two other sadhus gained access, Abhiram Das told his disciple.

When the Muslim guard came for his round of duty, the Hindu guard handed over the keys. Around 3 a.m., an auspicious time in Hinduism, Abhiram Das and the other sadhus started ringing small bells inside the mosque. They lit a lamp and sang to the tiny idol that was placed on the pulpit under the central dome: 'God appeared, compassionate and benevolent,' the sadhu told his disciple.[21]

This act of installation of the idol proved to be a milestone and also a turning point in the then nearly 421-year dispute over the Ram

---

[20]Pokharel, Krishna, and Paul Beckett, 'Ayodhya, the Battle for India's Soul: The Complete Story', *The Wall Street Journal*, 10 December 2012, https://tinyurl.com/3ys863ss. Accessed on 2 August 2024.
[21]Ibid.

Janmabhoomi–Babri Masjid structure. The book *Gita Press and the Making of Hindu India*, authored by Akshaya Mukul, has quoted noted Hindi journalist and RSS insider Ram Bahadur Rai to point towards an RSS connection with the sudden appearance of the idol in Ayodhya.

> Rai wrote that he had been told by RSS leader Nanaji Deshmukh that the idol had been introduced into Ayodhya complex after holy immersion in the Saryu river … When Rai expressed a wish to record this fact, Deshmukh did not agree, though he maintained it was the truth. Deshmukh's claim has not found any mention in scores of published works on Ayodhya, but points at a web of conspiracy whose threads are yet to be untangled.[22]

Chanting Begins

The chanting of couplets '*Bhaye pragat kripala, Deen Dayala* (The God who bestows kindness and compassion has appeared)' continued to celebrate what they called the appearance of Lord Rama at the spot under the central dome of the disputed mosque. The 'mysterious' emergence of the idol became the talk of the town by early morning.

A large crowd gathered there amid the chanting of religious couplets and the puja of Lord Rama. The Vishva Hindu Parishad (VHP), in the mid-1980s, put up a display board at the workshop near Karsevakpuram in Ayodhya, narrating a story about the 'appearance' of the idol of the deity. It said that Abul Barkat, the Muslim guard on duty that night, saw the whole area under the central dome illuminated with a golden light as Lord Rama appeared there.

The first information report (FIR) lodged under Sections 147, 295 and 448 of the Indian Penal Code (IPC) for rioting, intentional defilement to a sacred place, and trespassing at 7.00 a.m. on 23 December 1949 records that a crowd of 50–60 people broke the locks and placed the idol inside the sanctum sanctorum. Ram Deo Dubey, the sub-inspector

---

[22] Mukul, Akshaya, *Gita Press and the Making of Hindu India*, HarperCollins Publishers India, 2017, p. 320.

in charge of Ayodhya police station who lodged the FIR, said that the names of Hindu deities were inscribed on the walls, and about 5,000 people had gathered there to perform the chanting thereafter. It named Abhiram Das, Ram Shukul Das, Sheo Darshan Das and about 50 or 60 persons for trespassing and desecration of the mosque by installation of the idol therein. The Ayodhya plan execution worked to perfection. A series of letters were exchanged at various levels.

Nehru Gets Upset

A senior police officer reached the site in Ayodhya with a message from Bhagwan Sahay, Uttar Pradesh chief secretary, in Lucknow, to K.K. Nayar, deputy commissioner, Faizabad, by about 2.30 p.m. In his message to Nayar, the chief secretary conveyed that no change could be allowed at the spot without consent of both the communities. He asked for minimum use of force, if necessary, to deal with the issue. He, however, left the final decision about handling of the situation to Nayar.

Prime Minister Jawaharlal Nehru was upset when he came to know about the unfolding developments, and so was Sardar Vallabh Bhai Patel, the deputy PM. Nehru, who was then in New Delhi, sent a telegram to Govind Ballabh Pant, premier of the United Provinces, Lucknow, on 26 December 1949: 'I am disturbed at developments at Ayodhya. Earnestly hope you will personally interest yourself in this matter. Dangerous example being set there which will have bad consequences.'[23]

Nayar Opposes Removal of Idol

A number of meetings were held in Lucknow and Ayodhya on a day-to-day basis to take stock of the unfolding situation. Nayar resisted

---

[23]*Selected Works of Jawaharlal Nehru: 15 November 1949 – 8 April 1950*, Series 2, Vol. 14, Part 1, Jawaharlal Nehru Memorial Fund, p. 445, https://tinyurl.com/4p47k6mp. Accessed on 28 June 2024.

the state government's directives to deal with the situation strictly and remove the idol. He said any action using force might lead to loss of lives. On 26 December 1949, he wrote to Bhagwan Sahay, saying:

> Installation of the idol was carried out in the night between 22nd and 23rd instant. It was an act of which there was no forewarning. The last CID report which I received regarding Ayodhya affairs reached me on the 22nd. Neither in that report nor in any previous report was it ever indicated that there was a move to install an idol in the mosque either surreptitiously or by force....
>
> The question of removing the idol is not one which Superintendent of Police and I can agree with or carry out on our initiative. I would, if the government decided to remove the idol at any cost, request that I be relieved and replaced by an officer who may be able to see in that solution a merit which I cannot discern.[24]

Nayar was not willing to remove the idol under any circumstances. He had categorically told the state government that he be removed from the deputy commissioner's post if it insisted on the removal of the idol. He wrote another letter to Sahay on 27 December 1949, and categorically said that he was not ready to shift the idol on his own initiative; doing so would ignite flames of communal violence:

> Today rumour is rife that removal of the idol is being contemplated and Hindus are reported to have decided to attack Muslim habitations and burn and pillage if this ... it will not be possible to protect the lives of the Muslims in all places if the storm breaks out, would it be possible to protect even my officers and their property. I have so far failed to find any Hindu even among Congressmen who is ready to support the move for removal of the idol.

---

[24]Noorani, A.G., (ed.), *The Babri Masjid Questions 1528-2003*, Tulika Books, New Delhi, 2003, pp. 212–14.

With the feeling in this state a step of this character would be like setting a lighted match to a powder magazine and I certainly cannot contemplate the results with equanimity or feeling of justification.[25]

Nehru Plans to Visit Ayodhya

Nehru referred to the issue in a letter to C. Rajagopalachari, Governor-General of India, on 7 January 1950. Nehru, in his letter, said,

> My dear Rajaji,
>
> I wrote to Pantji last night about Ayodhya and sent this letter with a person who was going to Lucknow. Pantji telephoned to me later. He said he was very worried, and he was personally looking into this matter. He intended to take action, but he wanted to get some well-known Hindus to explain the situation to people in Ayodhya first. I told him on the telephone about your letter to me, which you sent this morning. Vallabhbhai is going to Lucknow the day after tomorrow at Pantji's request. This is in connection with the elections to Parliament.
>
> Yours, Jawaharlal.[26]

Nehru was keeping an eye over the situation from New Delhi and was ready to visit Ayodhya if the situation so warranted. He wrote a letter to G.B. Pant on 5 February 1950, saying,

> My dear Pantji,
>
> I shall be glad if you will keep me informed of the Ayodhya situation. As you know, I attached great importance to it and to its repercussions on all-India affairs and more especially Kashmir.

---

[25]Ibid. 215.
[26]*Selected Works of Jawaharlal Nehru: 15 November 1949–8 April 1950*, Series 2, Vol. 14, Part 1, Jawaharlal Nehru Memorial Fund, p. 445, https://tinyurl.com/4p47k6mp. Accessed on 28 June 2024.

I suggested to you when you were here last that, if necessary, I would go to Ayodhya. If you think this should be done, I shall try to find the date, although I am terribly busy.

Yours sincerely, Jawaharlal Nehru.[27]

Time Not Ripe for Nehru's Visit

A note given along with this letter points out that Pant replied to Nehru's letter on 9 February 1950 and said that there was no marked change in the Ayodhya situation. He said Muslims wanted to move the High Court on the issue. Pant informed Nehru about the transfer of local officials. About Nehru's visit to Ayodhya, he wrote, 'I would have myself requested you to visit Ayodhya if time were ripe.'[28] Deputy PM Sardar Patel, who was also keeping an eye over unfolding developments, wrote to Pant and referred to the telegram sent by Nehru and the discussions held on the issue during the visit that Patel undertook to Lucknow. He was concerned about the communal situation. He was clear about the fallout of the incident and felt the issue should be resolved amicably.

Patel in his letter to Pant on 9 January 1950 wrote:

My dear Pantji,

The Prime Minister has already sent you a telegram expressing concern over the developments in Ayodhya. I spoke to you about it in Lucknow. I feel that the controversy has been raised at a most opportune time both from the point of view of the country at large and of your own province in particular. The wider communal issues have only been recently resolved to the mutual satisfaction of the various communities. So far as the Muslims are concerned, they are just settling down to their new loyalties ... In your own province, the communal problem has always been a difficult one.

---

[27]Ibid.
[28]Ibid.

I think it has been one of the outstanding achievements of your administration that, despite many upsetting factors, communal relations have generally improved very considerably since 1946.[29]

Patel Against Resolving the Dispute Forcibly

Patel, in the same letter to Pant, asked that the issue should be resolved amicably with the spirit of toleration and goodwill between the Hindus and the Muslims.

We have our own difficulties in the United Provinces organizationally and administratively as a result of group formations. It would be most unfortunate if we allowed any group advantage to be made on this issue. On all these grounds, therefore, I feel that the issue is one which should be resolved amicably in a spirit of mutual toleration and goodwill between the two communities.

I realize there is a great deal of sentiment behind the move which has taken place. At the same time, such matters can only be resolved peacefully if we take the willing consent of the Muslim community with us. There can be no question of resolving such a dispute by force. In that case, the forces of law and order will have to maintain peace at all costs. I am, therefore, quite convinced that the matter should not be made such a live issue and that the present inopportune controversies should be resolved by peaceful (methods) and accomplished facts should not be allowed to stand in the way of an amicable settlement. I hope your efforts in this direction will meet the success.

Yours sincerely,

Vallabhbhai Patel[30]

---

[29]Das, Durga (ed.), *Sardar Patel's Correspondence, 1945–50, Vol. 9: Political Controversies—Refugees from East Bengal Territorial Integration of Princely States*, Navajivan Publishing House, 1974, pp. 310–11, https://tinyurl.com/4beas6d9. Accessed on 28 June 2024.
[30]Ibid.

Pant, replying to Patel on 13 January 1950, said that efforts to find a peaceful solution were ongoing and he was hopeful of a solution. He stated, 'I have to thank you for your letter about the Ayodhya affair. It will be of great help to us here. Efforts to set matters right in a peaceful manner are still continuing and there is a reasonable chance of success, but things are still in a fluid state, and it will be hazardous to say more at this stage. With best regards, Yours sincerely, GB Pant.'[31]

Pant's letter indicates that the communal atmosphere continued to be fragile across the country. Nayar's refusal to follow the directives to remove the idol from under the central dome was taken seriously. The plan to shift the idol, however, was shelved. Others who opposed the removal of the idol included Congress member of legislative assembly (MLA) from Faizabad, Baba Raghav Das.

Receiver Appointed

The additional city magistrate (ACM), Faizabad, ordered attachment of the disputed site on 29 December 1949 on apprehension of breach of peace. He appointed Priya Datt Ram, chairman of the Faizabad municipal board and leader of the Kayastha Party, as the receiver. Priya Datt was considered close to Gopal Narain Saxena, also known as Pallanji, whom the Congress had chosen to handle the campaign against Acharya Narendra Dev in the by-election to Faizabad legislative assembly seat.[32] The ACM asked an Ayodhya station officer to carry out the attachment. He ordered Priya Datt to take charge and arrange for the care of the property in dispute, and asked the receiver to submit a plan for management of the property for approval.

Priya Datt took charge of the property on 5 January 1950. The Hindu Mahasabha general secretary V.G. Deshpande, meanwhile, undertook visits to Ayodhya more than once. A circular of the Hindu Mahasabha was sent to all its activists calling them to celebrate Ram

---

[31] Ibid. 311–12.
[32] Gould, Harold A., *Grass Roots Politics in India: A Century of Political Evolution in Faizabad District*, Oxford and IBH Publishing Company, 1994, p. 179.

Navami on 27 March 1950 as Ram Janmabhoomi Day. This circular was followed by a personal note from Deshpande 'implying that the "beautiful structure" of the temple was still standing, although the only remains attributable to it were 14 carved pillars in the fabric of the mosque.'[33]

Ram Prakat Utsav

Ayodhya subsequently started celebrating Ram Prakat Utsav to mark the anniversary of the 'appearance' of the idol. Nayar, who was placed under suspension and reinstated later, resigned from service and joined the BJS. In 1965, he was elected MLA and in 1967, Member of Parliament (MP) from Bahraich on a Jan Sangh ticket.[34] His wife Shakuntala Nayar was elected an MP from Gonda in 1952 on a Hindu Mahasabha ticket.[35] Guru Dutt Singh, who also resigned from service later, joined the BJS and became its Faizabad district chief. At the same time, attempts to foment communal trouble continued in Ayodhya. Several preventive arrests were made, and those arrested included Ayodhya Hindu Mahasabha secretary Gopal Singh Visharad.[36] Visharad was the first to file a legal suit before a civil judge in Faizabad on 16 January 1950 as a Hindu worshipper. He contended that he was not being allowed to enter the disputed site to offer worship. He urged the court to allow him to offer prayers at the birthplace of Lord Rama. On 5 December 1950, Mahant Ramchandra Das Paramhans filed another suit before the civil judge, Faizabad, seeking the same relief as sought by Visharad. However, this suit was withdrawn on 18 September 1990.

Visharad was a regular visitor to the then disputed site to worship the idol of Ram Lalla that had been placed under the central dome

---

[33]Jaffrelot, Christophe, *The Hindu Nationalist Movement and Indian Politics (1925–1990)*, Penguin Books India Ltd, 1996, p. 95.
[34]Ibid. 93.
[35]Ibid. 94.
[36]Ibid. 95.

on the intervening night of 22–23 December 1949. Some security officials stopped Visharad from entering the disputed site to perform puja where the idol was placed. So, Visharad filed a plea before the Faizabad court for his right to perform worship at the site. He urged the court that the idol should not be removed from the site. The court issued an *ex-parte* injunction. On 19 January 1950, the court modified the injunction preventing removal of the idol and interference in worshipping. The trial court confirmed the injunction on 3 March 1951. The Allahabad High Court dismissed the appeal against the order of the trial court.

The Nirmohi Akhara, an order of Hindu saints, filed another suit on 17 December 1959 for getting the charge and management of the temple. The Uttar Pradesh Sunni Central Waqf Board filed a suit on 18 December 1961, urging the court to declare the disputed area a public mosque and for removal of the idol. Another suit was filed by the deity Lord Rama (Bhagwan Shri Ram Lalla Virajman at Shri Ram Janmbhumi, Ayodhya) and the birthplace of the deity (Asthan Shri Ram Janam Bhumi, Ayodhya) on 1 July 1989 through a 'next friend' for the purpose of declaring the entire premises of Ram Janmabhoomi as belonging to the deities and preventing any interference in construction of a Ram temple. The Indian law recognizes a deity, such as Ram Lalla Virajman, as an individual entity capable of legal action. Deoki Nandan Agarwal, a retired High Court judge, served as the initial 'next friend' of Ram Lalla from 1986 to 1996. Thakur Prasad Verma, a history professor, assumed the role from 1996 to 2009, followed by Triloki Nath Pandey until his demise in 2021.[37]

VHP Founded

The VHP, a Hindu organization having roots in the RSS, was founded on the occasion of Krishna Janmashthmi on 29 August 1964 to

---

[37] Bajpai, Namita, 'Ram Lalla Virajman Bereft of "Next Friends" for Ayodhya Consecration Ceremony', *The New Indian Express*, https://tinyurl.com/ytdp9wc2. Accessed on 26 August 2024.

propagate the Hindu religion, unite and consolidate the Hindu society, and protect its core values, beliefs and traditions. The VHP began working to bring various Hindu sects together. This was the time when activities of Christian missionaries like religious conversions were being brought into focus. Various Hindu organizations were looking for opportunities to consolidate the Hindus. The Congress government in Madhya Pradesh decided to set up an inquiry commission, led by M.B. Niyogi, in view of the complaints regarding Christian missionaries resorting to inducements to convert the people. The M.B. Niyogi Commission submitted its report titled 'Report of the Christian Missionary Activities Enquiry Committee, Madhya Pradesh' in 1956. The commission's findings gave a new twist to the debate on religious conversions.

Another factor that led to the formation of the VHP was the need to have an umbrella organization to connect with Hindus living in different parts of the world. This was pointed out in an article published in *The Print*.

> There are two major developments that were the catalysts for the setting up of the VHP—the Niyogi Committee report of 1956, which highlighted the growing conversions of tribals into Christianity by missionaries in the state of Madhya Pradesh, and the Nehru government's rebuff to Trinidad MP Dr Shambunath Kapildeo who visited India in 1950s.
>
> Kapildeo wanted the then government to help in strengthening the cultural identities of Hindus in Trinidad and other places outside India but the Nehru government's response was lukewarm as it perceived his agenda to be a communal one.
>
> So he met the second RSS *sarsanghchalak* M.S. Golwalkar and shared his concerns. The RSS realized that there was a need to connect with Hindus living abroad as they sought to retain their cultural identity.[38]

---

[38] Anand, Arun, 'VHP Struggle for Ram Mandir in Ayodhya Didn't Begin in 1983. It Started 19 Years Earlier', *The Print*, 13 August 2020, https://tinyurl.com/2p9vha74.

Virat Hindu Sammelan

A large number of religious conversions of Dalits (to Islam) were reported in Meenakshipuram, Tamil Nadu, in 1981. This turned out to be a trigger for moves to consolidate the Hindus amid the growing rhetoric of Islam resurging on the strength of petrodollars, a term used for the money earned by oil-exporting countries by selling oil. Senior Congress leader Karan Singh, son of Hari Singh, the last Hindu king of Kashmir who acceded to India, organized the Virat Hindu Sammelan at the Boat Club Lawns in New Delhi on 18 October 1981. Singh founded the Virat Hindu Samaj that organized the large congregation of Hindus. The RSS played an important role in making the Virat Hindu Sammelan a success. Those owing allegiance to the RSS were made the organization's key functionaries. Hans Raj Gupta was appointed one of its top leaders, V.H. Dalmia was made its treasurer, and Ashok Singhal was appointed as general-secretary.[39] It was envisaged as a social reform organization and the apparent cause was the conversions reported in Meenakshipuram.

Senior Congress leaders, including ministers from states, attended the Virat Hindu Sammelan. Those seen at the Boat Club congregation included Vir Bahadur Singh, Uttar Pradesh's minister for transport, and Surendra Singh, minister of state for home affairs.[40] It was during the tenure of Vir Bahadur Singh as the CM of Uttar Pradesh that the locks of the Babri Masjid were opened on 1 February 1986. Prime Minister Indira Gandhi handled the issue tactically. Karan Singh informed PM Indira Gandhi about the success of the Virat Hindu Sammelan, claiming it to be a huge gathering of about a million people. Indira Gandhi, in a letter to Karan Singh on 13 October 1982, indicated that she thought the latter was being identified as a VHP leader. So,

---

Accessed on 3 August 2024.
[39]Noorani, A.G., 'Karan Singh's Career', *Frontline*, 10 February 2012, https://tinyurl.com/mr3zyykc. Accessed on 26 June 2024.
[40]Mitra, Sumit, 'Virat Hindu Samaj Holds Massive Rally to Protest against Conversion of Harijans to Islam', *India Today*, 15 November 1981, https://tinyurl.com/3rayxvyy. Accessed on 3 August 2024.

Karan Singh, in a letter dated 17 October 1982 to PM Indira Gandhi, categorically stated that he was not associated with the VHP.[41]

Ashok Singhal rose to the top in the VHP, becoming the organization's chief and ultimately turning into a key figure of the Ram temple movement. He belonged to a well-off family of Allahabad (now Prayagraj). His family had an ancestral mansion named Mahavir Bhawan in Allahabad. He was known to RSS's Prof. Rajendra Singh alias Rajju Bhaiya, Department of Physics in Allahabad University. He pursued a bachelor's degree in metallurgical engineering from Banaras Hindu University (BHU), Varanasi, in 1950. There was no public demand at any forum about the disputed structure till 1980. The Liberhan Ayodhya Commission of Inquiry, appointed by the Union government following the demolition of the disputed Ram Janmabhoomi–Babri Masjid structure on 6 December 1992, observed in its report:

> Only claim made or demands raised up to this time were confined to removal of receiver, right to collect religious offerings and possession of land etc. These demands remained confined to civil courts. There was no demand by the public at large at any forum. There is no iota of evidence to hold contrary to this.[42]

Muzaffarnagar Meeting

The VHP had been looking for opportunities to build a larger network of Hindus. It had no inkling about the potential of the Ram temple issue. It did not, thus, have any major plans for the Ram temple till this time. A meeting was organized under the banner of Hindu Jagaran Manch in Muzaffarnagar on 23 March 1983. Muzaffarnagar, a district in western Uttar Pradesh, was in focus for witnessing large-scale riots between Hindus and Muslims in 2013. The Ram temple issue was

---

[41] Alam, Jawaid (ed.), *Kashmir and Beyond: 1966-84—Select Correspondence between Indira Gandhi and Karan Singh*, Penguin Random House, 2011, India, pp. 330, 344–5.
[42] Liberhan Ayodhya Commission of Inquiry, 'Mobilisation of Kar Sevaks', *Report of the Liberhan Ayodhya Commission of Inquiry*, para 58.1, https://tinyurl.com/mtartfek. Accessed on 4 August 2024.

raised for the first time at a public platform in Muzaffarnagar. Former PM Gulzari Lal Nanda, Prof. Rajendra Singh and other RSS and VHP leaders were among those who reached Muzaffarnagar to attend the meeting. Dau Dayal Khanna from Moradabad, who earlier worked as the health minister in the Congress government in Uttar Pradesh, wrote a letter to PM Indira Gandhi raising the issue of liberation of Ram Janmabhoomi.

Ayodhya, Mathura and Kashi

Khanna tagged the Ram temple issue of Ayodhya with that of the Krishna Janmabhoomi, the birthplace of Lord Krishna in Mathura (a temple town situated on the banks of the Yamuna in western Uttar Pradesh), and the Kashi Vishwanath Temple, the shrine dedicated to Lord Shiva in Varanasi (considered to be one of the oldest cities in the world, situated on the banks of the Ganga in eastern Uttar Pradesh).

The Congress government's Muslim appeasement policy and the utter neglect of places of worship for Hindus came under attack at the meeting. The VHP began focusing on Ayodhya along with Mathura and Kashi shrines. It reached out to the saints to seek their guidance and called upon them to lead society. The VHP began convening meetings of the Dharam Sansad, a conference of some religious leaders of Hindus, and the Kendriya Margdarshak Mandal, an apex decision-making body of select prominent saints. The VHP convened meetings of the two bodies to push the Ram temple agenda and get a stamp of approval from the prominent saints for wider acceptability.

Ayodhya was already celebrating Ram Pragat Utsav every year with enthusiasm. But the thirty-fourth anniversary of Ram Pragat Utsav was different. A Hanuman Pataka (pennant) was planted for the first time on the top of the central dome of Babri Masjid on 4 January 1984, giving a boost to the VHP's temple movement.[43] A large crowd gathered near the disputed structure to get a glimpse of

---

[43]Rao, P.V. Narasimha, *Ayodhya: 6 December 1992*, Penguin Random House, India, 2006, p. 23.

the Hanuman Pataka and have darshan of Ram Lalla there. A hawan was also performed inside the central dome, which was the sanctum sanctorum. This made the RSS leadership realize the political potential of the Ram temple issue.[44] They began working on ways to achieve the objective of mass mobilization on the Ram temple issue. Agitation for construction of the Ram temple was launched in 1984.

First Dharam Sansad

The VHP organized the first Dharam Sansad at Vigyan Bhawan in New Delhi on 7–8 April 1984 and decided to start the movement for the liberation of Ram Janmabhoomi in Ayodhya and Krishna Janmabhoomi in Mathura, and settlement of the Kashi Vishwanath–Gyanvapi Mosque dispute in Varanasi.

A call for opening of the lock at Ram Janmabhoomi was also given at a conference held in New Delhi. The Faizabad administration had put locks on the two gates of the disputed Ram Janmabhoomi complex. Pujaris could go inside from one of the two gates, and devotees were only allowed a glimpse of Ram Lalla from a distance behind the grill-brick wall as this gate was always locked. This was projected as the captivity of Ram Lalla. So, the demand for his liberation by opening of the locks was drawing attention.

At the next conference in Ayodhya, the Ram Janmabhoomi Mukti Yagya Saniti was set up. Dau Dayal Khanna was appointed its convenor.[45] Mahant Avaidyanath, who succeeded Mahant Digvijaya Nath as the chief priest of Gorakhnath Temple following the latter's death in 1969, was unanimously appointed president of the committee constituted to steer the campaign for the Ram temple on 1 July 1984. Mahant Nritya Gopal Das of the Mani Ram Chawani (an important centre for the Ram temple movement), Ayodhya, and Mahant Ramchandra Das Paramhans of Digambar Akhara (a dominant *akhara*[46] in Ayodhya,

---

[44]Ibid.
[45]Ibid.
[46]*Akhara* is a Hindi word for wrestling arena. Adi Shankaracharya is believed to have

one associated with the Ram temple movement) were declared vice presidents of the committee.[47]

The Ram–Janki Rath Yatra Rolls

The VHP launched a programme to awaken people to the Ram Janmabhoomi issue. It decided to take out the Ram–Janki Rath Yatra (chariot procession), beginning from Sitamarhi (believed to be Sita's birthplace) in Bihar to New Delhi, on 25 September 1984. The demand for opening of locks was gaining momentum. Slogans like '*Aage badh kar jor se bolo, janmabhoomi ka taala kholo* (Move forward and shout for opening of lock on Lord Rama's birthplace)' were being raised aggressively along the route of the Rath Yatra that reached Ayodhya on 6 October 1984. At Ayodhya, saints made a pledge to liberate Ram Janmabhoomi along with the two other shrines in Mathura and Kashi. The VHP then flagged off another Rath Yatra for its onward journey to New Delhi. It was scheduled to publicize the VHP's demands for the Ram temple, and a convention of the Hindus was planned in New Delhi in December 1984. Soon, the news broke on 31 October that PM Indira Gandhi had been assassinated in New Delhi. By this time, the Rath Yatra had reached Ghaziabad. Therefore, its onward journey was suspended. The VHP relaunched the Rath Yatra programmes only in 1985. These proved to be a phenomenal way to reach out to the masses and take the organization's agenda ahead in different regions of the country. It encouraged the VHP to plan more such programmes in future. These included senior BJP leader Lal Krishna Advani's Rath Yatra from Somnath to Ayodhya (1990) to mobilize support for *kar seva* (service for the construction of the Ram temple) for the Ram temple

---

set up akharas in eighth century to create a warrior class entrusted with the job of protecting Hinduism. Over the years, the akharas have evolved as centres for physical and spiritual training of seers. They follow a religious tradition and debate upon spiritual and religious issues as well.

[47]Rao, P.V. Narasimha, *Ayodhya: 6 December 1992*, Penguin Random House, India, 2006, p. 23.

and to counter PM V.P. Singh's Mandal[48] agenda. His repeat Rath Yatra (1992) was undertaken to build pressure on the Rao government in favour of the Ram temple in Ayodhya.

The VHP was, however, not new to the yatras. It had organized several yatras to push various causes before the launch of the Ram Janmabhoomi movement.

> Much before the various 'yatras' were carried out for Ramjanmabhoomi from mid-1980s onwards, the VHP had already gained enough experience by testing the waters successfully with 'Jnan Ratham Yatra' in Kerala in 1982, the 'Dharma Yatra' again in Kerala in 1983 and most importantly, the maiden 'Ekatmata Yatra' in 1983.
>
> The 'Ekatmata Yatra' was aimed at creating awareness about nationalism through symbols of *Bharat Mata* (Mother India) and *Ganga Mata* (Mother Ganga).[49]

VHP Intensifies Demand to Open the Lock

The VHP's demand for opening the locks of Ram Janmabhoomi was gaining momentum. The Congress government was exploring options. It worked behind the scenes to chalk out a solution as Ayodhya was taking the centre stage in politics. Several meetings were being held at top levels of the state government in Lucknow and also in New Delhi. President Giani Zail Singh visited Faizabad on the day of Ram Navami on 20 April 1983. His visit was, however, limited to Kanak Bhawan and he did not visit the Ram Janmabhoomi complex. Then CM of Uttar Pradesh Sripati Mishra accompanied him. Zail Singh first went to the Hanuman Garhi Temple in Ayodhya. He then wanted to visit Ram Janmabhoomi. He was told that the birthday celebrations of

---

[48]Virk, Aviral, 'Ayodhya Part 5: Mandal's Caste & Quota vs BJP's Rath & Ram', *The Quint*, 11 November 2017, https://tinyurl.com/279kw9hy. Accessed on 26 August 2024.
[49]Anand, Arun, 'VHP Struggle for Ram Mandir in Ayodhya Didn't Begin in 1983. It Started 19 Years Earlier', *The Print*, 13 August 2020, https://tinyurl.com/2p9vha74. Accessed on 3 August 2024.

Lord Rama were organized at Kanak Bhawan in Ayodhya. Thereafter, he was taken for a visit to Kanak Bhawan, where he briefly addressed the public.[50] The purpose of his visit remains a mystery.

A Workable Option

The Congress considered unlocking of the disputed spot a workable option to counter the VHP's agitation plans on the Ram temple issue. Advocate Umesh Chandra Pandey, on 21 January 1986, moved an application before a local court in Faizabad praying for opening of the lock placed on the grill-brick wall[51] gate outside the sanctum sanctorum and allowing unrestricted puja, darshan, etc., to Hindus, and removal of police force from the disputed structure.[52] On 25 January 1986, another application was moved by Pandey before the court of Munsif Sadar, Faizabad, as regular Suit Number 2 of 1950, praying for the same relief.[53] He referred to the order of the Faizabad civil judge, on 16 January 1950, which stated that no hindrance would be caused in the way of performing puja of Ram Lalla (at the disputed site). He said that the locks put up there were in violation of the city magistrate's order. The munsif magistrate, on 28 January 1986, turned down the request.

Umesh Chandra Pandey then filed an appeal in the court of Faizabad district judge K.M. Pandey. The district judge summoned senior district officers before passing any order.

Faizabad DM Indu Kumar Pandey, IAS, who later became chief secretary of Uttarakhand, and the senior superintendent of police (SSP) of Faizabad, Karamvir Singh, who later rose to be Uttar Pradesh's

---

[50]Singh, Sheetla, *Ayodhya: Ramjanmabhoomi-Babri Masjid ka Sach (Ayodhya: Truth about Ramjanambhoomi-Babri Masjid)*, Kaushal Publishing House, Faizabad, 2019, pp. 51–2.
[51]*M Siddiq (D) Thr Lrs vs Mahant Suresh Das & Ors*, (2019), CA 10866-10867/2010, p. 18, https://tinyurl.com/bdfjzf3k. Accessed on 25 August 2024.
[52]Rao, P.V. Narasimha, *Ayodhya: 6 December 1992*, Penguin Random House, India, 2006, p. 32.
[53]Ibid.

director general of police (DGP), were asked to record their statements in court on 31 January 1986. Neither of the officers raised any objection to opening the locks. Pandey informed the court that locks had been there on the gates for a long time. He said the lock on one of the two gates there had never been opened and added that the priest had been using another gate to get inside. The city magistrate allowed entry of some people there from time to time. He said that there was no apprehension of breach of peace if the locks were opened. Karamvir Singh said that he did not see any problem on the law-and-order front.

The Lock Is Opened

Pandey ordered the opening of the locks at about 4.15 p.m. on 1 February 1986. Within an hour, the district administration made the compliance. At last, the locks were opened. 'Yes, the court's order came in the afternoon. We asked the Inspector, Kotwali police station Ayodhya, to get the locks opened. We did not apprehend any threat to the law-and-order situation. After the court's order for opening of the lock, the district administration made compliance. The locks were opened by the evening,' said Pandey over phone from Dehradun. The key to the lock on the grill-brick wall gate could not be traced, so the local officials used hammer and stones, said another retired officer aware of the developments 1 February 1986.[54]

A team of Doordarshan camerapersons was present at the time of opening of the locks, and the event was telecast by the official channel leading to tension in some places.[55] Pandey said that district administration had not invited the Doordarshan team, and he does not remember it being present in Ayodhya at that point. But the news about the opening of locks soon spread like wildfire, and a large crowd gathered outside the disputed complex for darshan.

---

[54]Telephonic interview with Indu Kumar Pandey (retired IAS).
[55]Rao, P.V. Narasimha, *Ayodhya: 6 December 1992*, Penguin Random House, India, 2006, p. 35.

Another Turning Point

The opening of locks was another turning point in the Ram temple movement after the installation of the idol in 1949. Mohammad Hashim, a resident of Faizabad, filed a writ petition in the Allahabad High Court challenging the district judge's order. An interim order was passed on the same on 3 February 1986, which read: 'Until further orders of the court, the nature of property in question as existing today shall not be changed.'[56]

This was the time when religious fervour was rising across the country. The VHP's focus on Lord Rama being under 'lock and key' or captivity was striking an emotional chord with the people. It was considered to symbolize the threat that Hinduism faced in India. *India Today*, in its issue dated 31 May 1986, observed: 'Slowly but surely, a resurgent and increasingly militant movement of Hindu revivalism is sweeping across the country. The message in the new militancy is that the minorities are being pampered while the majority has been restrained from asserting Hindu nationalism.'[57] The Congress obviously was left with limited choice. It opted for opening of locks to pulling the rug from under the feet of the RSS and the VHP leaders. It wanted to take the initiative of the Ram temple away from them. Its move, however, boomeranged and eventually proved advantageous to the saffron brigade.

---

[56]Ibid. 33.
[57]Badhwar, Inderjit, 'Resurgent and Increasingly Militant Movement of Hindu Revivalism Sweeps across India', *India Today*, 31 May 1986, https://tinyurl.com/bdev2a2h. Accessed on 28 June 2024.

4

The Congress Role

When the senior BJP MLA Fateh Bahadur Singh thanked his father and the then Indian National Congress (INC) CM of Uttar Pradesh, Vir Bahadur Singh, for their contribution to the cause of the construction of the Ram temple in Ayodhya in the state's legislative assembly, not many were surprised.

Those who have watched the unfolding of political developments in Uttar Pradesh over the years often refer to Vir Bahadur Singh's direct or indirect role in opening the locks of the disputed Ram Janmabhoomi complex.

'I want to pay my respects, through you (chair), to all those who sacrificed their lives for the great cause of the construction of the temple at Bhagwan Sri Ramjanmabhoomi Dham, Mahant Avaidyanath Ji Maharaj, former Uttar Pradesh CM the late Vir Bahadur Singh, the late Ashok Singhal and Nana Saheb (Nanaji Deshmukh). We can't forget their contribution,' Fateh Bahadur Singh said while speaking in the Lower House of the Uttar Pradesh Legislature on 2 March 2021.[1]

A senior Congress leader, Vir Bahadur Singh held office as the Uttar Pradesh CM from 24 September 1985 to 24 June 1988. The present CM and chief priest of Gorakhnath Math, Mahant Yogi Adityanath, is the disciple of Mahant Avaidyanath. Both are connected with Gorakhpur, a district on the Indo-Nepal border in eastern Uttar Pradesh. Gorakhnath Math played a pivotal role in building up the

---

[1] Doordarshan Uttar Pradesh, 'Uttar Pradesh Vidhan Sabha Proceedings on March 2, 2021, Uttar Pradesh Vidhan Sabha Satra 2021 Ki Karyavahi Ka Sidha Prasaran', *Youtube*, https://tinyurl.com/bdm2zevr. Accessed on 16 August 2024.

agitation for the Ram temple. Ashok Singhal, an RSS member, was the VHP chief and led the Ram temple movement. Nanaji Deshmukh, a social reformer and politician from the RSS who was conferred with India's highest civilian honour Bharat Ratna, is understood to have been aware of the developments about placing of the idol under the central dome of Babri Masjid in 1949, which proved to be a turning point in the Ram temple movement.

Vir Bahadur Singh's Contribution

Fateh Bahadur Singh, who represents the Caimpiyarganj constituency of Gorakhpur, has been vocal about his father's contribution and commitment to the cause of the Ram temple in Ayodhya. He has been frequently making such observations about his father, who rose to the position of CM of Uttar Pradesh and a Union minister in Rajiv Gandhi's government. He also held important portfolios in the Congress government as a minister in the state before becoming the CM. The Congress always spoke about a mutually agreed formula (by both Hindus and Muslims) or a court order as an acceptable solution to the Ram Janmabhoomi–Babri Masjid dispute. It, therefore, did not accept such direct or indirect role of any of its leaders in paving way for the construction of the Ram temple.

Vir Bahadur Singh held the CM's office when the Faizabad district judge ordered the opening of locks of the then disputed complex on 1 February 1986. A Kshatriya by caste, Singh is understood to have had a natural bonding with the then Gorakhnath Peethadheeshawar, Mahant Avaidyanath, a leader of the Ram temple movement. Vir Bahadur Singh is said to have worked actively to ensure that the locks on the gates of the disputed Ram Janmabhoomi–Babri Masjid complex were opened. As the CM, he sometimes spoke—in private conversations—about his concern for the Ram temple and the locks put up on the gates of the disputed structure. The removal of the locks, which kept the common pilgrims away from darshan of Ram Lalla's idol, may have been at the top of his mind when he assumed office as the CM of Uttar Pradesh.

Locked Ancestors

Vir Bahadur Singh came from a family of Suryavanshi Rajputs (solar race) of Gorakhpur district in eastern Uttar Pradesh. '*Purkhe band hain* (Our ancestors are locked inside)'[2] was his oft-repeated observation in private conversations with his close friends with whom he shared his concern for the locks at the gate of the disputed structure, amid the moves of the RSS and the VHP to intensify agitation for the construction of the Ram temple. However, he did not admit or discuss in public if he had any concrete plans to get his ancestors released from captivity by opening the locks at the gates of the disputed complex.

'Yes, my father wanted the locks to be opened,' said Fateh Bahadur Singh. 'God appeared in his dreams and said: "You have become a Raja (CM) of Uttar Pradesh, and I (idol of Lord Rama as a child) am still behind the locks." Opening of the locks was one of the reasons for my father's removal from the CM's post,' he said while explaining his father's concern for the Ram temple.[3]

Changing CMs

The Congress has had the tradition of appointing CMs as per the instructions from the top, and PM Rajiv Gandhi was the top party leader at that point of time. Veteran Congress leader N.D. Tiwari, who preceded Vir Bahadur Singh as the CM of Uttar Pradesh, also succeeded him. When Rajiv Gandhi was visiting a flood-affected Lucknow (capital city of Uttar Pradesh), he whispered something in the ears of both Vir Bahadur Singh and N.D. Tiwari. This conversation was stated to be Rajiv Gandhi's signal for a change of leadership, asking Tiwari to resign in order to get inducted as a Union minister and Singh to take over as the CM of Uttar Pradesh.

---

[2]Telephonic interview with Fateh Bahadur Singh.
[3]Ibid.

Singh's Private Visit

'Whenever my father had any conversation with Mahant Avaidyanath, it was about the construction of Ram temple. What the BJP is doing today, my father thought about and worked to execute the same long back,' added Fateh Bahadur Singh.[4]

The issue of the Ram temple came up for discussion during one such meeting between Vir Bahadur Singh and Gorakhnath Math chief Mahant Avaidyanath in Lucknow. Singh has been quoted (by a former police officer) to have conveyed to Mahant Avaidyanath that Rajiv Gandhi wanted a magnificent Ram temple in Ayodhya. Devendra Bahadur Rai (who later became Faizabad SSP) was Vir Bahadur Singh's security officer. He resigned and was elected MP from the BJP. D.B. Rai said:

> One day Vir Bahadur Singh called me and asked, can you drive? I said, yes. He asked me to send my car, driver, security and secretary all on leave. I have to go somewhere. I will go with you in your car. That night quietly, Vir Bahadur Singh went to a retired income tax officer, Mohan Singh's Lucknow home. Mohan Singh took us to a room, there president of Ram Janmabhoomi Mukti Yagya Samiti Mahant Avaidyanath Nath was already sitting. Mohan Singh left after escorting us to the room. Now there were only three of us. Vir Bahadur Singh started, 'Rajiv ji wants, like the Somnath, a magnificent temple to be constructed at Ayodhya. But the central government will construct it. There are only three conditions to it. First, the central government will pay for the expenses of temple construction. Second, BJP will have nothing to do with temple construction. And third, the disputed structure will not be demolished. A roof will be put over pillars from all sides. And a temple will be constructed on its roof. The structure will remain as it is. The plan is that the disputed structure is already weak. Without repair it will fall by

---
[4]Ibid.

itself in some days. After which only Ram Janmabhoomi temple will remain there.

Avaidyanath laughed at Vir Bahadur Singh's proposal and questioned, 'How will BJP and VHP gain from this?' 'Congress will get its political benefit.' Then the conversation ended at a point where it was agreed that Avaidyanath Ji will speak with other leaders of VHP and then inform about his views. But Avaidyanath Ji never spoke on the matter again and this opportunity was missed in assessing gains and losses.[5]

Muslim Appeasement

Fateh Bahadur Singh insists that the then PM Rajiv Gandhi was aware of the unfolding developments and the move of opening the locks.[6] Wazahat Habibullah, an IAS officer and friend of Rajiv Gandhi, however, felt otherwise. In his book *My Years with Rajiv: Triumph and Tragedy*, he narrates that the question had been troubling him, and so he asked this to Rajiv Gandhi while flying to drought-hit Gujarat in the PM's cabin of a Boeing 737 in September 1986:

> So my question to Rajiv was: 'Since the removal of the locks was not going to change the status quo in any way, but would earn the support of sections of the Hindu community for your party, was it not realized that such a benefit could only be limited? After all, with the core of Congress remaining secular, the development could not be exploited to the maximum, and the right wing would hijack the outcome, which it could trumpet as its triumph.' That is what had happened.
>
> Rajiv's answer was direct and instant: 'No government has any business to meddle in matters like determination of the functioning of places of worship. I knew nothing of this development until I was told of it after orders had been passed and executed.'

---

[5]Sharma, Hemant, *Ayodhya: A Battleground*, Rupa Publications, 2020, pp. 167–8.
[6]Telephonic interview with Fateh Bahadur Singh.

I was, as might be imagined, completely taken aback. 'But, sir, you were PM.'

'Of course, I was. Yet I had not been informed of this action, and have asked Vir Bahadur Singh (under whose watch, and under whose instructions, it was rumoured, the magistrate had taken this fateful—or shall I call it fatal—decision) to explain. I suspect it was Arun (Nehru) and Fotedar (Makhan Lal) who were responsible, but I am having this verified. If it is true, I will have to consider action.' In the coming month, Nehru was dropped from the cabinet.

I did, of course, know that the communication between the Uttar Pradesh CM and the PM was as a rule conducted through Arun Nehru, who had retained a hold over state politics.[7]

Vijay Shankar Pandey, a former IAS officer, who worked for long with the Uttar Pradesh government and the Government of India before retiring as a secretary in the Union government, was posted as a joint secretary to CM Vir Bahadur Singh in 1986 when the locks were opened. Pandey said he felt the decision enjoyed the support of the Congress leadership. When asked about Habibullah's observations on the issue, he said he was not aware if there was any communication between Vir Bahadur Singh, Arun Nehru and Rajiv Gandhi on the issue. But if a wrong decision was taken without holding consultation, it should have been immediately reversed, he added.[8]

Surya Pratap Singh, also a former IAS officer who held various important positions in state government, including with CM Vir Bahadur Singh, said the latter had called him soon after the district court's order to open the locks.

'Chief Minister asked me to rush to Ayodhya and get aarti performed there. I reached Ayodhya. As no key of the lock (on the gate of disputed structure) was available, some officials had to break

---

[7]Habibullah, Wajahat, *My Years with Rajiv: Triumph and Tragedy*, Westland Publications, 2020, pp. 108–9.
[8]Telephonic interview with Vijay Shankar Pandey (former IAS).

open the lock,' said Singh. About whether Rajiv Gandhi was aware of these developments, he stated, 'There is no reason to believe that Rajiv Gandhi was not aware of developments about opening of locks. Without the PM's knowledge, the CM would not have acted so swiftly to get the locks opened.'[9]

Nehru to Rao

The Congress leaders consistently maintained that the construction of the Ram temple should be done either by a court order or through a negotiated settlement between Hindus and Muslims. The Congress was in power when all the major developments concerning Ayodhya unfolded, barring when the Supreme Court of India pronounced its verdict on 9 November 2019, clearing all the decks for construction of the Ram temple in Ayodhya.

The grand old party cannot shy away and has to own direct or indirect responsibility for apt or inept handling of the issue. The sequence of events starting from the time of placing of the idol on the intervening night of 22–23 December 1949 to the opening of locks on 1 February 1986, and from laying of the foundation stone of the Ram temple on 9 November 1989 to the demolition of Babri Masjid on 6 December 1992 throw light on the Congress's confusing signals. The Congress found itself in a dilemma and adopted the 'one step forward and two steps back' approach for various issues.

India's first PM, Jawaharlal Nehru, was in office when the idol was placed in 1949. The demand for the liberation of Ram Janmabhoomi was first raised during the tenure of Indira Gandhi as PM in 1983. Rajiv Gandhi held the office of PM when the locks at the gate of the disputed structure were opened in 1986 and the foundation stone was laid for the first time for the construction of the Ram temple. Senior Congress leader Rao held the office of PM when the disputed structure was demolished in 1992. The sympathetic approach of then

---

[9]Telephonic interview with Surya Pratap Singh (former IAS).

Uttar Pradesh CM Govind Ballabh Pant at the state level had provided a conducive atmosphere for placing of the idol under the central dome of the disputed structure in 1949. Pant had failed to act immediately against Faizabad deputy commissioner K.K. Nayar, who refused to take action for the removal of the idol despite PM Jawaharlal Nehru's instructions to do so.

Indira Gandhi's Soft Approach

Prime Minister Indira Gandhi adopted a soft approach when the issue of liberation of the three shrines of Ayodhya, Mathura and Kashi was first raised at the Muzaffarnagar meeting in 1983. Former Congress minister Dau Dayal Khanna, who raised the issue at the Muzaffarnagar meeting, also wrote to her raising the demand for liberation of the three shrines. *India Today*, in an article published in 1986, spoke about the prevailing mood in the society in the mid-1980s.

> The communal divide—now almost out of the control of the mainstream political parties—began with the patronage of Singh's (Uttar Pradesh CM Vir Bahadur Singh) own party. It took an emotional turn in 1983, during the Kashmir polls, when hardcore RSS elements in Jammu forgot their Bharatiya Janata Party (BJP) candidates and joined hands with the Congress (I) in a bid to end Farooq Abdullah's regime. Mrs Gandhi had herself openly exhorted Hindus in the Jammu region to vote for her party. After 1980, Mrs Gandhi began to refrain from attacking the RSS or BJP on communal issues. And in 1984, the Congress (I) joined hands with the Shiv Sena's Bal Thackeray in Maharashtra to fight the panchayat poll.[10]

---

[10]Badhwar, Inderjit, 'Resurgent and Increasingly Militant Movement of Hindu Revivalism Sweeps across India, *India Today*, 31 May 1986, https://tinyurl.com/bdfzccjn. Accessed on 29 June 2024.

The Congress Manoeuvring

The Congress's behind-the-scenes manoeuvring and attempts to take initiative away from the VHP at the time of opening of locks is another example of lack of a clear strategy on the part of the grand old party. So it did not work for the party. The Congress had to pay a heavy price for its failure to read the consequences at the time of the *shilanyas* (foundation stone-laying ceremony) and the indifference at the time of demolition of the disputed structure on 6 December 1992.

The party now faces charges of doing nothing for the cause of the Ram temple. Lord Rama is revered by all and the Congress leaders are no exception to this. But over the years, most of them have refrained from visiting the Ayodhya shrine in public glare after the idol was placed under the central dome of the disputed structure, locks were opened, and the makeshift temple was put up after the demolition of the disputed structure. Most senior Congress leaders stayed away from the consecration ceremony (Pran Pratishtha) of Ram Lalla's idol at the newly constructed Ram Temple in Ayodhya on 22 January 2024. Most of the party had not visited the new temple even after the consecration ceremony. On the other hand, the BJP leaders, including CMs, have consistently visited the disputed structure in Ayodhya, with the BJP's first CM Kalyan Singh making a point to be there along with his council of ministers soon after taking oath of office in 1991. Current CM Yogi Adityanath has been doing so frequently, and has made several trips to Ayodhya. The BJP leaders from different states attended the consecration ceremony and have been visiting Ayodhya thereafter. The Congress leaders have stayed away, apparently feeling that their act may displease the Muslim community. It should be noted that PM Rajiv Gandhi was not in Ayodhya when the VHP laid the symbolic foundation stone for the Ram temple. On the other hand, PM Narendra Modi himself performed Bhoomi Pujan and laid the foundation stone on 5 August 2020 for construction of a grand Ram temple in Ayodhya. He performed the rituals to complete the Pran Pratishtha on 22 January 2024, and visited the Ram Temple to offer prayers on 5 May 2024 when the 2024 Lok Sabha elections were underway.

Mahatma Gandhi Visits Ayodhya

Mahatma Gandhi had paid a visit to Ayodhya in 1921 and offered prayers at a Ram temple there. He worshipped Lord Rama and himself made a reference about his visit to a small temple at the lord's birthplace in Ayodhya. (Ram Lalla's idol was not placed under the central dome of the disputed structure at the time).

> When I arrived in Ayodhya, I was taken to a small temple that stands at the place where Shri Ramchandra is believed to have been born. The devout among non-cooperators had suggested to me that I should request the temple priest to use Khadi for dressing the idols of Rama and Sita. I did make the suggestion, of course, but is hardly likely to have been acted upon. When I went for darshan, I saw them dressed in ugly muslin with brocades. If I had Tulsidas's strength of profound devotion, I too would have been as insistent as he had been. Tulsidas had vowed, in a Krishna temple, that unless Lord Krishna took visible form as Rama with bow and arrow, he would not bow (to the deity). Devout writers say that when Goswami (Tulsidas) took this vow, his eyes saw images of Ramchandra standing on every side and he bowed his head most readily. I often feel like insisting that I would bow my head only when the officiating priests made our Thakoreji swadeshi by dressing him in Khadi. But I must first do the tapascharya which Tulsidas did and acquire his unique devotion.[11]

Bengaluru-based historian Ramachandra Guha, however, has made the following observations in an article titled 'Mahatma Gandhi Would

---

[11]*Collected Works of Mahatma Gandhi, Vol. 22: 15 November 1920–5 April 1921*, Gandhi Sevagram Ashram, p. 441, https://tinyurl.com/2s3mvj7u. Accessed on 4 August 2024.

Not Have Wanted a Temple in Ayodhya', published in the *Hindustan Times* in February 2019:

> In 1921, Gandhi visited Ayodhya for the first and last time. He did not care to enter any of the town's many temples. However, while addressing a public meeting, Gandhi said he 'condemned violence most strongly and unequivocally, and said he considered it a sin against God and man'. Several decades later, northern and western India experienced an orgy of violence committed by men speaking in the name of a God said to be born in Ayodhya.[12]

Communal Views of Congress Leaders

Jawaharlal Nehru also wanted to pay a visit to Ayodhya after the idol of Ram Lalla was placed under the central dome on the night of 22 and 23 December 1949. He said he felt disturbed after hearing about the recent developments. He indicated this in a telegram communique sent to Uttar Pradesh Premier Govind Ballabh Pant.[13] He favoured removal of the idol. Whether Nehru would have paid a visit to the disputed site in Ayodhya or would have stayed away from doing so is another question.

Nehru was in New Delhi when the idol was placed surreptitiously. He indicated that a section of Congress leaders was supporting the move of placing the idol. Nehru expressed his unhappiness about the situation to Congress leaders, and even wrote about the same in his letters. In one such letter dated 5 March 1950 to Kishorilal Ghanshyamlal Mashruwala, an independence activist, Nehru observed that he was not happy with the way the state government of the day was handling the issue in Ayodhya.

---

[12]Guha, Ramachandra, 'Mahatma Gandhi Would Not Have Wanted a Temple in Ayodhya', *Hindustan Times*, 9 February 2019, https://tinyurl.com/yfrt2exd. Accessed on 30 June 2024.

[13]*Selected Works of Jawaharlal Nehru: Second Series 2, Vol. 14, Part 1 (15 November 1949– 8 April 1950)*, Jawaharlal Nehru Memorial Fund, p. 458, https://tinyurl.com/4r33r9yy. Accessed on 30 June 2024.

My dear Kishorilal Bhai,

You refer to the Ayodhya mosque. This event occurred two or three months ago and I have been very gravely perturbed over it. The U.P. Government put up a brave show, but actually did little. Their District Officer in Fyzabad rather misbehaved and took no steps to prevent this happening. It is not true that Baba Raghav Das instigated this, but it is true that after this was done, he gave his approval to it. So also some other Congressmen in the U.P. Pandit Govind Ballabh Pant condemned the act on several occasions, but refrained from taking definite action probably for fear of a big scale riot. I have been greatly distressed about it and have repeatedly drawn Panditji's attention to it.[14]

As discussed earlier, Baba Raghav Das (1896–1958), who joined the INC in 1920, was fielded as a Congress candidate from the Faizabad-Ayodhya seat. Baba Raghav Das, who used to work for political, moral, social and educational uplift of the people, made Gorakhpur his headquarters. In order to ensure defeat of the socialist leader Acharya Narendra Dev and victory of Baba Raghav Das, Govind Ballabh Pant had sought help from the saints of Ayodhya. Uttar Pradesh's Congress government looked sympathetic towards the Ram temple issue, but most of the party's leaders appeared to be adopting a neutral stance, at least in public. The Congress governments often refrained from making any moves that could be questioned by the minorities. The BJP benefitted from this as and when the accusations of Muslim appeasement became louder amid threats of communal polarization.

The Congress Role Comes into Question

The Congress leaders began working out strategies that could deprive the BJP of any political advantage on the issue. They reached out to Hindu leaders to find an acceptable solution to it. They feared

---

[14]Ibid. 459–60.

accusations of taking steps of placating the majority community and thus angering the Muslims. The opening of locks of the disputed structure on 1 February 1986 obviously fell under this category.

The Congress's role came into question again when Faizabad district judge K.M. Pandey, on 1 February 1986, ordered the opening of the locks of the disputed structure. The judge pronounced his order when an appeal was filed before him on 30 January 1986. Applications urging that Muslims be given an opportunity to be heard in the case were rejected. The Congress faced accusations of playing an invisible role in opening of the locks. These accusations gained ground from the manner in which the Congress government in Uttar Pradesh implemented the orders soon after being passed. The Allahabad High Court, which heard a petition from the Muslims on 3 February 1986, did not give any relief on the issue observing that there should be no change in the nature of property in question existing on that day.

Rao, in his book *Ayodhya: 6 December 1992*, has mentioned that a writ petition was filed against the said order of district judge, Faizabad, for opening of the lock, and that an interim relief application seeking stay of the said order was sought. He said that this was not accepted by the High Court. He further stated that opening the locks shook the Muslim community. Rao questioned the move of opening the locks and said that many described the move a stage-managed affair, as the order was implemented speedily to pre-empt the VHP's plans.[15]

Pranab Mukherjee, former President of India, who was witness to or even a participant in many of the decisions between 1980s and 1990s as a Congress leader and Union minister, called the move an 'error of judgement'. 'The opening of Ram Janmabhoomi temple site on 1 February 1986 was perhaps another error of judgement. People felt these actions could have been avoided,' Pranab Mukherjee wrote in *The Turbulent Years: 1980–1996*.[16]

---

[15]Rao, P.V. Narasimha, *Ayodhya: 6 December 1992*, Penguin Random House, India, 2006, p. 35.
[16]Mukherjee, Pranab, *The Turbulent Years: 1980–1996*, Rupa Publications, 2016, p. 129.

Mishandling of Issues

Many other acts of omission and commission by the Congress government came into question, making PM Rajiv Gandhi and the party unpopular. Mukherjee further wrote: 'Rajiv's actions on the Shah Bano judgement and the Muslim Women (Protection of Rights on Divorce) Bill drew criticism and eroded his modern image... The Bofors issue proved to be one of the causes of his undoing in the 1989 Lok Sabha elections, though no charge has been substantiated against Rajiv till date.'[17] The Rajiv Gandhi-led government had moved the Muslim Women (Protection of Rights on Divorce) Bill to enact a new law to nullify the Supreme Court's order in the Shah Bano case. The Congress's move to open the locks at the gates of the disputed structure was obviously to please the Hindus. It, however, angered the Muslims.

The Rajiv Gandhi-led government's moves did not work in its favour. It was feeling the pressure of the accusations of corruption being levelled against it on various other fronts. Its mishandling of the issues gave the RSS and the VHP a tool to hammer with and build public opinion against the Congress. It became evident from the outcome of the 1989 Lok Sabha elections. The VHP struck an emotional chord with the people by issuing a call to donate bricks for the construction of the Ram temple. By agreeing to do so, people found an emotional connect with the cause of the Ram temple. The VHP used this as an opportunity to reach out to people and collect bricks along with token funds, if any. Its workers also transported the bricks to Ayodhya.

Nod to the Ram Temple Foundation Stone

With this, the VHP obviously wanted to mount pressure on the Congress government for taking steps towards the construction of the temple. The Kumbh Mela is considered the largest gathering of pilgrims on Earth. It attracts a large number of saints as well. It is held on a rotation basis by the four pilgrimage centres, namely Allahabad,

---

[17]Ibid.

Haridwar, Nasik and Ujjain. After 12 years, it was Allahabad's turn in January 1989. The VHP used the opportunity to send a strong message to the Congress government. The Dharam Sansad, at a meeting held in Prayag Kumbh (Allahabad) and convened by the VHP, decided to begin the kar seva for construction of the Ram temple in Ayodhya from 9 November 1989. Under these circumstances, the Rajiv Gandhi-led government decided to allow the VHP to lay the foundation stone on the disputed site on 9 November 1989, and go for the 1989 Lok Sabha elections. Union Home Minister Buta Singh was sent to Ayodhya to handle and supervise the work related to shilanyas ceremony of the Ram temple. Singh, who has been holding various meetings with Uttar Pradesh CM Narayan Dutt Tiwari in Lucknow to work out a solution to the issue, held discussions with him again to ensure a smooth foundation-laying ceremony in Ayodhya.

This was considered an act out of Rajiv Gandhi's desperation to check his waning popularity. He was committing blunders one after the other. The VHP considered the Rajiv Gandhi-led government's decision regarding the foundation stone as a victory of sorts. Hence, on the morning of 9 November 1989, the VHP leaders and saints assembled for the laying of the Ram temple foundation at the spot designated for the purpose, following obvious clearance from the Congress government's bosses in Lucknow and New Delhi. This too was a disputed spot, notwithstanding the claims made to the contrary. The kar sevaks carried displays of *trishul* (trident), mace, and bow and arrow as they moved to the foundation-laying spot, all the while raising slogans in favour of the Ram temple. The Ram temple agitation saw a large participation of Shiv Sainiks, the activists and members of the Shiv Sena founded by Balasaheb Thackeray on 19 June 1966. It included representations from different castes of society and the regions.

A Dalit Lays the Foundation Stone

The VHP leaders obviously wanted to make the Ram temple movement all-inclusive. In order to ensure participation of the downtrodden classes, Kameshwar Chaupal, a Dalit, was selected to lay the foundation for the Ram temple. He laid the first brick at the spot dug out for laying the foundation. This spot was close to the disputed Ram Janmabhoomi–Babri Masjid complex. Kameshwar is now the Dalit member of the Ram Janmabhoomi Teerth Kshetra Trust, which was set up following the Supreme Court's verdict in favour of construction of the Ram temple in Ayodhya. Mahant Avaidyanath was the first to pick the spade to dig the ground, after which others followed. Those who dug the ground for the foundation stone-laying ceremony included Mahant Ramchandra Das Paramhans, Mahant Nritya Gopal Das and Ashok Singhal, amid others.

The Election Commission of India (ECI) had already announced Lok Sabha elections, on 17 October 1989. The elections were held in two phases on 22 and 26 November 1989. So, the first phase of 1989 Lok Sabha elections was scheduled within two weeks post the foundation stone-laying ceremony of the Ram temple. Rajiv Gandhi launched his 1989 poll campaign in Ayodhya (Faizabad) and gave a call for Ram Rajya. The five-week poll campaign was marked by widespread violence.[18] The Rajiv Gandhi-led government had taken a big risk. It was a gamble. It came as a huge surprise to many Congress leaders. They failed to find any logic in holding the foundation stone-laying ceremony ahead of the 1989 Lok Sabha elections.

The Congress Loses the Poll

The Congress lost badly in the 1989 Lok Sabha elections. It lost the 1989 Uttar Pradesh legislative assembly elections too. It has not returned to power in Uttar Pradesh after being voted out in the 1989 Uttar Pradesh legislative assembly elections. The Congress failed to feel the pulse of the people. Its actions reflected the party's ideological dilemma. It apparently acted in the manner that the RSS and the VHP had probably wanted it to. The RSS and the VHP proposed and

---

[18]'India Parliamentary Chamber: Lok Sabha, Elections Held In 1989', https://tinyurl.com/3j2a3jn3. Accessed on 4 August 2024.

the Congress disposed. The year 1989 also marked the beginning of a turbulent period in India's politics. The Congress did not learn its lessons from the failures of the experiments made in 1986 and 1989. P.V. Narasimha Rao's government's acts of commission and omission later in 1992 gave a jolt to the party.

Did PM Rao fail to read the writing on the wall? Was the demolition of the disputed structure on 6 December 1992 a foregone conclusion? The Rao-led government failed to take preventive steps well in time. It had limited options. It continued to watch the situation closely and acted only after the demolition of the disputed structure was completed on 6 December 1992.

Pranab Mukherjee, who was not part of Rao government at that time, felt that the government was confronted with a Hobson's choice. The Uttar Pradesh government, led by BJP leader Kalyan Singh, had assured the Supreme Court that the disputed structure would be protected.

Mukherjee took up the issue with Rao later.

He wrote further that he had later questioned Rao on the issue:

> Later, in a private meeting with PV, I did not mince words. I burst out, 'Was there no one who advised you of the danger? Did you not understand the global repercussions of any damage to the Babri Masjid? At least now take concrete steps to quell communal tensions and assuage the feelings of Muslims through affirmative action.'
>
> PV looked at me as I said this, and in his characteristic style did not let any emotion cross the face. But I had known and worked with him for several decades. I did not need to read his face. I could feel his sadness and disappointment.
>
> I have often wondered later if it was this outburst of mine which finally led to the call I received from him on 17 January 1993, inviting me to join the Cabinet.[19]

---

[19]Mukherjee, Pranab, *The Turbulent Years: 1980–1996*, Rupa Publications, 2016, p. 155.

Pranab Mukherjee Joins Rao's Cabinet

Pranab Mukherjee joined the cabinet of PM P.V. Narasimha Rao. The Congress continued to face questions about the handling of the Ram temple issue. Muslims were losing faith in the Congress and so were other sections of society for different reasons.

What went behind the Rajiv Gandhi-led government's decision to allow the VHP to lay the foundation stone near the disputed complex on 9 November 1989? This has remained a mystery over the years. The developments that preceded it days before the shilanyas might, however, throw some light on the issue. A senior IPS officer (now retired), who was privy to the developments, recollected the sequence of events ahead of the shilanyas in 1989. He said that PM Rajiv Gandhi, along with Union Home Minister Buta Singh and then Uttar Pradesh CM N.D. Tiwari, had visited the ashram of Devraha Baba. Devraha Baba was a saint who lived on an erected platform in the Maath area of Mathura. He blessed the visitors with the touch of his big toe on their head. The former IPS officer said that Rajiv Gandhi's visit, along with Buta Singh and Tiwari, came a few days before the proposed shilanyas programme on 9 November 1989.

Devraha Baba's Blessings

The retired IPS officer added that many saints and senior VHP leaders, including Ashok Singhal, were visiting Devraha Baba regularly to seek the latter's guidance on the Ram temple issue. The Congress leaders, including Rajiv Gandhi, certainly wanted Devraha Baba's blessings and to convince him to put pressure on the VHP leaders to get the shilanyas deferred post the 1989 Lok Sabha elections. Upon hearing their request, Devraha Baba said, '*Bachcha, ho jane do. Isi main kalyan hai* (Let the shilanyas take place. This is for the well-being of humanity).'

At this, Tiwari asked Devraha Baba as to how this was going to benefit the Congress. Devraha Baba was a saint; he asked Tiwari not to talk about the interests of any political party. 'This is for the well-being of India,' replied Devraha Baba. Rajiv Gandhi, thus, followed what Devraha Baba told him to do.[20]

The Congress and Kalyan Singh

The Congress was in a dilemma not only on the issue of laying the foundation stone of the Ram temple, it was also in a fix at almost every step before and after demolition of the Babri Masjid. It, however, always maintained a safe distance from Kalyan Singh, who emerged as the hero of the Ram temple movement. It also continued to maintain a distance from Mohammad Azam Khan, who was one of the main voices of Muslims on the mosque issue and worked as the convenor of the Babri Masjid Action Committee (BMAC). The Congress distanced itself from them even when Kalyan Singh and Azam Khan were upset with their political parties, the BJP and the Samajwadi Party (SP), respectively. The Congress's move was obviously to disassociate itself from any controversy. This became evident when possibilities of an alliance between the Congress and the SP were being explored before the 2009 Lok Sabha elections. The SP had joined hands with Kalyan Singh's Rashtriya Kranti Party ahead of the 2009 Lok Sabha elections. The Congress then made it clear that the party would not have any deal with the SP till the time the latter had links with Kalyan Singh. Mulayam Singh Yadav, SP chief, later regretted his decision and agreed that aligning with Kalyan Singh was a big mistake, as it caused divisions in the SP. Mulayam Singh Yadav, however, never denied his relationship with the latter, who was considered to be a principled leader. Kalyan Singh was instrumental in the installation of Mulayam Singh Yadav as CM of Uttar Pradesh in 2003. He apparently sent signals of softening his stance towards the Congress when he defended Sonia Gandhi amid accusations that she was responsible for tapping phones of SP leaders like Mulayam Singh Yadav and Amar Singh.

---

[20]Telephonic interview with the now-retired IPS officer.

Kalyan Singh Defends Sonia Gandhi

Kalyan Singh refused to subscribe to this view and called Sonia Gandhi a mature politician. 'Sonia Gandhi is now a mature politician. It is not possible that she will stoop down to the level of tapping phones and that too of leaders like Mulayam Singh Yadav and Amar Singh,' he said while speaking to media persons informally at a function on his birthday on 5 January 2006. Mulayam Singh Yadav, as CM of Uttar Pradesh, had, on 30 December 2005, accused Sonia Gandhi of getting phones of senior SP leaders tapped in order to destabilize the SP government led by him. He had absolved PM Manmohan Singh, Union Home Minister Shivraj Patil and Defence Minister Pranab Mukherjee of being involved in the phone-tapping fiasco and said the phones of SP leaders were being tapped at the behest of 10, Janpath, the residence of Sonia Gandhi.

The Congress's stance of supporting Mulayam Singh Yadav and yet disassociating from Kalyan Singh (when the former joined hands with the latter) remains, by and large, unexplained barring the reason of the latter's questionable role in the demolition of Babri Masjid. The Congress's continued support to the Mulayam Singh Yadav-led government—which led a breakaway group of Janata Dal—even after the firing on kar sevaks in Ayodhya on 30 October and 2 November 1990 also remains questionable. When Vishwanath Pratap Singh became the PM of India, heading the National Front (NF) government comprising the Janata Dal as its main constituent after the 1989 Lok Sabha elections, Mulayam Singh Yadav was installed as the CM of Uttar Pradesh.

'Maulana Mulayam'

As CM, Mulayam Singh Yadav ensured that Babri Masjid was protected despite the VHP's aggressive campaign for construction of the Ram temple. When the V.P. Singh-led government fell following the withdrawal of support by the BJP in the wake of L.K. Advani's arrest in Bihar, the Congress extended its support to Mulayam Singh Yadav as CM of a Janata Dal breakaway group. Advani was arrested when he was leading the Rath Yatra to Ayodhya following the VHP's call for kar seva there on 30 October 1990. The Mulayam Singh Yadav-led government ordered firing on the kar sevaks to protect the disputed structure on 30 October and 2 November. Yadav's challenging tone and tenor in which he addressed the public meetings is attributed to be one of the major reasons that proved to be advantageous to the BJP on Ayodhya issue.

Yadav's assertions in public meetings—'*Parinda bhi par nahin maar paayega* (Not a single bird will be allowed to fly over the mosque)'—and that he was being called 'Maulana Mulayam' may have worked for him.

> As a shrewd politician, he (Mulayam Singh Yadav) was aware that he desperately needed Muslim's support to completely oust the Congress from Uttar Pradesh and therefore began to belligerently press for communal harmony. By delivering one of the most iconic quotes which shall be associated with him for years—Masjid par ek parinda bhi par nahin maar sakega—he strongly provoked Hindu hardliners and further polarized the state. He was despised by many and disparagingly called Maulana Mulayam, which also became a term for endearment for several others! And there was more to follow even as he refused to tone down the rhetoric.[21]

The Congress Faces Ire of People

The Congress bore the brunt of people's ire in the 1989 Lok Sabha elections. Vishwanath Pratap Singh, who became PM with the support of the ideologically opposed BJP, lost the vote of confidence in Lok Sabha and resigned on 7 November 1990. Later, V.P. Singh, deposing before the Liberhan Commission, said, 'The VHP international president Ashok Singhal had opposed his efforts to solve the Ayodhya

---

[21] Aron, Sunita, *Akhilesh Yadav: Winds of Change*, Tranquebar Press, 2013, p. 147.

dispute through peaceful means by stating that the Congress had offered his organization a better deal by permitting shilanyas.'[22]

> Further, in his deposition, V.P. Singh agreed that the opening of the locks of the disputed structure in 1989 was a landmark in the Ayodhya movement. He felt that the Congress had allowed shilanyas to be performed with the intention of winning the Hindu vote because it saw the formation of an axis between the Janata Dal and the BJP, with the Left's support as a serious threat. He said that Rajiv Gandhi government had asked the VHP to go in for shilanyas because Congress circles were concerned about the possibility of a swing of the Hindu vote.[23]

The Congress obviously faced defeat in the 1989 polls for its questionable decisions and mishandling of issues that made the party unpopular. Its tally came down from 415 in 1984 to 197 in 1989 Lok Sabha elections. Its decline led to the beginning of a coalition era in the politics of India. It won 232 seats in the 1991 Lok Sabha polls, and P.V. Narasimha Rao was installed as the PM of the Congress-led minority government at the Centre. Rao, with his persuasiveness, political manoeuvring and the art of engineering defections, completed a full term. The Congress tally in the Uttar Pradesh legislative assembly polls, where it continued to support the Mulayam Singh Yadav government, came down from 94 in 1989 to 46 in 1991.

The Congress formed a party-led United Progressive Alliance (UPA) government at the Centre after the 2004 and 2009 Lok Sabha elections, with Manmohan Singh installed as the PM twice. It has, however, remained out of power, and its poll performance has dipped consistently since 1989 in Uttar Pradesh. Significantly, the Congress entered into an alliance with the SP, founded by Mulayam Singh Yadav and now led by his son Akhilesh Yadav, for the 2017 Uttar Pradesh assembly elections. The alliance, however, failed to work. In the 2019

---

[22]Kaur, Naunidhi Kaur, 'Of Ayodhya and the Congress', *Frontline*, 8 December 2001, https://tinyurl.com/y58dw2wv. Accessed on 1 July 2024.
[23]Ibid.

polls, the Congress won only one of Uttar Pradesh's 80 Lok Sabha seats. It won only one seat in the Uttar Pradesh legislative assembly in the 2022 polls. The Congress and the SP joined hands again and became INDIA bloc partners in Uttar Pradesh in the 2024 Lok Sabha polls. This time, the alliance did wonders. The Congress's tally improved, with the party winning six seats and the SP registering victory on 37 seats. But the road ahead is still not easy for the Congress in Uttar Pradesh, politically the most significant state in India.

5

Saffron Surge

India was witnessing growing anti-Congress sentiments in 1977. A strong anti-incumbency wave worked against Indira Gandhi, the first female PM of India. She was the daughter of India's first PM Jawaharlal Nehru. She was initially dubbed a *goongi gudiya* (mute doll), as she kept a low profile and remained non-assertive despite holding important positions in the government and the Congress party.

Indira Gandhi, however, consciously and consistently transformed her image over the years by taking many bold decisions, including some controversial ones, and thus earned the title of the Iron Lady of India. Her authoritarian and contentious move to impose Emergency in India on 25 June 1975, which remained in force till 21 March 1977, made her even more unpopular. Consequently, she lost the 1977 Lok Sabha elections and so did several Congress stalwarts.

The BJS Links

India's first non-Congress government led by the Janata Party, with Morarji Desai as the PM, was thus formed in 1977. The BJS, to which the BJP owes its origin, was founded on 21 October 1951. The BJS, also known as the Jana Sangh, had strongly opposed the proclamation of Emergency. It merged with the Janata Party, along with other opposition parties, to oppose Indira Gandhi.

Syama Prasad Mookerjee, the founder of the BJS, was the minister of industry in the cabinet headed by Jawaharlal Nehru. He met the then RSS *sarsanghchalak* (chief) Madhav Sadashivrao Golwalkar to work out the formation of the BJS. He was opposed to the Nehru government's decision of banning the RSS following the assassination of Mahatma Gandhi. He accused it of indulging in Muslim appeasement. Ultimately, he resigned from the ministry on 19 April 1950, with 'desire for alternative politics against the policies of Jawaharlal Nehru' brewing in his mind.[1]

The BJS, which won three seats in the first Lok Sabha elections in 1951, was growing slowly as a political party.[2] It won four seats in 1957,[3] 14 seats in 1962,[4] 35 seats in 1967[5] and 22 seats in 1971 Lok Sabha elections.[6] Several opposition leaders were put behind bars during Emergency. The BJS merged with the Janata Party to pose a united front in 1977 Lok Sabha polls against the Congress government's oppression during Emergency. The Janata Party came to power after the 1977 polls and decided to set up a number of commissions of inquiry to probe the excesses committed against the people. Indira Gandhi was sent to jail for a brief period.

The Janata Party Disintegrates

Morarji Desai announced his resignation as the PM in July 1979, as he was unable to handle the internal contradictions in the first non-Congress government in independent India. This brought an ignominious end to the efforts that were being made to pose a challenge

---

[1] Anand, Kabool, 'BJP's 43 Years: How It Emerged from Jana Sangh and Became World's Largest Party', *India Today*, 7 April 2023, https://tinyurl.com/aucbv8tc. Accessed on 21 August 2024.
[2] *General Election, 1951 (Vol I, II)*, Election Commission of India, https://tinyurl.com/yuykdaxw. Accessed on 21 August 2024.
[3] *General Election, 1957 (Vol I, II)*, Election Commission of India, https://tinyurl.com/yet4m95b. Accessed on 21 August 2024.
[4] *General Election, 1962 (Vol I, II)*, Election Commission of India, https://tinyurl.com/5fbvancf. Accessed on 21 August 2024
[5] *General Election, 1967 (Vol I, II)*, Election Commission of India, https://tinyurl.com/jjtwybdf. Accessed on 21 August 2024.
[6] *General Election, 1971 (Vol I, II)*, Election Commission of India, https://tinyurl.com/ycxnd3ps. Accessed on 21 August 2024.

to the Congress. Dual membership (senior Janata Party ministers owing allegiance to the RSS as well) was one of the main issues that led to serious differences within the Janata Party, and caused the subsequent fall of Desai government.

Indira Gandhi decided to extend the Congress's support to Charan Singh, who, as home minister in Morarji Desai's government, had got Indira Gandhi arrested. He was made the next PM of India on 28 July 1979.

Charan Singh's tenure as PM was short-lived. He could continue in office till 14 January 1980 and tendered his resignation only 23 days after being sworn in as the PM. He gave indications that the Congress leadership expected him to withdraw the cases filed against Indira Gandhi and her son Sanjay Gandhi for the excesses committed during Emergency.

Charan Singh, however, did not name anyone directly. In a statement, published in the *Indian Express* on 21 August 1979, he referred to the 'authoritarian forces' and the 'quarters which sought interference in the normal functioning of the judiciary' and remarked, 'The country would not have forgiven us if we had, for the sake of remaining in office, agreed to withdraw prosecutions against persons responsible for atrocities during Emergency.'[7]

Indira Gandhi returned to power following fresh elections and became the PM again on 14 January 1980. It was during this tenure of Indira Gandhi—also the last—that the issue of liberation of Ram Janmabhoomi in Ayodhya was first raised at a meeting held in Muzaffarnagar on 23 March 1983.[8] The demands for a solution to Krishna Janmabhoomi in Mathura and settlement of the Kashi Vishwanath Temple–Gyanwapi Mosque dispute in Varanasi were tagged along with the demand for liberation of Ram Janmabhoomi.

---

[7]'Forty Years Ago, August 21, 1979: Charan Govt Resigns', *The Indian Express*, 21 August 1979, https://tinyurl.com/2p9w2d93. Accessed on 2 July 2024.

[8]'Invoking Cultural Consciousness: Shri Ram Janmabhoomi Movement Is an Example that the Energy Generated in the Sangh Powerhouse Is Used for Betterment of the Society and Finding Solution to the Social Problems', *Organiser*, 5 December 2016, https://tinyurl.com/ywrk766u. Accessed on 2 July 2024.

BJP Is Launched

Charan Singh's exit as the PM without ever facing Parliament exposed fissures in the Janata Party. Despite the Jana Sangh's merger with the Janata Party, those owing allegiance to the RSS faced accusations of dual loyalty. The RSS membership issue had come to the fore, and its escalation resulted in the disintegration of the Janata Party. A resolution that the party's national executive passed on 4 April 1980 left no place for the continued presence of RSS members in the Janata Party. So, those associated with the Jan Sangh had to leave of the Janata Party. This ultimately led to the formation of the BJP.

The BJP was thus launched in New Delhi on 6 April 1980. Atal Bihari Vajpayee, a prominent BJS leader with extraordinary oratory skills, was declared its first president. Vajpayee, who worked as the minister of foreign affairs in the Morarji Desai-led government and later rose to become the PM of India, had evolved himself as a moderate Hindutva leader. Vajpayee received appreciation even from his adversaries. His acceptability bridged the political divide and crossed all barriers. Prime Minister Jawaharlal Nehru was mesmerized with Vajpayee's speech in Parliament in 1957 and foretold, 'This young man one day will become the country's PM.'[9]

The BJP adopted Gandhian socialism as its guiding political philosophy. This did not work for the party. A section of BJP leaders, most notably Rajmata Vijayaraje Scindia, resisted the move even at that point of time.[10]

The assassination of PM Indira Gandhi on 31 October 1984 sent shock waves across the country. Her son Rajiv Gandhi was installed as the next PM of India. Under Rajiv Gandhi's leadership, the Congress scored a landslide victory in the 1984 Lok Sabha elections. He became the youngest PM, riding the sympathy wave generated following the assassination of his mother. He was nicknamed 'Mr Clean'. With his

---

[9] Basak, Sanjay, 'This Young Man Will Be PM One Day, Nehru Had Said of Vajpayee', *Deccan Chronicle*, 16 August 2018, https://tinyurl.com/2uesxvph. Accessed on 2 July 2024.
[10] Advani, L.K., *My Country My Life*, Rupa and Co., 2008, p. 322.

popularity at its peak, Rajiv Gandhi's charismatic leadership raised new hopes.

BJP's Introspection

The BJP won only two seats in the 1984 Lok Sabha elections.[11] This was the BJP's first Lok Sabha election, and the poll results were much lower than the party's expectations. The BJP's tally was even lower than that of the Jana Sangh, which had won three seats in the first Lok Sabha elections in 1951. Those who won were not the BJP stalwarts Atal Bihari Vajpayee and L.K. Advani, the two politicians who together built the BJP from scratch into a strong political force in the country. Instead, A.K. Patel from Mehsana, Gujarat, and Chandupatla Janga Reddy from Hanamkonda, Andhra Pradesh, were the two elected members of the Lok Sabha.

The BJP was massively disappointed, and obviously wanted to introspect. A working group comprising senior leaders felt that the party was veering away from its core political philosophy. The BJP's 'ideological distinctiveness' had been blurred and the party was failing to gain acceptance among the masses. The BJP had its roots in the Jana Sangh, and thus in the RSS. Senior party leaders who were unable to identify with the Gandhian socialism wanted the party to follow its own ideology. It was felt that Integral Humanism, as propounded by Pandit Deen Dayal Upadhyay, should be the ideology of the party, and this was included in the BJP's constitution at its national council meeting in Gandhinagar on 9 October 1985. The council adopted a resolution restating the party's Five Basic Commitments: (1) nationalism and national integration; (2) democracy; (3) Gandhian socialist approach to socio-economic system—that is, a society based on equity and freedom from exploitation; (4) positive secularism—that is, *sarvpantha sambhav*; and (5) value-based politics.[12]

---

[11]*General Election, 1971 (Vol I, II)*, Election Commission of India, https://tinyurl.com/2tuvc85t. Accessed on 21 August 2024.
[12]Malhotra, Vijay Kumar, and J.C. Jaitli, *Evolution of BJP: Vol. 10*, p. 20, https://tinyurl.

Bofors Scam

As PM, Rajiv Gandhi spoke openly from public platforms about the prevailing corruption in the system. He spoke about how only 15 paisa out of a rupee spent by the government on the people's welfare was actually reaching the people at the grassroots level.[13] His image of Mr Clean, however, did not last long. It suffered badly following a major dent when India entered into a ₹1,437 crore deal with AB Bofors, the Swedish artillery manufacturer, to buy 400 155 Howitzer guns for the Indian army in 1986. A year later, the Swedish State Radio channel, in its report on 16 April 1987, accused Bofors of paying kickbacks in the deal.[14] The Rajiv Gandhi-led government mishandled the issue right from the beginning; it strongly defended the Bofors deal. It termed the reports about kickbacks as false and mischievous. Many questions remained unanswered.

Rajiv Gandhi's wife Sonia, who later became president of the INC, hailed from Italy. His adversaries used this Italian connection as an opportunity to discredit him. The Rajiv Gandhi-led government mishandled the Shah Bano case as well. A mother of five children, Shah Bano was married to Mohammad Ahmad Khan. He got married again after nearly 14 years of marriage without paying any maintenance to her. A five-judge bench of the Supreme Court, comprising then Chief Justice of India Y.V. Chandrachud, Justice Ranganath Mishra, Justice D.A. Desai, Justice O. Chinappa Reddy and Justice E.S. Venkataramiah, ordered unanimously on 23 April 1985 for payment of maintenance to Shah Bano. Muslim fundamentalists were upset with the Supreme Court's order. *India Today* observed: 'India's 7.5-crore strong Muslim community is in turmoil because of the controversy on the Supreme Court judgement in the Shah Bano case. The religious row has strengthened fundamentalism

---

com/4ev7k4xa. Accessed on 21 August 2024.
[13]Saksena, Devendra, 'The 85-Paise Riddle!', *The Statesman*, 10 August 2017, https://tinyurl.com/afx84x2t. Accessed on 21 August 2024.
[14]"What Is the Bofors Scam Case?', *The Indian Express*, 3 February 2018, https://tinyurl.com/bdhpw9jk. Accessed on 2 July 2024.

and caused a severe schism within the community.'[15]

Rajiv Gandhi was under pressure to take steps to undo the Supreme Court's decision, and he succumbed to it. The Muslim Women (Protection of Rights on Divorce) Act 1986 was enacted to nullify the impact of the apex court's ruling. This move invited accusations of Muslim appeasement. Rajiv Gandhi's popularity graph was on a decline. He was losing ground badly. Advani called the enactment of the new law a blatant act to appease the minority vote-bank. This provided the BJP an opportunity to train its guns at the Congress. So, the grand old party looked for an opportunity to please the Hindus too. It worked to get the locks of the disputed structure opened on 1 February 1986. This was considered the Congress's masterstroke and the BJP was compelled to rework its strategy.

Senior journalist Kanchan Gupta, in an article in *Open* magazine, observed:

> It took three years between 1986 and 1989 for the BJP to get its act together. Partly because there was resistance to Advani's attempt to steer the party towards a Hindu platform and largely because, apart from Advani, nobody could really foresee how the Ayodhya story would unfold. Finally Advani decided to force the party's hand. At the Palampur national executive meeting in 1989, he moved a resolution, a rare exercise of presidential power, adopting Ayodhya as a core political cause of the BJP. Since a resolution moved by the President is passed without debate or vote, the naysayers had to bite their tongue and keep quiet. Thus was Ram Mandir added to what was till then a single-issue (abrogation of Article 370) core agenda; the demand for a Uniform Civil Code followed.[16]

---

[15]Gupta, Shekhar, Inderjit Badhwar, and Farzand Ahmad, 'Shah Bano Judgement Renders Muslims a Troubled Community, Torn by an Internal Rift', *India Today*, 16 January 2014, https://tinyurl.com/ym6jbtn4. Accessed on 2 July 2024.
[16]Gupta, Kanchan, 'A Chariot in History', *Open*, 15 November 2019, https://tinyurl.com/yc4uk98z. Accessed on 7 August 2024

The Palampur resolution, adopted at the BJP's national executive meeting held at Palampur, Himachal Pradesh, in June 1989, was a major move that provided the much-needed connect with the people and the Hindutva edge to the party. The Ayodhya issue was turning out to be advantageous to the BJP. The VHP, a frontal organization of the RSS, decided to put all its energy on raising the demand for construction of the Ram temple.

The BJP realized that the agitation for the construction of the Ram temple was going to have a larger impact on the political horizons. It demanded that the Ram temple be constructed in the same manner in Ayodhya in which the Jawaharlal Nehru government constructed the Somnath Temple. The Palampur resolution said:

> The BJP calls upon the Rajiv Government to adopt the same positive approach in respect to Ayodhya that the Nehru Government did with regard to Somnath. The sentiments of the people must be respected and Ram Janmasthan must be handed over to Hindus—if possible through a negotiated settlement, or else, by legislation. Litigation is certainly no answer.[17]

Somnath Temple, believed to be 2,000 years old, is situated in Gujarat on the shores of Arabian Sea on the west coast of India. Somnath is believed to be the first among 12 famous Jyotirlingas, the Hindu shrines where Lord Shiva is worshipped. The Jyotirlinga also represents Lord Shiva as a pillar of light. The Somnath Temple remained a point of attraction for foreign invaders. Mahmud Ghazni, in the mid-1020s, indulged in plundering before destroying the temple. He took away precious jewels along with other valuable items from there. In 1297 and 1394, the temple was destroyed again. In 1706, Mughal ruler Aurangzeb also demolished the structure.[18] Sardar Vallabhbhai Patel, India's deputy PM in the Jawaharlal Nehru-led government, visited

---

[17]'Advani Wants Early Verdict on Ayodhya', *The New Indian Express*, 17 May 2012, https://tinyurl.com/4rrnjvnr. Accessed on 21 August 2024.
[18]'Shree Somnath Jyotirlinga Temple', *Gujarat Tourism*, https://tinyurl.com/mrvfrrc6. Accessed on 21 August 2024.

Junagarh, Gujarat, and promised on 12 November 1947 to rebuild the same.[19]

The Palampur resolution proved to be an important milestone for the BJP, as it brought both the party and the Ram temple issue to the centre-stage of Indian politics. The Congress government was already feeling the pressure of the support that the VHP was building up in favour of the Ram Janmabhoomi issue. The VHP's demand for construction of the Ram temple was gaining momentum. This was when the Congress had a strong leadership at the top.

The Rajiv Gandhi-led government thought it was time to stop the BJP from taking any further advantage. Besides opening the locks of the disputed structure, the Rajiv Gandhi government decided to allow the laying of the Ram temple's foundation stone at a spot close to the disputed structure ahead of the 1989 Lok Sabha elections.

Prime Minister Rajiv Gandhi obviously had a well-worked-out plan in his mind. He was aware of the importance of the Ayodhya issue. He was also aware of the public's growing support for the Ram temple movement and the advantage the BJP might garner on the issue in the elections. He knew of the mounting challenges the Congress was going to face in the elections. He decided to take up the gauntlet. On 16 October 1989, Rajiv Gandhi called his foreign minister P.V. Narasimha Rao to his residence in the morning and asked him to lead the Indian delegation at the Commonwealth summit in Kuala Lumpur beginning next day. He said that the ECI was about to announce Lok Sabha elections and so he was going to stay back in New Delhi. On 17 October 1989, the ECI announced the programme for Lok Sabha elections. The polls were scheduled for 22 and 26 November 1989. Prime Minister Rajiv Gandhi was to launch the poll campaign from the Faizabad Lok Sabha seat, of which Ayodhya was a part.

---

[19]"History', *District Gir Somnath*, https://tinyurl.com/5dcjcc7r. Accessed on 2 July 2024.

Ram Rajya

Launching the poll campaign, Rajiv Gandhi called upon people to vote for the Congress to be able to usher in Ram Rajya. Did the Congress's plan work? It failed miserably. The Congress had queered its own pitch. It wanted to win the support of both Muslims and Hindus. It lost the support of both communities and consequently the 1989 Lok Sabha elections.

The Congress emerged as the largest single party in 1989 Lok Sabha elections, winning 197 out of the 510 seats it contested. Vishwanath Pratap Singh had shifted from finance ministry to defence ministry but resigned as the defence minister on 11 April 1987—five days before the Bofors revelations. He parted ways with the party before the 1989 elections. Singh extensively campaigned for the Janata Dal; the party stood second, winning 143 out of the 244 seats it contested for the Lower House (Lok Sabha) of Parliament.

BJP Gains

The BJP's numbers showed a remarkable jump with the party winning 85 of the 225 seats contested. The BJP's increased numbers reflected how the party was gaining by riding the Ram temple wave that the VHP's temple-related agitation was generating on the political horizons. The Rajiv Gandhi-led government's moves had boomeranged and obviously helped the BJP. The Congress, despite being the largest single party, decided not to form the government. Vishwanath Pratap Singh replaced Rajiv Gandhi as the PM with the BJP's support. The poll outcome bolstered the BJP's confidence. It indicated that the agitation for construction of the Ram temple was moving in the right direction and that the same was not a distant dream. The VHP had linked the Ram temple issue to the identity of the Hindus. The VHP's agitation was not for any other temple; it was about the temple at the birthplace of Lord Rama.

Somnath Yatra

The VHP proposed to perform kar seva at the disputed site on 30 October 1990. Its call for kar seva in Ayodhya on 30 October created a buzz. The BJP was waiting to make use of the available opportunity. But PM Vishwanath Pratap Singh's announcement regarding the implementation of Mandal Commission's recommendations, on 7 August 1990, led to a nationwide agitation and consequently a sharp division in Hindu society. Those favouring the Mandal Commission recommendations and those opposing them came face to face.

The BJP was concerned about the deep divide among Hindus. It did not want to shift focus from the Ram temple issue. It obviously wanted to associate directly with and promote the cause of the Ram temple, apparently to divert attention from the Mandal issue. It proposed to reach out to the masses and mobilize public opinion in favour of the construction of the Ram temple in Ayodhya. The Rath Yatra—from Somnath, Gujarat, to Ayodhya—was considered a good idea. Senior BJP leader Advani, who was then the BJP president, was to lead the Rath Yatra. He was evolving as a hard-core face of Hindutva. The idea of a Rath Yatra was conceived early in September 1990. Advani was thinking of undertaking a *padyatra* (journey on foot) from Somnath on 25 September 1990, which was the birth anniversary of party's ideologue, Pandit Deen Dayal Upadhyaya. The birth anniversary of Mahatma Gandhi, 2 October 1990, was considered another option when it came to deciding the date.

The Rath Yatra was to reach Ayodhya to join the kar seva proposed on 30 October. Advani shared the idea with Pramod Mahajan, who suggested that a padyatra might not be a workable idea. Mahajan said Advani would not be able to cover the areas the latter wanted to. Advani said he did not want to travel by car, as this would not provide opportunity for interaction with the people on his way. He thought a jeep yatra may be a better idea. So, Mahajan came up with the idea of a Rath Yatra, as the journey was being undertaken for the cause of the Ram temple.

He also suggested that the rath could travel across at least a dozen states covering a large part of western, southern, central, northern and eastern India.

The Rath Yatra Rolls

An air-conditioned Toyota vehicle was converted into a chariot, powered with cultural and religious symbolism, for the journey ahead. The chariot was 'bedecked with a colourful picture of a bow-and-arrow-wielding Rama'.[20] The Rath Yatra finally started on 25 September 1990. Advani offered prayers at the Somnath Temple in the morning. Those who accompanied him included Pramod Mahajan and Narendra Modi, the latter now being the PM of India.

Frenzy was witnessed on the route as the Rath Yatra moved ahead. The Rath Yatra caught the people's attention as they shouted slogans of 'Ram Lalla hum aayenge, mandir wahin banayenge (We will come to build the Ram temple there)', rang bells and beat thalis. The Rath Yatra continued to hog limelight, evoking tremendous response along the route. There were reports of communal tension/violence at some places.

The V.P. Singh-led government was closely watching the unfolding developments, and so were other leaders of the Janata Dal, including Lalu Prasad Yadav and Mulayam Singh Yadav, then CMs of Bihar and Uttar Pradesh, respectively.

The Rath Yatra had to pass through Bihar and some districts of eastern Uttar Pradesh to reach Ayodhya. A series of consultations were held at various levels to work out a solution. Advani was in New Delhi for a brief period, as his Rath Yatra took a break for the festival of Diwali. He was scheduled to leave for Calcutta on 18 October 1990, to resume the Rath Yatra from Dhanbad in Bihar. He cancelled his trip to remain available for any further discussions in New Delhi and decided to proceed directly to Dhanbad on 19 October. Advani met

---

[20] Verma, Nalin, '"Mandir Wahin Banayenge" Said L.K. Advani 30 Years Ago, but Will Stay Home on August 5', *The Wire*, 4 August 2020, https://tinyurl.com/txesa92a. Accessed on 21 August 2024.

the PM at the Sundar Nagar Guest House of the *Indian Express* in the presence of the newspaper's owner Ramnath Goenka, on 19 October. Advani, at this meeting, made it clear to the PM that the BJP did not intend to withdraw its support to topple the V.P. Singh-led government. Senior BJP leader Murli Manohar Joshi, who along with Atal Bihari Vajpayee and L.K. Advani formed part of the BJP's well-known trio, later deposing before the Liberhan Ayodhya Commission of Inquiry, observed that Advani did not intend to withdraw the BJP's support to the V.P. Singh government. 'Advani said that it was not the intention of the BJP that the government should fall. He said that it was alright if the government brought an ordinance and handed over the disputed land to the RSS/VHP official as its receiver. He said that the ordinance was welcome,' Joshi told the Liberhan Commission.[21] There was no positive outcome in the end.

The V.P. Singh-led government enjoyed the BJP's support. However, soon some differences cropped up between the two. The PM felt that the BJP did not cooperate and hardly ever discussed the subject threadbare with him. He apparently realized that though the BJP took advantage of the Ram temple issue in the 1989 Lok Sabha elections, it wanted to give an impression that the party and the VHP were two different entities and sought to downplay any differences with the Janata Dal on the issue.[22]

Stopping the Rath Yatra

Advani's Rath Yatra continued its onward journey. A game of political one-upmanship was already going on in the Janata Dal. Mulayam Singh Yadav's differences with the PM on handling of the Ram temple issue came to the fore. Bihar CM Lalu Prasad Yadav, too, was turning ambitious, aspiring to establish himself at the national political

---

[21]Singh, Onkar, 'M M Joshi Blames it on V P Singh', *rediff.com*, 11 June 2001, https://tinyurl.com/53uv3pne. Accessed on 21 August 2024.
[22]Mukerji, Debashish, *Disruptor: How Vishwanath Pratap Singh Shook India*, HarperCollins Publishers, 2021, pp. 407.

horizons. Both Mulayam Singh Yadav and Lalu Prasad apparently wanted to score a political point. The former gave sufficient indications that his government might not allow the Rath Yatra to roll on once it reached Uttar Pradesh. The latter had a geographical advantage; the Rath Yatra had to pass through Bihar to reach Uttar Pradesh. Lalu Prasad wanted to stop it early in Dhanbad, apprehending communal trouble if the procession were to move any further.

In his book, *Gopalganj to Raisina: My Political Journey*, Lalu Prasad observed:

> Soon after the BJP leader (Advani) announced his programme, I went to New Delhi to meet him personally. I said bluntly, '*Aap danga phailane wala yatra rok dijiye. Bahut parishram se humne Bihar mein bhaichara kayam kiya hai. Agar aap danga yatra nikaliyega, toh hum chhodengein nahin!* (You must stop the yatra plan, which is aimed at fuelling riots. We have re-established brotherhood in Bihar after a great deal of effort. If you don't stop the communal march, we won't spare you).' Though I was candid, I spoke politely to him in one-on-one meeting. But Advani, who is sober and soft-spoken, became infuriated. He said, '*Dekhta hoon, kaun mai ka doodh piya hai jo mera rath yatra rokega* (Let's see which person who has had his mother's milk can stop the chariot).' I then shot back, '*Mainey ma aur bhains dono ka doodh piya hai… Ayiye Bihar mein batata hoon* (I have had the milk of my mother, as well as of a buffalo… Come to Bihar to see what can I do).[23]

Lalu Prasad, whose government finally stopped and arrested Advani, said he was under no pressure to stop the Rath Yatra. About Advani's arrest, he said:

> To be honest, nobody had asked me to stop the procession or arrest Advani. The PM had said nothing. Mufti Mohammad Sayeed, who was the Union minister for home affairs, called

---

[23] Yadav, Lalu Prasad, and Nalin Verma, *Gopalganj to Raisina: My Political Journey*, Rupa Publications, 2019, p. 75.

me to Delhi and enquired if I planned to detain Advani. When I remained non-committal, he said, 'Why are you taking it upon yourself (to block the procession)? Let the yatra go on.' I then retorted, '*Aap sab ko satta ka nasha chad gaya hai* (You people are intoxicated by power).'[24]

Lalu Prasad Dithers?

Afzal Amanullah, the son-in-law of Syed Shahabuddin, IFS officer-turned-politician and the then convenor of the All India Babri Masjid Action Committee (AIBMAC), was posted as the deputy commissioner of Dhanbad, a part of undivided Bihar and now in Jharkhand, where Advani was scheduled to begin the second phase of his yatra to Ayodhya following a Diwali break.

The Bihar CM was weighing his options. He had probably already made up his mind to stop the Rath Yatra and get Advani arrested. He was in touch with the PM in New Delhi about Advani's arrest. Lalu Prasad claimed he did not get any response to his question to the PM on the issue. His claim gets credence as Singh's government was being run with the BJP's support. He wanted to get Advani arrested in Dhanbad and had asked the officials there to do so. However, Advani was not arrested there.

Did the officials refuse to arrest Advani at Dhanbad or did Lalu Prasad start having second thoughts? Afzal Amanullah clarified his position on the issue in 2007. According to a report published in the *Hindustan Times*, Afzal Amanullah indicated that RJD chief Lalu Prasad had dithered before ordering the arrest of L.K. Advani in October 1990, when the BJP leader's Rath Yatra was rolling to Ayodhya from Somnath. Amanullah, who was posted as home secretary of Bihar in November 2007, said, 'Lalu Prasad himself told me not to arrest Advani as it would have wider political ramifications. He had told me that he was in touch with V.P. Singh—then PM—and that arresting

---

[24]Ibid. 76.

Advani could lead to the fall of the government at the Centre.'[25] Advani's Rath Yatra did not stop at Dhanbad.

Advani Changes Route

Lalu Prasad clarified later that he planned to detain Advani at Sasaram, but this plan was leaked and Advani changed his route. Speaking to *NDTV*, Lalu Prasad said,

> Our original plan was to arrest him (Advani) the moment his train, the Howrah Rajdhani, entered Bihar around 2 a.m. somewhere near Sasaram. My DM of Rohtas, Manoj Srivastava took railway officials into confidence and the plan was to stop the train at a railway cabin and arrest L.K. Advani. But this plan was leaked, so we needed a new one. It was with great difficulty that we could reach Srivastava, who was already near the railway track. Those were days when there were no mobile phones.[26]

A decision was thereafter taken to detain him at Dhanbad, but this plan too did not materialize.

Amid rising communal tension and apprehensions about the fate of the V.P. Singh-led government, Advani's Rath Yatra reached Patna on 23 October 1990. Advani addressed a large public meeting in Patna and left for his journey to reach Samastipur. This place was part of Lalu Prasad's detention plans for Advani. The latter, along with other leaders, stayed there for the night. Lalu summoned IAS officer R.K. Singh, who later became the Union minister for power in the Narendra Modi government, and Deputy Inspector General (DIG) Rameshwar Oraon to his Anne Marg residence to discuss the modalities for Advani's arrest.

Both the officers were tasked with arresting Advani at Samastipur.

---

[25] Roy, Anirban Guha, 'Who Arrested Advani?', *Hindustan Times*, 3 November 2007, https://tinyurl.com/f8her6y9. Accessed on 2 July 2024.
[26] Yadav, Lalu, 'Why and How I Arrested LK Advani - By Lalu Yadav', *NDTV*, 7 December 2017, https://tinyurl.com/2fnsnjs2. Accessed on 21 August 2024.

Advani Arrested

Lalu Prasad kept his plans a closely guarded secret. He did not share anything with other officials, including the DM and SP of Samastipur. He called the pilot to get ready for an early flight the next day. He did not tell the pilot about the destination. He wanted to ensure that his plan was executed this time. He spoke to Sudhir Kumar, the DM of Dumka (now in Jharkhand), and asked him to get the Masanjore (about 30 km from Dumka) guesthouse ready for the next day. Lalu dropped hints that he might visit Dumka the following day. He also called the Samastipur government house as a journalist to enquire whether Advani was alone there and whether there were any journalists outside the guesthouse. He was told that Advani was alone sleeping in his room. R.K. Singh and Rameshwar Oraon knocked at the door of Advani's room in the guesthouse and arrested him. Both the officers informed Lalu that they had made the arrest and the BJP leader was being taken to Masanjore by chopper. Lalu ensured that appropriate security was deployed around the Masanjore guesthouse where Advani was being taken.

Advani's arrest in Samastipur on 23 October 1990 brought an abrupt end to the Rath Yatra. His arrest triggered communal tension at many places.

BJP Withdraws Support

Within hours of Advani's arrest, the BJP decided to withdraw its support to the V.P. Singh-led government. Senior BJP leader Atal Bihari Vajpayee handed over a letter to then President R. Venkataraman, informing him about the withdrawal of support to the central government. The President asked PM V.P. Singh to prove confidence in the Lok Sabha on 7 November 1990. The latter lost the confidence motion by a vote of 142 to 346 in the Lok Sabha, with eight abstentions. His government needed 261 votes to survive.[27]

---

[27]'Three Prime Ministers Who Lost No-Confidence Motions in the Past', *Hindustan*

Singh handed over his resignation to the President, marking the end of the 11-month V.P. Singh-led NF government of which the Janata Dal was a major constituent. The Rath Yatra eventually catapulted Advani to the position of a national Hindutva icon, and turned out to be an important milestone in the BJP's journey towards becoming a strong political force.

The Young Turk

By this time, the kar sevaks had begun arriving at Ayodhya. On 30 October 1990, the police opened fire to stop the kar sevkas; it resulted in the death of several kar sevaks in Ayodhya. Another attempt was made to reach the then disputed Ram Janmabhoomi–Babri Masjid structure on 2 November 1990. The police opened fire again to stop the kar sevaks. On one hand, the BJP blamed Uttar Pradesh CM Mulayam Singh Yadav and PM V.P. Singh for the violence. On the other hand, the BJP was being blamed for violating the prohibitory orders and fomenting communal trouble. However, the Rath Yatra, the subsequent arrest of Advani, the firing and continued agitation for the Ram temple drove a point home: why can't there be a Ram temple at the birthplace of Ram in Ayodhya?

There was a split in the Janata Dal. Chandra Shekhar, who led a breakaway faction of Janata Dal (Samajwadi Janata Party), became PM with the support of the Congress on 10 November 1990. He was active in politics from his student days and was known as a 'Young Turk' owing to his conviction and courage. He began working on finding a solution soon after assuming office as PM of India. But he resigned as PM in less than four months, accusing the Congress of sabotage; the Congress had targeted his government following allegations of police surveillance at the residence of the Congress leader and former PM Rajiv Gandhi. With the resignation of the Chandra Shekhar-led government, India faced the 1991 Lok Sabha elections.

Times, 20 July 2018, https://tinyurl.com/26xs8p33. Accessed on 21 August 2024.

BJP Wins Uttar Pradesh

The BJP's numbers rose again with the party winning 120 out of the 468 seats it contested in 1991 Lok Sabha elections. The Congress—which had refused to form government despite being the largest single party in 1989—won 232 out of the 487 seats contested in 1991. The Liberation Tigers of Tamil Eelam (LTTE) executed a well-worked plan to kill former PM Rajiv Gandhi, who was assassinated by a suicide bomber at Sriperumbudur in Tamil Nadu on 21 May 1991. P.V. Narasimha Rao became the PM of India, the first PM from the South. Uttar Pradesh assembly elections, too, were held in 1991, along with elections to the Lok Sabha following Mulayam Singh Yadav's resignation and recommendation to State Governor B. Satya Narayan Reddy to dissolve the legislative assembly. The BJP won the assembly elections in Uttar Pradesh, getting 221 out of the 415 assembly seats the party contested in the then 425-member assembly. Senior BJP leader Kalyan Singh, who emerged as the hero of the Ram temple movement, was installed as the CM of the first BJP government in Uttar Pradesh.

At Lord Rama's Doorstep

A new chapter began in the history of the temple movement as senior BJP leader Kalyan Singh began his innings as CM of Uttar Pradesh. The BJP used the formation of its government in Uttar Pradesh to send a message to the masses on the Ayodhya issue. After being sworn in as Uttar Pradesh CM on 24 June 1991, Kalyan Singh, along with his council of ministers, went for darshan of Ram Lalla at the disputed site in Ayodhya the following day, raising slogans of '*Saugandh Ram ki khate hain, mandir yahin banayenge* (We swear to Lord Rama to build the temple at the disputed spot)' to reaffirm the BJP's commitment to the cause of the Ram temple.

Both the central government led by P.V. Narasimha Rao and the state government of Kalyan Singh in Lucknow appeared to be working at cross purposes right from the beginning on the Ayodhya issue. There was a complete lack of coordination between the two. The demolition of the disputed structure on 6 December 1992 came as a big setback to both of them.

The BJP CM of Uttar Pradesh, Kalyan Singh, whose government was dismissed following the demolition, was a tall leader of the Ram temple movement. President's rule was imposed in Uttar Pradesh by the evening of 6 December. The BJP emerged stronger after the demolition jolt, and it was voted as the largest single party winning 177 of the 422 seats contested in the 1993 assembly elections. The BJP was, however, deprived of the opportunity of forming a government. This was the time of the beginning of the coalition era in Uttar Pradesh. Mulayam Singh Yadav, who had worked out a coalition with the Bahujan Samaj Party (BSP), was installed as the next CM with support of the Congress and other parties. The SP, which was an unrecognized party, won 109 of the 256 seats it contested, while the BSP, then a state party, won 67 out of the 164 assembly seats it contested in Uttar Pradesh.

Prime Minister Vajpayee

Then came the 1996 Lok Sabha elections. The P.V. Narasimha Rao-led government had lost its credibility. Questions were raised about the way they had handled the situation in Ayodhya on 6 December 1992. This election gave a fractured mandate. The BJP, which had established itself as the sole crusader of the cause of Hindutva, did not push the temple issue as aggressively as it did till the demolition of the disputed structure in the 1992. The party worked hard to spread its base. The BJP emerged as the largest single party in the 1996 Lok Sabha elections. It won 161 out of the 471 seats it contested in the elections. The Congress won only 140 out of the 529 seats it contested.[28] This marked the beginning of short-lived governments. The BJP formed its first-ever government at the Centre led by Atal Bihari Vajpayee. The first BJP government, however, lasted only for 13 days, as the party failed to prove its majority in the Lok Sabha.

---

[28]*General Election, 1996 (Vol I, II)*, Election Commission of India, https://tinyurl.com/57a3m69e. Accessed on 21 August 2024.

Short Tenure

Though Vajpayee's tenure remained short, it was considered an achievement for the BJP—it had come a long way following its formation.

The Janata Dal's H.D. Deve Gowda succeeded Vajpayee as the new PM of the United Front government on 1 June 1996, and remained in office till 21 April 1997. Inder Kumar Gujral of the United Front became the next PM and remained in office for less than one year. The 1998 Lok Sabha elections also saw a hung Parliament. The BJP won 182 out of the 388 seats the party contested. The Congress could only win 141 out of the 477 seats the party contested.[29] Atal Bihari Vajpayee became the PM of the National Democratic Alliance (NDA) government with the help of different political parties, and his government lasted 13 months this time.

Vajpayee Again

In the 1999 Lok Sabha elections, the BJP won 182 of the 339 seats it contested. The Congress tally came down to 114 out of 453 seats.[30] Atal Bihari Vajpayee was again installed as PM of the NDA government, and this government lasted a full term. Vajpayee made efforts to find a solution to the temple issue. But an amicable solution was hard to hammer out.

There was hope that the BJP would enact legislation to construct the Ram temple. People felt the party was not fulfilling its commitment. The BJP-led coalition, the NDA, was voted out in the 2004 Lok Sabha elections. The BJP won 138 out of the 364 Lok Sabha seats in 2004. The Congress won 145 out of the 417 seats it contested. The BJP's numbers came down to 116 seats in 2009. The Congress won 206

---

[29] *General Election, 1998 (Vols I, II)*, Election Commission of India, https://tinyurl.com/bde2mje7. Accessed on 21 August 2024.
[30] Election Commission of India, *Statistical Report on General Elections*, 1999, Volume 1, p. 90, https://tinyurl.com/mr38773n. Accessed on 28 November 2024.

seats in the 2009 Lok Sabha polls. It entered into alliances and the UPA government was formed in 2004 as well as 2009.

The Congress PM in both the UPA governments, Manmohan Singh, was known for his unassuming demeanour and worked to strengthen the economy and introduced schemes, like the Mahatma Gandhi National Rural Employment Guarantee Scheme However, his second term as PM was shrouded in controversies amid charges of policy paralysis, which became the hallmark of the government, along with a number of scams being reported one after the other.

BJP's Game Changer

The BJP, taking advantage of the situation, worked out a move announcing then Gujarat CM Narendra Modi as its prime ministerial candidate for the 2014 Lok Sabha elections. This proved to be a game changer for the party. It broke all its records, getting 282 seats in the 2014 polls. The Congress's number came down to 44 out of 464 in 2014. In 2019, the BJP won 303 out of the 436 seats contested; the Congress won 52 out of the 421 seats.

The Supreme Court of India, in the meantime, delivered its verdict, paving the way for the construction of the Ram temple, on 9 November 2019. The construction of the first phase of a grand Ram temple is complete; work to complete the remaining phases continues. At an event led by PM Narendra Modi, Ram Lalla's idol was consecrated at the newly built Ram Temple in Ayodhya on 22 January 2024, ahead of the 2024 Lok Sabha elections. The BJP, however, got only 240 Lok Sabha seats in the 2024 polls and lost the Ayodhya Lok Sabha seat. The party remained below the majority mark of 272 in the Lower House of Parliament. However, PM Modi secured a third term and now leads the NDA government at the Centre.

The BJP Rises

Year	BJP's Tally in Lok Sabha Elections
1984	2
1989	85
1991	120
1996	161
1998	18+2
1999	182
2004	138
2009	116
2014	282
2019	303
2024	240

6

Mandal vs Kamandal Politics

Held amid a raging controversy over the Bofors deal and rising Sikh militancy in Punjab, the 1989 Lok Sabha elections led to the exit of the Rajiv Gandhi-led Congress government at the Centre five years after it had won by a landslide.

The Janata Dal leader Vishwanath Pratap Singh, who spearheaded an aggressive poll campaign, relentlessly accusing the Rajiv Gandhi-led government of indulging in corruption, was installed as the next PM.

V.P. Singh led the NF government, the second coalition government after the Janata Party that came to power in 1977 general elections. Rajiv Gandhi, who launched his poll campaign on the Ram Rajya poll plank from Ayodhya, had lost his charisma. Meanwhile, V.P. Singh, who emerged as a formidable anti-corruption crusader, had begun his campaign from Bhagalpur (Bihar), which witnessed large-scale anti-Muslim violence.[1]

Muslims Rally behind Janata Dal

V.P. Singh's opposition to the VHP sent a message to the Muslims to rally behind the Janata Dal, which had joined hands with the BJP in terms of an informal seat adjustment in the 1989 Lok Sabha polls. The Congress, despite being the single largest party, failed to take along both Hindus and Muslims. Rajiv Gandhi decided to stay away

---

[1]Badhwar, Inderjit, and Prabhu Chawla, 'Rajiv Gandhi Loses His Charismatic Touch, V.P. Singh Proves to be a Formidable Campaigner', *India Today*, 30 November 1989, https://tinyurl.com/4h9bpjtb. Accessed on 14 June 2024.

from forming government, taking the 1989 poll results to be the people's mandate against his party. As V.P. Singh's campaign against the Congress had led to the exit of the Rajiv Gandhi-led government, he was being considered as the obvious choice by the Janata Dal for the PM's post. Drama, however, unfolded when the Janata Dal MPs gathered at the central hall of Parliament to elect the new leader of its parliamentary party who, by established convention, would take over as the PM. When the proceedings began, V.P. Singh proposed the name of Haryana CM Chaudhary Devi Lal as the Janata Dal parliamentary party's leader. Soon the journalists waiting outside flashed the news that Devi Lal was to be the next PM. This was not to be the scripted end of the story. When Devi Lal rose to speak, he nominated V.P. Singh as the Janata Dal parliamentary party leader, withdrawing his own name for the post. Singh was thus elected and sworn in as the PM of India on 2 December 1989. The BJP extended support to the V.P. Singh-led NF government; so did the two communist parties.

NF Contradictions

The NF government was full of internal contradictions. Chandra Shekhar, who later replaced V.P. Singh in the country's top political seat of power following the BJP's move to withdraw support from the latter's government, was considered a strong claimant for the PM's post. Devi Lal, too, considered himself a candidate for the country's top political post. Chandra Shekhar supported Devi Lal.

V.P. Singh chose Devi Lal to be the deputy PM in an obvious bid to balance the pressures within the NF government. The latter's aspirations soon began to run high. He had given up his claim to be elected the Janata Dal leader as an apparent compromise formula to pave way for V.P. Singh to become the PM. The NF government enjoyed the support of the ideologically opposite parties. He had to strike a balance and ensure coordination between the opposite and asymmetrical ideologies.

BJP Cadres Felt Isolated

Though the BJP and the Janata Dal worked out a seat adjustment, V.P. Singh strategically maintained distance from the former during his poll campaign. Singh always called the left parties his natural allies. He did not say so about the BJP. Senior BJP leader L.K. Advani felt V.P. Singh's behaviour towards the BJP at some public meetings was not acceptable and reflected his double standards. Advani, in his autobiography *My Country My Life*, recounted a 'distasteful' incident that took place at an election rally in favour of a Janata Dal candidate in Mathura. Advani said that the Janata Dal and the BJP had made seat adjustment and supported each other's candidates, and that the BJP was campaigning for the Janata Dal's candidate in the temple town of Mathura. However, V.P. Singh objected to the BJP's flags being put up alongside the flags of the Janata Dal at the venue when he came to address the election rally in Mathura. He refused to address the public meeting unless the BJP's flags were removed from there. This made the BJP workers angry.

Advani stated,

> 'Our party workers were flabbergasted and angry. After all, it was the Janata Dal that had sought seat sharing and a joint election campaign with the BJP. Even after the election, when it was time for government formation, VP Singh had no compunction in seeking and accepting the support of the BJP. Simultaneously, he had this tendency of projecting himself as an 'uncompromising secularist' who would have nothing to do with the BJP. This was certainly a blatant display of double standards.'[2]

V.P. Singh Feels the Pressure

V.P. Singh was facing mounting pressure from the VHP's campaign for the Ram temple. He faced pressure from Devi Lal too. The politics that

---

[2]Rao, P.V. Narasimha, *Ayodhya: 6 December 1992*, Penguin Random House, India, 2006, p. 442.

V.P. Singh followed to deal with the pressure from both sides changed the course of politics in the country. The BJP, too, worked out ways to deal with V.P. Singh. The party and Singh continued to make moves and counter-moves, and this subsequently came to be called the 'politics of Kamandal and Mandal', which continued to dominate the political horizons of India for at least the next four decades. *Kamandal* is an oblong water pot carried by sages. This term is often used, mainly in the Hindi heartland, when talking about the BJP's politics of Hindutva and pushing the cause of the liberation of the three shrines at Ayodhya, Mathura and Kashi. The term 'Mandal' owes its origin to the name of former chairman of Backward Classes Commission, B.P. Mandal, who submitted his report recommending quota in jobs for the Other Backward Classes (OBCs) on 31 December 1980. The Mandal issue, thus, is linked to the OBCs' fight for social justice, focusing on empowerment and the politics of caste.

The Fault Lines

The Janata Dal had included the promise of implementation of the Mandal Commission recommendations in its 1989 Lok Sabha elections manifesto. The Mandal Commission issue had the potential of derailing the BJP's and the VHP's Ram temple plans that the 1989 Palampur resolution had brought to the centre stage. V.P. Singh resorted to the Mandal card to manage the pressures within the Janata Dal. It was considered to be a tool to manage the pressure from the BJP as well.

The caste lines or the fault lines clearly existed in society. The political aspirations of the Janata Dal leaders were bringing them to the fore.

Mayhem at Meham

The NF began to feel the pinch of internal contradictions within a few months after V.P. Singh's installation as the PM. Devi Lal was seen as an important power centre that posed a threat to V.P. Singh's leadership.

The unease between Singh and Devi Lal came to public domain during by-election to Haryana's Meham legislative assembly constituency that Devi Lal represented till the 1989 Lok Sabha elections. The CM of Haryana had resigned from this seat when he became the Deputy PM in the V.P. Singh-led government. His son O.P. Chautala replaced him as CM of Haryana. As Chautala was not an MLA, he had to get elected to the Haryana legislative assembly from any seat within a period of six months. The choice obviously turned out to be the Meham assembly seat. The by-election to the Meham assembly seat on 27 February 1989 was held amid reports of rigging and booth capturing. The ECI announced re-polls for eight booths next day. Ten persons were killed in violence on the re-poll day and the election was subsequently countermanded.[3] This caused embarrassment to V.P. Singh, who eventually sought the resignation of O.P. Chautala.

This aggravated the situation further as relations between Singh and Devi Lal soured. Growing differences between them were an open secret. This had the potential to lead to fall of the NF government. Some of the NF leaders like Lalu Prasad Yadav saw the Mandal Commission report as an opportunity to settle inner contradictions. This was also apparently an effective tool to divert attention from the Ram temple issue. Former Bihar CM Lalu Prasad Yadav, in his memoir *Gopalganj to Raisina: My Political Journey*, said that he was worried about the differences between Singh and Devi Lal because the fall of the NF government could have an impact on Bihar. So he came up with the idea of implementation of the Mandal Commission's report. Yadav met V.P. Singh and requested him to take action against Devi Lal.

Yadav wrote:

> V.P. Singh had a sharp mind and good political instincts. He replied, 'Devi Lal Ji is a leader of the Jats and the backwards. If I act against him, he might fan out in India, propagating that I

---

[3]Verma, Nivedita, 'Dus Point Mein Samjhein Meham Kand (Know about Meham in 10 Points)', *Amar Ujala*, 27 May 2022, https://tinyurl.com/sj8d63em. Accessed on 12 August 2024.

am anti-backward and anti-poor.' He was right, of course. But I had come fully prepared. I responded, 'There is a way out. The Mandal Commission gave its report in 1983 recommending a 27 per cent quota for the backward classes in government jobs.[4]

Advani Wanted Consultation

Yadav put forth his point effectively to V.P. Singh. The latter, having the BJP's support to his government, maintained lines of communication with the party's leaders. V.P. Singh used to have weekly dinners for BJP leader Advani and CPI (M) general secretary Harikishan Singh Surjeet. Advani had made it clear to Singh that the Mandal Commission report should be implemented after proper discussions with his party and other coalition partners. But the PM apparently felt otherwise. He had to take a call on the issue soon. He dropped Deputy PM Devi Lal from his cabinet on 1 August 1990.

Singh Makes Up Mind

V.P. Singh had made up his mind to implement the Mandal Commission recommendations. He was a shrewd politician. He inducted Devi Lal as deputy PM to keep him in good humour. But he failed to foresee how Devi Lal could turn out to be the trouble maker for his government. However, he was ready to take on Devi Lal. This became evident six days after he dropped the latter from his cabinet. On 7 August 1990, he announced in Parliament that the central government will provide 27 per cent reservation in jobs of government and public-sector undertakings (PSUs) to socially and educationally backward classes. This led to nationwide agitation by the youths against the central government's move. Delhi University student Rajiv Goswami committed self-immolation against the Union government's move. Singh's move had hit and shaken the BJP badly.

---

[4]Yadav, Lalu Prasad, and Nalin Verma, *Gopalganj to Raisina: My Political Journey*, Rupa Publications, 2019, pp. 55–6.

Opinions of CMs Sought

Singh held consultations with the CMs of different states and got favourable response from Mulayam Singh Yadav and Lalu Prasad Yadav, the CMs of Uttar Pradesh and Bihar, respectively. It was, however, only after Devi Lal's exit from the cabinet that the issue was expedited, and a decision to implement the report was taken. Senior journalist Debashish Mukerji, in his book *Disruptor: How Vishwanath Pratap Singh Shook India*, has noted:

> Barring Sharad Pawar and Paswan, most ministers were surprised. '*Pehle se koi build-up nahin tha, pata bhi nahin tha kisiko* (There was no previous build-up, no one knew it was coming),' said Arif Khan (Governor of Kerala). But with the report's implementation having been promised in the Janata Dal manifesto, no one dissented on that day either. Arif Khan, however, presciently worried about how their supporting parties—the BJP and communists—would respond, though he realized that no party would risk opposing the decision, publicly, given the size of the OBC vote bank.[5]

Singh announced the decision to implement the Mandal Commission report without consulting the BJP, which was extending outside support to the NF government led by him. The BJP was not happy with the way he decided to implement the report. Advani had requested Singh for consultation before making the final move. The Left parties were also not apparently happy with the way the government went ahead with the implementation of the Mandal Commission report, and wanted economic backwardness instead of caste as the criteria for reservation.[6] The VHP was building pressure on the NF government to begin the kar seva for construction of the Ram temple, and the Mandal report

---

[5]Mukerji, Debashish, *Disruptor: How Vishwanath Pratap Singh Shook India*, HarperCollins Publishers, 2021, p. 394.
[6]Nair, Sobhana K., *Ram Vilas Paswan: The Weathervane of Indian Politics*, Roli Books, 2024, p. 85.

was diverting attention from the Ram temple issue. The BJP obviously wanted to divert attention from the politics of Mandal to Kamandal. It thought of reaching out to the people to give a push to the Ram temple agenda. It was against this backdrop that the idea of organizing a Rath Yatra was conceived.

An article in *Frontline* has observed:

> In 1990, the RSS was demanding that the BJP publicly denounce the Mandal Commission report. While the party's upper-caste leaders agreed in private, they could not say it publicly lest it alienate the party's middle castes.
>
> The VHP was desperate to begin the construction of the Ram temple in Ayodhya and had announced October 30 as the appointed date. It was then that BJP leader Lal Krishna Advani came up with the perfect foil for the Mandal agitation—the kamandal politics of Hindutva.[7]

Another article published in *The Statesman* noted that the RSS was not comfortable with the implementation of OBC quota in jobs. It stated:

> The RSS castigated the V.P. Singh government's decision to implement OBC reservation. Dr Rajendra Singh, who was the RSS chief between 1994 and 2000, called for gradual reduction in job quotas. (Mohan) Bhagwat (who is the RSS chief now) himself in 2016 just before the Assembly elections in Bihar proposed a review of reservation policy. Publicity chief of the RSS, Manmohan Vaidya, too in 2017, speaking at the Jaipur Literature Festival, suggested fixation of a time limit for continuation of reservation. Faced with backlash, the RSS quickly distanced itself from the statements made by Bhagwat and Vaidya. But the discomfort of the RSS with the idea of caste-based reservation has become apparent.[8]

---

[7] '1990: Lal Krishna Advani Embarks on Rath Yatra', *Frontline*, 15 August 2022, https://tinyurl.com/yc5xhxe8. Accessed on 9 August 2024.

[8] Guha, Ayan, 'RSS and the Reservation Riddle', *The Statesman*, 4 October 2019, https://tinyurl.com/9pur9cuc. Accessed on 9 August 2024

The RSS has now clarified its stance on the reservation issue. It has reiterated that 'anybody whoever has been given reservations should continue to have them, as long as societal inequality exists.'[9]

The Caste System

It is important to mention the existing caste system in which India has remained caught up for ages. It has been responsible for the inequalities in society. There has been discrimination on the basis of caste in society, and the Mandal report issue finds its origin in the same. Did the caste divide exist in ancient India? The Purushasukta, considered a hymn in the Rigveda, refers to the origin of the 'varnas' or the caste system.[10] According to this, the gods created the world from the cosmic being—the Purusa—the primeval male whose body was offered at a Vedic sacrifice. His mouth became scholars, teachers and priests (Brahmins); his arms were made into the warriors (Kshatriyas); his thighs the common people (Vaishyas); and from his feet came the servants or labourers (Shudras).[11]

The caste system was, however, not hereditary and rather based on division of work. There are various other theories too about the origin and the time of origin of the caste system. Some foreign travellers have referred to the caste system in ancient India. Its origin is also linked to the arrival of Aryans in India. *The Cambridge History of India* has dealt with the issue of the existence of the caste system in the Rigveda period:

> In one sense, its (caste system's) presence in the Rigveda cannot be disputed. In the Purushasukta the four castes of the later texts, Brahmana (priest), Rajanya (prince or more broadly

---

[9]The Wire Analysis, 'Mohan Bhagwat Says RSS Always Supported Reservations. But Is That True?', *The Wire*, 29 April 2024, https://tinyurl.com/mpp8dxkx. Accessed on 9 August 2024
[10]Wendy Doniger O'Flaherty (trans.), *The Rig Veda*, Page 2000, Penguin Random House, India, pp. 29-30.
[11]Ibid. 29-31.

warrior), Vaisya (commoner) and Sudra are mentioned. But this hymn is admittedly late and can prove nothing for the state of affairs prevailing when the bulk of Rigveda was composed. On the other, as we have seen, the distinction between the Aryan colour (varna) and that of the aborigines is essential and forms the basis of caste. The question is thus narrowed down to the consideration of the arguments for and against the view that in the Aryans themselves caste divisions were appearing. On the other hand, it is argued that in the period of Vashistha and Visvamitra, when the great poetry of the Rigveda was being produced, neither the priestly class nor the warrior class was hereditary.[12]

First Backward Classes Commission

The caste system gradually became more rigid over the years. Certain sections of society were denied basic rights on the basis of their castes. The caste system thus became the root cause of inequalities in society that still persist. The Constitution of India came into force on 26 January 1950, providing equality to all citizens. It bars any discrimination against any citizen on the basis of religion, race, caste, sex and place of birth. The Union government decided to set up the First Backward Classes Commission on 29 January 1953. The commission headed by Kaka Kalelkar made efforts to study the situation at the grassroots level and toured extensively before submitting its report on 30 March 1955. It analysed the information thus received and worked out the criteria for identification of socially and educationally backward classes. It also worked out a large list of backward castes and classified the most backward among them.

---

[12]Keith, A. Berriedale, 'The Age of the Rigveda', *The Cambridge History of India, Volume 1: Ancient India*, Edward James Rapson (ed.), Cambridge University Press, London, 1922, p. 92.

Mandal Commission Set up

When the Janata Party came to power, PM Morarji Desai made an announcement on the floor of Parliament on 20 December 1978 about setting up a Backward Classes Commission. Babu Bindeshwari Prasad Mandal, former MP and former CM of a non-Congress government for a brief period in Bihar in 1968, was appointed chairman of the commission. Four members of this commission, popularly known as the Mandal Commission, included Dewan Mohan Lal, R.R. Bhole, Dina Bandhu Sahu and K. Subramaniam. Dina Bandhu Sahu resigned from his membership on 5 November 1979 on grounds of health. L.R. Naik (a former MP) replaced him as a member. The commission was expected to investigate the conditions of socially and educationally backward classes in India.

Mandal Commission Submits Report

The Indira Gandhi-led government gave two extensions to the commission and delivered her valedictory address on 12 December 1980. The Mandal Commission, in its report submitted on 31 December 1980, identified 3,743 castes as socially backward. B.P. Mandal, while submitting the commission's report, wrote to the President of India on 31 December 1980, observing,

> On the basis of our extensive tour throughout the length and breadth of India the response received from the general public at large, I would like to state that the Backward Classes of this country repose high hopes in the Government's positive response to our recommendations. Apprehensions were rightly expressed before us that in case the report of my Commission also meets the same fate as that of Kaka Kalelkar's Commission, the legitimate hopes and aspirations of the socially and educationally backward classes, which constitute a bulk of the population, will be dashed to ground.[13]

---

[13]*Report of the Backward Classes Commission, First Part (Vols 1 and 2)* 1980, https://tinyurl.com/yjdx2n38. Accessed on 9 July 2024.

Mandal's apprehensions were not baseless. The Indira Gandhi government did not act on the report. It remained buried in the Union government's files for nearly a decade. The Rajiv Gandhi-led government chose not to act. The state governments expected the Centre to take a call to implement its recommendations. Mandal may not have been aware of the impact that the commission's recommendations would have on the politics of the country in the years to come. A demand for reservation for backward castes, however, was being consistently raised. This was coming into focus in the Hindi heartland where the VHP was intensifying its agitation for the construction of the Ram temple.

The Centre Seeks Opinion

Senior Congress leader N.D. Tiwari, who had the distinction of working as CM of undivided Uttar Pradesh and Uttarakhand, was CM of Uttar Pradesh at the time of the 1989 Lok Sabha elections as well. He spoke on the issue of reservation for backward classes in the state legislative assembly during the question hour on 28 September 1989. He wanted to make the point that his government had taken an initiative on the issue even before the setting up of the Mandal Commission, and that the Centre had sought opinion of the state government on the issue. Tiwari said:

> The Mandal Commission was set up by the central government and so the main responsibility of implementing the same lies with the Union government. The central government has taken steps in this regard and has asked for opinion… In 1977 this humble servant (Tiwari) got an opportunity to announce, for the first time, 15 per cent reservation (for backward classes). Later, orders in this regard were issued when Ram Naresh Yadav was the CM (of the Janata Party). But the court took the view that the orders were not well thought out, not considered deeply and were not in accordance with the aspirations of the Constitution. The orders were thus called invalid. I have constituted a sub-committee of the state cabinet and it has held nine meetings.

The sub-committee collected a lot of facts to consider whether the Mandal Commission's list of backward classes is correct or not whether mind was applied to make the list. We accepted the sub committee's report, and an ordinance was promulgated, and it has been implemented w.e.f. 1977 to ensure that the appointments made in the intervening period have some basis and those appointed get seniority. This house will get an opportunity to pass the replacing bill against the ordinance.[14]

Tiwari's observations indicate that the Mandal Commission report was turning out to be an important issue on the political horizons, and the Rajiv Gandhi-led government had sought the state government's opinion on the same.

The Backlash

V.P. Singh's announcement to implement the Mandal Commission recommendations led to countrywide protests, and reports of incidents of self-immolation began pouring in. Soon representatives of different sections of society, including engineers, doctors and teachers, joined the agitating groups of students one after the other. As there was backlash against the decision of implementing the recommendations, the V.P. Singh-led government's move came into question.

Pranab Mukherjee, former President of India, felt that the V.P. Singh-led government was under pressure of managing contradictions within and the rising demand for the Ram temple in Ayodhya. He wrote:

> Beset by internal contradictions and the growing stridency of the BJP/VHP demand for a mandir in Ayodhya, the VP Singh-led NF government announced in Parliament, on 7 August 1990, that it would go ahead with the implementation of the Mandal Commission's recommendations to implement a

---
[14]'Proceedings and Synopsis', *Uttar Pradesh Legislative Assembly*, 28 September 1989, p. 4, https://tinyurl.com/mr3hcbn2. Accessed on 12 August 2024.

27 per cent reservation quota for OBCs in government jobs and central universities. A violent and widespread student's agitation exploded against this decision. One of the agitators, Rajiv Goswami, attempted self-immolation in October 1990 shocking the nation.[15]

The Face of Rage

Rajiv Goswami, a Delhi University student, was the first to set himself on fire, on 19 September 1990. He became the face of rage and agitation against the Mandal Commission recommendations. The agitation spread like wildfire, with more students attempting self-immolation. Former bureaucrat Anil Swarup, who worked in senior positions in the Uttar Pradesh government, in the Union government, and also with Uttar Pradesh CM Kalyan Singh, observed:

> With a view to countering the 'Kamandal' agitation, a large political group led by Vishwanath Pratap Singh who eventually became the PM of India, announced reservation for backward castes in government jobs. 'Kamandal' was an epithet assigned to describe the agitation launched by right-wing organizations like the VHP to build a Ram temple at Ayodhya during the late 1980s. Horrific scenes of self-immolations during those agitations still remain etched in the memory of many.[16]

The BJP's Dilemma

As mentioned earlier, the RSS wanted the BJP to publicly denounce the V.P. Singh-led government's decision amid apprehensions of the saffron party losing its upper-caste support base.

But both the RSS and the BJP refrained from doing so. They had to walk a tightrope. Both organizations were aiming at consolidating

---

[15]Mukherjee, Pranab, *The Turbulent Years: 1980–1996*, Rupa Publications, 2016, pp. 117–19.
[16]Swarup, Anil, *Ethical Dilemmas of a Civil Servant*, Unique Publishers, 2021, p. 59.

the Hindu votes on the Ram temple issue. The implementation of the Mandal Commission recommendations had far-reaching consequences for society. The OBCs, together with the Dalits, formed a formidable political force.

The BJP had been pushing for the cause of the temple at the birthplace of Lord Rama, revered by Hindus regardless of class and caste. The party and its affiliate organizations, such as the VHP, had been pursuing the politics of aggressive Hindutva. Any division among Hindus on the lines of caste, when it came to an issue like Mandal Commission recommendations, posed a threat to this. The BJP, however, had no other choice. It had to welcome the decision to implement the Mandal Commission recommendations. It did raise questions over the manner in which the Mandal report was implemented. L.K. Advani noted in his book: 'Here, sadly, was a classic case of a socially progressive measure earning a bad name because of its blatant politicization.'[17] At its national executive committee meeting held in New Delhi on 17 October 1990, the BJP adopted a resolution stating:

> The BJP has been in favour of reservations to socially and educationally backward classes. However, the manner in which the Government announced its decision about the Mandal Commission Report without any consultation with supporting parties, and without qualifying it with any economic criteria, was utterly wrong. The decision was prompted not by any concern for the backward classes, but by considerations of political expediency. The Government's decision can only lead to dividing and sub-dividing society. The result has been not only serious disturbance of peace and enormous loss of life and property, but also the immolation by some of the flowers of our youth.
>
> The issue of Ram Janmabhoomi Mandir–Babri Masjid has been hanging fire for long. The people want the Ayodhya sites restored to close the old unhappy chapter of the Mandir, desecrated and converted into a Mosque. This is not a communal

---

[17] Advani, L.K., *My Country My Life*, Rupa and Co., New Delhi, 2008, pp. 447.

issue. It is a matter of national honour, calculated to promote national reconciliation. But instead of seeing the matter in this positive light, the Government has communalised the issue. Some leaders of the ruling party have even whipped up communal passions, leading to serious rioting.[18]

After pointing towards the politicization of the Mandal Commission report, and how the Ram Janmabhoomi–Babri Masjid issue had remained unresolved for years, the BJP national executive committee felt there was a need to respect the Hindu sentiments. It felt that the Hindu sentiment could be satisfied only with the construction of a temple at the Ram Janmasthan. It pointed out that the mosque built by Babur was abandoned in 1936, and thus no namaz had been offered at the place thereafter. Since at least 1949, pujas and *parikrama*s (a ritual performed by clockwise circumambulation of entities, objects or places) had been going on there regularly. The dispute was in fact between a mandir and a non-masjid. 'Even so, in deference to Muslim sentiment, the VHP has offered to relocate the Masjid structure elsewhere.'[19]

The BJP national executive warned the Union government of withdrawal of support if any attempts were made to stop the Rath Yatra led by L.K. Advani. It resolved that the Union government should respect the sentiments of the people and allow construction of the Ram temple at his birthplace, in Ayodhya.[20]

Questions Raised

Prime Minister V.P. Singh's move to implement the Mandal Commission's recommendations did not leave other leaders with any choice. Major political parties were aware that any semblance of opposition to the move, on any pretext, would deprive them of support of the OBCs, a sizeable chunk among the Hindus. A sharp division persisted in society

---

[18]'BJP—Political Resolutions', *BJP e-Library*, pp. 290–1, https://tinyurl.com/44mjpzke. Accessed on 9 August 2024.
[19]Ibid.
[20]Ibid.

on the issue. Those from upper castes who strongly opposed the move did not command a majority. Those belonging to the deprived sections, on the other hand, supported the move. Hence, the senior-most leaders had to indulge in a balancing act. While welcoming or supporting the implementation of the Mandal Commission recommendations, they questioned the way the report was implemented without taking the student community into confidence.

Rajiv Gandhi Makes His Point

V.P. Singh's predecessor Rajiv Gandhi, who was then the Leader of Opposition in Lok Sabha, made his point clear on the issue of reservations. He accused the PM of creating rift in the society. Speaking in Lok Sabha on the Mandal Commission report on 6 September 1990, he said:

> We, the Congress, are in favour of a comprehensive action plan, an affirmative action plan for the backward communities. We need that. The problem cannot be solved by playing politics or by limited politically motivated manipulations... Both of them, whether it is the Kalelkar Commission or the Mandal Commission, talk of very wide ranging, sweeping action that needs to be taken. We must remember that. The Congress is for such assistance to 'Socially and Educationally Backward Classes'. That is what the constitution had said. But having said that we are in favour of all such measures. I am including 'all' because I believe some questions were raised yesterday in this House. The Congress is in favour of all such measures.[21]

Rajiv Gandhi made it clear that the Congress was in favour of assisting the socially and economically backward classes (SEBCs). The grand old party would like the benefits to reach all the people who needed them and not remain confined to the privileged lot. He obviously wanted

---

[21]'Discussion under Rule 193', *Lok Sabha Debates, Third Session*, 6 September 1990, pp. 486–8, https://tinyurl.com/msj5xzkm. Accessed on 10 August 2024.

exclusion of those who did not fall in the category of socially and educationally backward classes.

He questioned how the benefits for SEBCs could be given to the children of a person who occupied a high constitutional office like that of a Supreme Court judge for 10 or more years and became a cabinet minister. Did the children of such persons really need help, or were the benefits given by the government being cornered by landlords and the people who owned property, he asked.[22]

L.K. Advani, in his autobiography, has made a reference to Rajiv Gandhi's speech as an important one and one of the longest speeches heard in Parliament. Advani observed that on the question of excluding the 'creamy layer', there was unanimity among the BJP, the Communist parties and the Congress.

V.P. Singh responded to Rajiv Gandhi's observations about the individuals in the higher economic strata getting the benefits. He said that the issue was about the whole section of society—the SEBCs—and not about socially and educationally backward persons. 'When a class moves up, then, of course, weaning out can be there. But when the whole class is under just zero and one per cent, that is not the issue. The issue is whether the whole class has gone up or not. That is the issue,' he stated.[23]

V.P. Singh Unhappy

V.P. Singh was not happy with the BJP leadership. He was critical of the party's stance on the Mandal Commission implementation. He observed that the decision to implement the recommendations led to Advani's Rath Yatra from Somnath to Ayodhya. The *Frontline* reported V.P. Singh's deposition before the Liberhan Commission on 20 November 2001: 'To my mind, it was the implementation of the Mandal report that led to the Rath Yatra. It was at that point that the BJP abandoned its stand that the Ayodhya issue is not on their agenda,

---
[22]Ibid.
[23]Ibid. 492.

and it was to counter Mandal that they took Ayodhya on their agenda.'[24]

V.P. Singh also felt that it was not the Shah Bano case (as stated by Advani before the Liberhan Commission) but the implementation of the Mandal Commission recommendations announced by him that triggered Advani's Rath Yatra.

Singh's government saw an exit when the BJP decided to withdraw its support following Advani's arrest in Bihar. Mulayam Singh Yadav, who was the Janata Dal CM in Uttar Pradesh, disassociated himself from V.P. Singh. Chandra Shekhar replaced V.P. Singh as the PM with the Congress's support. Mulayam Singh Yadav continued to be the CM of the Janata Dal breakaway group with the Congress's support. However, senior Congress leader N.D. Tiwari, who was the Leader of Opposition in the Uttar Pradesh legislative assembly, questioned the intentions of the V.P. Singh-led government over the manner in which it implemented the Mandal Commission recommendations.

Tiwari Questions NF Government

Speaking on the motion of confidence moved by CM Mulayam Singh Yadav in the Uttar Pradesh legislative assembly, N.D. Tiwari said:

> The manner in which the central government implemented reservation to indulge in politics of reservation and make vote banks can't be justified. Its bad outcome is being reflected on the youths who are setting them on fire. Self-immolation is sad. About 100 youths have set themselves on fire. These 'Lomharshak' (deeply moving) self-immolations took place right under the nose of the NF government. Besides the self-immolations, why were police bullets fired on the youths at a number of places? If the students and youths had been taken into confidence on the issue such a situation would not have occurred.[25]

---

[24]Kaur, Naunidhi, 'Of Ayodhya and the Congress', *Frontline*, 8 December 2001, https://tinyurl.com/3rdz58z3. Accessed on 10 July 2024.
[25]Uttar Pradesh Vidhan Sabha Proceedings, Tenth Legislative Assembly, Fourth Session, 20 November 1990, p. 37, https://tinyurl.com/mr3hcbn2. Accessed on 12 August 2024.

The Congress continued to support Mulayam Singh Yadav whose acts of omission and commission in a way helped the BJP in intensifying the agitation for the construction of the Ram temple. Any reference to the politics of Kamandal and Mandal will remain incomplete without a mention of his relationship with the BJP leadership. He maintained a cordial relationship with the leaders of all political parties. The BJP leadership was no exception to this rule. This often led to the accusation that Mulayam Singh Yadav and the BJP were hand in glove with each other. He did not hesitate in admitting his cordial relations with the BJP leaders. He became the CM of Uttar Pradesh for the third time in 2003, about a decade after his government had opened fire on the kar sevaks in 1990 and the demolition of the disputed structure on 6 December 1992 in Ayodhya. This was when the BSP and the BJP coalition (formed after the 2002 assembly elections) failed. The two parties had reached an understanding to have a CM in a rotation of six months. The BSP chief, Mayawati, was the first to assume office under this agreement that required her to vacate the seat for the BJP's nominee after completion of her six-month term. She, however, resigned as CM of Uttar Pradesh without giving the BJP a chance, thereby ending the BJP–BSP coalition.

Mulayam Did Not Arrest BJP Leaders

Mulayam Singh Yadav recalled his cordial relationship with the leaders of the Sangh Parivar and how his government did not arrest them when some of them went underground. Speaking on the confidence motion he moved in the state legislative assembly on 8 September 2003, Yadav said:

> We feel the pain of Uttar Pradesh today. Dr Govind Ballabh Pant, Dr Sampoornand and Purushottam Das Tandon have worked here. We should follow the practice and conduct ourselves in such a manner so that we become source of inspiration for coming generations. People all over India are saying that the dignity of Uttar Pradesh has suffered a setback. We have Rama and

Krishna in our magnificent Uttar Pradesh, we have Deobandis. We have everything. We have a mixed culture and love among the people even if there are attempts to create a division. Tandonji (reference is obvious to Lalji Tandon, the senior BJP leader and a close associate of former PM Atal Bihari Vajpayee), you also know it well, when you were absconding (BJP leaders had gone underground to intensify the Ram temple agitation ahead of 30 October 1990 kar seva) we used to talk to each other. I knew—we talked over telephone. But we did not touch (arrest) you. You used to give us suggestions. Nana Saheb Deshmukh led the Kar Seva. He (Nana Saheb Deshmukh) said Mulayam Singh ji you are right. But these people are also right. Allow Kar Seva. Talks were held between 10 PM to 3AM. This way I tried to find a solution to resolve Ayodhya dispute. We never entered into any confrontation.[26]

SP–BJP Relations

Lalji Tandon or other BJP leaders did not counter Mulayam Singh Yadav's observations. This only gave credence to theories that Mulayam Singh Yadav and the BJP were supplementary and complementary to each other in the politics of Uttar Pradesh. Mulayam Singh Yadav won the confidence motion. Speaker Keshri Nath Tripathi, who was from the BJP, announced that the house had voted in favour of the motion. 'There are 244 votes in favour motion moved by the CM and 154 votes have been cast against the motion. As the number of votes in favour of motion is more, this motion is accepted,' said Tripathi.[27]

---

[26]Uttar Pradesh Vidhan Sabha Proceedings, Fourteenth Legislative Assembly, Second Session, 8 September 2003, p. 106. https://tinyurl.com/mr3hcbn2. Accessed on 12 August 2024.
[27]Ibid. 110.

Mulayam Stood by Friends

Mulayam Singh Yadav was known for standing by his friends. He decided to install his son Akhilesh Yadav as CM following the SP's victory in 2012 assembly elections. The former whispering into PM Narendra Modi's ears in 2017 is often quoted to make a point about his personal relations with leaders of other political parties, including those of the BJP. Modi was in Lucknow to attend the swearing-in ceremony of CM Yogi Adityanath who had replaced Akhilesh Yadav following the SP's defeat in the 2017 assembly elections. The PM, while paying tribute to Mulayam Singh Yadav at a public rally in Gujarat in 2022, spoke about seeking Yadav's blessing and advice when he was declared the BJP's prime ministerial candidate for the 2014 Lok Sabha elections.[28]

Mulayam Singh Yadav passed away in a Gurugram hospital on 10 October 2022, after a prolonged illness. He had left everybody stunned when, on the last day of the outgoing Lok Sabha in 2019, he wished that all the members of the house were re-elected and PM Narendra Modi came back to power post 2019 Lok Sabha elections. This was the time when the SP, led by Mulayam Singh Yadav's son Akhilesh Yadav, had joined hands with the BSP to defeat the BJP in 2019 Lok Sabha polls. Mulayam Singh Yadav's words came true, and the BJP government led by PM Narendra Modi won the poll. Incidentally, the Modi-led government decided to confer the Padma Bhushan on Mulayam Singh Yadav posthumously in 2023.

---

[28] 'PM Remembers Mulayam Singh Yadav's Remark That Stunned Opposition', *NDTV*, 10 October 2022, https://tinyurl.com/4ef62zmu. Accessed on 30 September 2024.

7

The Build-Up to the Demolition, Rising Pitches

An aggressive movement to awaken and unite Hindus on the issue of the construction of the Ram temple in Ayodhya was building up across the country. A message about Hinduism being in danger in India was doing the rounds. If Hindus can't have a Ram temple in Ayodhya, where will they? This was the question the newly formed Hindu organizations were repeatedly posing.

Ayodhya has been revered as the birthplace of Lord Rama over the ages. Any dispute over a temple at Lord Rama's birthplace became a cause of concern for the Hindus.

Questions about Hindus being denied construction of the Ram temple were drawing the attention of a section of people. The organizations raising such questions started getting acceptability. It was an apparent reaction to the VHP's campaign and what a section of people perceived as minority appeasement by successive governments over the years. A sharp reaction to the moves and countermoves over the Ram temple–Babri Masjid issue was thus striking an emotional chord with the people.

The Congress's Soft Approach

A growing realization in the Congress about the call these organizations were giving in the name of awakening of the Hindus resulted in the party having a rather soft approach towards them. The party's soft stance towards the Ram Janmabhoomi–Babri Masjid issue was reflected in the actions of the Congress-led government. These included opening of locks of the disputed structure on 1 February 1986. Its changed stance vis-à-vis the Hindu bodies was just a beginning. The demand for liberating all prominent Hindu temples that had been converted into mosques by Muslim rulers was gaining ground. *India Today*, in an article published on 31 May 1986, called this phenomenon a militant movement of Hindu revivalism:

> Slowly but surely, a resurgent and increasingly militant movement of Hindu revivalism is sweeping across the country. The message in the new militancy is that the minorities are being pampered while the majority has been restrained from asserting Hindu nationalism.[1]

A Bolt from the Blue

The VHP's mobilization of public opinion in favour of the Ram temple had begun to pay. The Congress leaders thought the opening of the locks of the disputed structure would ease the pressure and pull the rug out from under the VHP's feet. The move to unlock the disputed structure came as a complete surprise to the VHP. P.V. Narasimha Rao called the move a bolt from the blue for the VHP.[2] The BJP felt otherwise; its White Paper on Ayodhya and the Ram temple movement that came in April 1993 noted that the unlocking on 1 February 1986 was the outcome of mass movement and the ultimatum given by the VHP:

> It was the mass movement, and not just points of law, which obviously moved the intransigent government through a subterfuge to undo the original wrong, and a legal perversity,

---

[1] Badhwar, Inderjit, 'Resurgent and Increasingly Militant Movement of Hindu Revivalism Sweeps across India', *India Today*, 31 May 1986, https://tinyurl.com/bdev2a2h. Accessed on 10 July 2024.
[2] Rao, P.V. Narasimha, *Ayodhya: 6 December 1992*, Penguin Random House, India, 2006, p. 37.

of keeping the sanctum sanctorum of Ram Lala and Ram Lala Himself under lock on the pretext of a law and order problem. Till then, no attempt had been made to grant the genuine and legitimate plea of the Hindus for unrestricted worship of the idol. However, once the ultimatum was given, things started moving at lightning speed...

Why did the District Court pass the order to direct unlocking? Simple. The Congress Government told the court through the DM, Faizabad, that there would be no law and order problem if the temple was unlocked. It took the Government 36 years to state the obvious. It is this that had held up the judicial order so long. Thus, it was the threat of direct action by the mass movement, and the deadline that made the Government respond in the manner it did.[3]

VHP Intensifies Agitation

The VHP stepped up its efforts to intensify the agitation for construction of the Ram temple after the opening of the locks. A day after the locks were opened, Mahant Avaidyanath presided over a meeting of the VHP. Ramchandra Das Paramhans and Mahant Nrityagopaldas of Maniram Chhavani attended the meeting, welcoming the move. The VHP continued to organize meetings of saints and hold various programmes to push the cause of the Ram temple. Its demand for opening of the locks had gradually turned into an agitation in favour of building a Ram temple. Slogans like '*Aage badhkar jor se bolo, janmabhoomi ka taala kholo* (Move forward and shout loudly, open the locks of gates to birthplace of Ram)' were replaced with 'Saugandh Ram ki khate hain, mandir wahin banayenge'.

---

[3]Bharatiya Janata Party, 'BJP's White Paper on Ayodhya and Rama Temple Movement', *BJP e-Library*, April 1993, pp. 29–30, https://tinyurl.com/2s3nzrva. Accessed on 11 August 2024.

BMAC Is Formed

The VHP's intensified agitation evoked sharp reactions among Muslims as well. They decided to organize protests that included a call for wearing black bands and observing a bandh against opening of the locks. They felt there was now a need to have an organization to oversee the agitation in favour of Babri Masjid and to consolidate the community's moves. Zafaryab Jilani, who argued the Babri Masjid case up to the Supreme Court, was a Lucknow-based advocate. He recollected how Ali Miyan, a noted Islamic scholar and the head of Islamic seminary Nadwa College in Lucknow, called him to have discussions on the Ayodhya issue in 1983. 'It was then that Ali Miyan gave me ₹2,000 and asked me to get the files from Ayodhya and prepare a note on the historical position of the mosque,' he said while speaking with a news channel.[4]

This turned out to be a major initiative that eventually led to the formation of the BMAC when the locks of the main gate of the disputed structure were opened on 1 February 1986. A report by senior journalist Pranshu Mishra read:

> An urgent meeting of the AIMPLB (All India Muslim Personal Law Board) was held, where it was decided to chalk out a campaign strategy in support of mosque. A meeting of Muslim leaders was held at the residence of noted lawyer Abdul Mannan in Lucknow... Those present included Azam Khan, the current MP from Rampur and a senior leader of the SP. Also present was the then Congress MLA Saiduzzaman. Two days later, a larger meeting was called at a house located in one of the narrow byways of Aminabad in Lucknow with around 200 people in attendance. It was in this meeting that the BMAC was formed.[5]

---

[4]Mishra, Pranshu, 'Ayodhya Case Verdict | Rs 2,000 from Islamic Scholar, Meeting in Lucknow: How Babri Masjid Action Committee Was Born', *News 18*, 9 November 2019, https://tinyurl.com/kfkjcy9y. Accessed on 10 July 2024.
[5]Ibid.

The BMAC was thus formed on 6 February 1986 to oversee a counter-movement in view of the VHP's stepped-up campaigns. Jilani and Mohammad Azam Khan were declared the BMAC convenors, and Maulana Muzaffar Hussain was named its president.

Ram Janmabhoomi–Babri Masjid Issue to the Centre Stage

The Rajiv Gandhi-led government allowed the laying of the foundation stone of the Ram temple on 9 November 1989, under the pressure of public opinion. The foundation stone-laying ceremony was only symbolic. It failed to make any headway towards working out a solution. The VHP's pressure building and consistent efforts had brought the Ram Janmabhoomi–Babri Masjid issue to the centre stage of politics in the country.

The BJP, which extended support to the V.P. Singh-led government at the Centre, was in favour of allowing some time to the newly elected government to resolve the Ram Janmabhoomi–Babri Masjid issue. The VHP, at the same time, wanted to use the opportunity to put more pressure on the government. V.P. Singh, who also wanted time to resolve the issue, did not favour any direct confrontation with the VHP and the saints. The VHP convened a meeting of Kendriya Margdarshak Mandal, a group of saints, in Allahabad on 27 January 1990. It decided that the kar seva would begin for construction of the Ram temple on 14 February 1990. The VHP worked out a plan for a long agitation beginning 14 February. A resolution passed in the same meeting expressed concern over the V.P. Singh-led government's apathy towards the cause of the Ram temple and warned it of dire consequences.[6]

---

[6]Rao, P.V. Narasimha, *Ayodhya: 6 December 1992*, Penguin Random House, India, 2006, p. 60.

V.P. Singh Seeks Time

The PM soon invited the saints for talks. He felt he needed at least four months, but the saints did not agree. The doors were, however, kept open for talks. Further meetings were scheduled for 4, 5 and 6 February in New Delhi. The BMAC gave a call to Muslims to reach Ayodhya on 13 February 1990, a day before the proposed commencement of VHP's agitation.[7] The PM was eventually given time to find a solution. The kar seva was extended by four months. The VHP, however, decided to continue its agitation.

Mulayam Singh Yadav, who was installed as the CM of Uttar Pradesh following the 1989 state legislative assembly elections, was not happy. He felt marginalized, as the PM was in direct touch with the VHP and the saints. Yadav adopted a tough stance against the VHP's agitation programmes. Dwarka Peeth Shankaracharya Swarupanand Saraswati, nicknamed 'Congress Swamy',[8] was known for his leanings towards the grand old party. He later supported Congress leader Sonia Gandhi when she took a holy dip in Allahabad during the Kumbh Mela in January 2001, amid opposition on the grounds of her foreign origin.[9]

Dwarka Peeth Shankaracharya announced that he would lay the foundation stone for the Ram temple again on 7 May 1990, saying that the foundation stone-laying ceremony conducted on 9 November 1989 was held at an inauspicious time. He was detained in Azamgarh on way to Faizabad on 30 April 1990. His detention sent a strong message that the Mulayam Singh Yadav government would not tolerate any nonsense. The four-month reprieve that the VHP and saints had given to V.P. Singh was about to end. The VHP, in consultation with the saints, issued a fresh deadline for beginning kar seva in Ayodhya on 30 October 1990, and the time for parikrama, with Kartik Purnima

---

[7] Ibid. 61.
[8] Kidwai, Rasheed, 'Swaroopanand, "Congress Swamy" Who Tried to Upstage VHP on Ram Mandir', *India Today*, 12 September 2022, https://tinyurl.com/45jupmv4. Accessed on 10 July 2024.
[9] Ibid.

falling on 1 November 1990. Ayodhya attracted large crowds on both days. This was advantageous to the VHP. Some other saints, however, were not in favour of waiting till 30 October and instead wanted kar seva to begin in July 1990 for the construction of the Ram temple.[10]

The VHP Builds Pressure

A parliamentary delegation led by then Lok Sabha Speaker Rabi Ray, with L.K. Advani as a member, left for London in the last week of June 1990. Advani was interviewed by Tarun Vijay, editor of *Panchjanya*, before the former's departure to the UK. Advani in this interview reaffirmed the BJP's support to the kar seva, which was scheduled to begin on 30 October. He said the V.P. Singh-led government had four months' time (June to October) to find a solution to the Ram Janmabhoomi–Babri Masjid dispute. He said a mass movement would be launched on a large scale (never seen before in the history of independent India) if any attempts were made to stop the kar seva. Media took this as a threat by Advani. Recalling the days, Advani noted in his autobiography that he forgot about the interview in London till his wife called from India, as he was busy defending the V.P. Singh government on various issues there. Advani noted:

> When I was about to depart from London, my wife called me up and said, 'What have you said? The papers here have reported with blaring headlines: "On Ayodhya, Advani threatens the biggest mass movement in the history of independent India."'
> The die had been cast. Relations between leaders of the kar seva and the government were souring.[11]

---

[10]Rao, P.V. Narasimha, *Ayodhya: 6 December 1992*, Penguin Random House, India, 2006, p. 65.
[11]Advani, L.K., *My Country My Life*, Rupa and Co., New Delhi, 2008, pp. 370.

Souring Relationship

The Centre's relations with the Uttar Pradesh government were also souring. Both V.P. Singh and Mulayam Singh Yadav belonged to the same party, the Janata Dal. They, however, appeared to be working at cross purposes. Singh's direct interactions with the VHP leaders and the saints displeased Yadav. Singh and Yadav did not have a cordial relationship right from the beginning.

Yadav distanced himself from the meetings V.P. Singh was holding to work out a solution to the Ram temple issue. He began challenging the VHP and the BJP, delivering fiery speeches at public meetings across the state. As mentioned in another chapter, he adopted a tough stance towards the VHP's proposed kar seva, declaring, '*Masjid par parinda bhi par nahin maar paayega.*' By delivering this, one of his most iconic quotes, he strongly provoked Hindu hardliners and further polarized the state. 'He was despised by many and disparagingly called Maulana Mulayam, which also became a term of endearment for several others! And there was more to follow even as he refused to tone down the rhetoric.'[12]

An Impregnable Fortress

The Mulayam Singh Yadav-led state government made tight security arrangements for the kar seva scheduled to begin on 30 October 1990. It virtually sealed all the entry and exit points to and from Ayodhya, well before the appointed day. The kar sevaks took rural roads and travelled at night to avoid police check posts and reach their respective destinations in villages nearby or in Ayodhya.

The VHP's call for kar seva on 30 October 1990 had created a buzz. The Mandal Commission recommendations, when implemented, left a trail of self-immolations and protests involving large-scale violence across India. This resulted in a divide in the society. Any mobilization for the kar seva was bound to lead to a consolidation of Hindus.

---

[12]Aron, Sunita, *Akhilesh Yadav: Winds of Change*, Tranquebar Press, 2013, p. 147.

Senior BJP leader L.K. Advani, against this backdrop, led the Ram Rath Yatra from Somnath, Gujarat, to join the kar seva in Ayodhya on 30 October 1990. Advani noted that the call for kar seva to mobilize the devotees of Lord Ram evoked a good response:

> People from all across the country were eager to converge at Ayodhya, from villages, far-off hamlets and urban slums. I had an intuition that history was about to be made.[13]

There was an aggressive mood all around and throughout the route as Advani's rath moved on; people raised slogans of 'Jai Shri Ram', 'Jai Somnath' and 'Saugandh Ram ki khate hain, mandir wahin banayenge', and '*Bachcha bachcha Ram ka, janmabhoomi ke kaam ka* (Every child is devoted to the cause of Rama's birthplace)'.

Temporary Jails

The Uttar Pradesh government had set up temporary jails to detain and place under house arrest the kar sevaks and the VHP leaders. A large posse of Central Paramilitary Forces was deployed around the disputed structure, and there was movement of paramilitary forces on the streets across Ayodhya. Some of the kar sevaks stayed in adjoining districts and reached Ayodhya via village routes, fields, or through the river route. The kar sevaks interacted in a friendly manner with the policemen. So a large number of kar sevaks, mainly youths, including women, were out on the streets on 30 October. This reflected the VHP's successful campaign and acceptance of the cause of the Ram temple. Senior journalist Sheetla Singh wrote:

> The VHP's sole objective was to challenge the government and focus on show of strength. The difference between the commoners and policemen had ceased to exist on trucks carrying the 'shilas' (bricks) during the VHP's 'shila pujan' programme and this reflected the police's soft stance towards this agitation (VHP's

---

[13] Advani, L.K., *My Country My Life*, Rupa and Co., New Delhi, 2008, p. 372.

agitation for the Ram temple). Slogans of *'police sipahi, bhai bhai'* (policemen are brothers) were raised. It was because of this soft attitude that allowed the kar sevaks to reach the disputed structure despite the restrictions. The presence of a large number of retired army and police personnel helped in turning the agitation (for the Ram temple) into a movement.[14]

Kar Sevaks Clash with the Police

Such observations assume significance as former DGP, Uttar Pradesh, Shirish Chand Dixit was one of the VHP's main functionaries along with VHP chief Ashok Singhal, Bajrang Dal founder president Vinay Katiyar, and others. Dixit, along with Singhal and others, had reached Ayodhya despite the ban on their entry.[15] V.P. Singh resigned as the PM following the BJP's withdrawal of support from his government when the Lalu Prasad Yadav-led state government stopped his Rath Yatra and detained him at Samastipur, Bihar. Advani's detention was no good news for the kar sevaks, but it added to their resolve. Many VHP and BJP leaders went underground while the police searched for them.

A large number of kar sevaks gathered on the streets of Ayodhya on 30 October. The groups began surging towards the disputed structure. A clash soon occurred between the kar sevaks and the police. The Mulayam Singh government ordered the police to open fire. By then, some of the kar sevaks had reached the top of the disputed structure.

In three days, a large number of kar sevaks regrouped and assembled in Ayodhya. As and when the police stopped the kar sevaks, they sat on the ground and began chanting in the name of Lord Rama. The kar sevaks divided themselves into smaller groups, made humble requests to the policemen to get away, only to regroup later on the streets of Ayodhya.

---

[14]Singh, Sheetla, *Ramjanmabhoomi–Babri Masjid Ka Sach*, Kaushal Publishing House, Faizabad, 2019, p. 147. Author's translation.
[15]Ibid. 153.

Another Clash

The kar sevaks were determined to reach the disputed structure. The police firing on 30 October did not deter them. The police were adamant about not allowing them to move towards Ayodhya. Those who were in Ayodhya were not being allowed to move towards the disputed structure. The police wanted to ensure that no kar sevak was able to reach Ayodhya this time. Another clash was witnessed on 2 November when the kar sevaks began making a move towards the disputed structure. The police initially lobbed tear gas shells. They opened fire on the crowd when the latter started increasing in number in an area close to Hanuman Garhi, instead of dispersing. Those who died in the police firing included the Kothari brothers (Ram Kothari and Sharad Kothari, aged around 22 and 20, respectively) from Calcutta. Both of them wore saffron-coloured cloth, with the word *kafan* (shroud) visible at the back. They were among the first kar sevaks who were seen mounting saffron flags atop the disputed structure on 30 October, thereby marking the event in history. Both of them were killed in the firing on 2 November 1990.[16] The street in which they were killed came to be known as Shaheed Marg in Ayodhya.[17] There was blood on the streets. Sixteen persons were killed in the firing incidents on 30 October and 2 November. The district administration's report said 14 persons died in Ayodhya while two were killed in Gonda, an adjoining district.[18]

L.K. Advani later said he was happy to know that the kar sevaks entered Ayodhya on 30 October 1990. He recalled the moment while deposing before the Liberhan Ayodhya Commission of Inquiry in 1990. A report published in *Outlook* quoted Advani as saying he was in detention at Mata Tila near Jhansi and was allowed to use a transistor. He said all modes of transportation to Ayodhya had been stopped, and

---

[16]'Ayodhya: From Saints to Lawyers, 15-Lesser Known Figures behind Ram Mandir', *The Economic Times*, 22 January 2024, https://tinyurl.com/244b4ptx. Accessed on 11 July 2024.
[17]Ibid.
[18]Singh, Sheetla, *Ramjanmabhoomi–Babri Masjid Ka Sach*, Kaushal Publishing House, Faizabad, 2019, p. 161.

hearing the news on *BBC* about the kar seva was 'one of the happiest moments' of his life. An article in *Outlook* states, 'Despite all these barriers, the manner in which the *kar sevaks* entered Ayodhya and performed *kar seva* represented a kind of symbolism of great value, he said adding when he heard this over radio (*BBC*) he felt it was one of his happiest moments in life.'[19]

The V.P. Singh-led government, meanwhile, worked on ways to find a solution to the dispute as the VHP's kar seva scheduled for 30 October 1990 inched closer. They consulted Advani, who was in New Delhi for a brief period following the Diwali break of his Rath Yatra, to promulgate the Ram Janmabhoomi–Babri Masjid (Acquisition of Area) Ordinance 1990 on 19 October to acquire 67 acres of land around the disputed structure. The V.P. Singh-led government was, however, compelled to withdraw the ordinance within hours. Advani felt the ordinance was withdrawn on 21 October 1990 following obvious opposition to the move by Mulayam Singh Yadav.[20]

Chandra Shekhar Becomes PM

With Congress's support, Chandra Shekhar took over as PM, replacing V.P. Singh on 10 November 1990, and Mulayam Singh Yadav survived as Uttar Pradesh CM and as a leader of the Janata Dal breakaway group. In order to prove his majority, Yadav moved a motion of confidence in the Uttar Pradesh legislative assembly. Speaking on the motion of confidence, Yadav justified his decision of ordering police firing to protect the disputed complex. Speaking on the motion of confidence, he said:

> I want to make it clear that even if Advaniji (Lal Krishna Advani) had been the CM, the Babri Masjid would not have been demolished. Advani would also not have done less than

---

[19] 'The Happiest Day of My Life', *Outlook*, 13 June 2001, https://tinyurl.com/2rzmnp2j. Accessed on 11 August 2024.
[20] Rao, P.V. Narasimha, *Ayodhya: 6 December 1992*, Penguin Random House, India, 2006, p. 385.

what I did to protect the Babri Masjid. And if Maulana Bukhari (Shahi Imam of Delhi's Jama Masjid) had been the CM, he would not have done more than my government did to save the Babri Masjid. By protecting the Babri Masjid the Uttar Pradesh government has saved thousands of temples and the lives of lakhs of Hindus. This is not an issue of Ayodhya but of entire Uttar Pradesh. If the mosque had fallen then we can't imagine what would have been the shape of the state Legislative Assembly, where we are sitting (Uttar Pradesh Legislative Assembly), and Delhi's Parliament. It was said the Centre is looking into the issue… I became cautious. I am grateful that they made me cautious.[21]

Yadav stated that unfortunately the person who occupied the highest office (PM V.P. Singh) sided with the communal forces. He added that the Ram Janmabhoomi issue had been on the backburner since 1949 and questioned why this issue was being raised after 35 years. He also said that he had been raising certain questions and not getting answers to them either from the BJP or from the VHP. These organizations, he noted, did not have any answers. Additionally, he made the point that when elections were about to take place in 1984, the VHP leaders raised the issue but did not push it for five years; they tried to play with the sentiments of many Hindus by raising the issue of laying the foundation of the Ram temple in 1989.[22]

Differences in Janata Dal

Yadav's assertions in the state legislative assembly reflected the differences within the Janata Dal. There may have been various reasons for the widening differences between Mulayam Singh Yadav and V.P. Singh. Their origin may also be traced back to the

---

[21] Uttar Pradesh Vidhan Sabha Proceedings, Tenth Legislative Assembly, Fourth Session, 20 November 1990, p. 37, https://tinyurl.com/mr3hcbn2. Accessed on 12 August 2024.
[22] Ibid.

developments that took place in the period preceding and succeeding the November 1989 elections to the Lok Sabha and the state legislative assembly.

Mulayam Singh Yadav was an ambitious politician. He played an important role in uniting Uttar Pradesh's opposition to a large extent against the Rajiv Gandhi government that was losing popularity. Yadav led the Janata Dal's election campaign in Uttar Pradesh aggressively. He was considered Janata Dal's obvious choice for the post of CM. Ajit Singh, MP from Baghpat and son of former PM Chaudhary Charan Singh, also entered the race for this post. The leader of legislature party is elected via a consensus, and Mulayam Singh and Ajit Singh came face to face for the post. The legislators were given a slip to mark their choice at the Uttar Pradesh Janata Dal legislature party meeting convened at Tilak Hall of Vidhan Bhawan in Lucknow in December 1989. Mulayam Singh Yadav defeated Ajit Singh. He was elected as the leader and the next CM of Uttar Pradesh.

V.P. Singh did not directly support Mulayam Singh or Ajit Singh in the contest. The former was, however, not happy with the way the PM handled the situation in his home state. He felt that V.P. Singh favoured Ajit Singh. Mulayam Singh was also not happy with the developments at the convention of saints that the VHP had convened in Allahabad on 28 and 30 January 1990. He had objections to the PM's move of sending two emissaries to the convention and claimed that one of the two emissaries, who was an MP, conveyed there that a dialogue for finding a solution to the Ram temple issue would be held only with the PM, and that there was no question of holding any talks with the Uttar Pradesh government.

Yadav, speaking in the Uttar Pradesh legislative assembly, made a reference to this and said that he had called the VHP leaders for talks on 3 February 1990. He added that after having discussions with him for nearly three-and-a-half hours at the Raj Bhawan in Lucknow, the VHP leaders said that they would not hold talks with the CMs and would only do so with the PM. According to Yadav, a meeting of leaders of all the political parties was called, but the BJP leaders did not turn up there, so the meeting had to be deferred. He acknowledged that the BJP's Rajendra Kumar Gupta turned up when the meeting was convened again.

Mulayam Singh Yadav also took strong exception to the manner in which the V.P. Singh government handled the Ram temple issue. He said that the VHP gave PM V.P. Singh four months to find a solution to the Ram temple dispute without the knowledge of the Uttar Pradesh government. He alleged that a committee comprising three ministers from Uttar Pradesh was constituted without his knowledge, and his name was dropped from the committee, though one of his colleagues was made a member.

'I have no regrets about this. But I feel bad that the PM (V.P. Singh) did not use the opportunity of the four months that the VHP gave to resolve the issue,' said Yadav in the state legislative assembly. In his message on Doordarshan and Akashvani (All India Radio [AIR]) on 9 February 1990, he asked whether the temple of Maryada Purushottam Lord Rama would be built by breaking the constitutional norms. He reiterated that the VHP and the BJP had given all the responsibility to the PM, and that the three of them (Singh, the VHP and the BJP) did not feel the need to take his government into confidence. According to him, the focus of a resolution passed on June 23 and 24 was only to convey '*Mandir banao, Mulayam Singh hatao* (Construct Ram temple and remove Mulayam Singh)'.[23]

The Son of Soil

The VHP held a meeting of saints in Haridwar on 23 and 24 June 1990, and Yadav apparently gave indications towards this meeting. A decision to begin kar seva for the construction of the Ram temple in Ayodhya from 30 October 1990 was taken there. Yadav obviously considered the VHP's move a conspiracy to dislodge his government. He said, 'I did not get any opportunity and no talks were held with

---

[23]Ibid.

me. Former PM Vishwanath Pratap Singh is to be blamed for this.'[24] His tough stance had a long-term impact and catapulted his image to that of a strong leader who could effectively look out for the interests of Muslims. It was for his tough stance and connect with the people at grassroots level that he was often called 'Dharti Putra' (son of the soil) by his followers. Yadav obviously acted tough; his action was in sharp contrast to the stand taken by senior BJP leader Kalyan Singh who, as the CM, refused to use any force against kar sevaks on 6 December 1992 when the disputed structure was demolished.

Mulayam Felt Humiliated

Yadav said V.P. Singh humiliated him because he demanded an inquiry into affairs of the Dahiya Trust. (V.P. Singh was born to the royal household of Dahiya and was later adopted by the ruler of Manda). 'I was among those who demanded an inquiry into irregularities in Dahiya Trust. The PM was upset with me because of the demand for an inquiry into wrongdoings by Dahiya Trust,' Yadav said.[25] He felt that his backward caste origin was the reason behind him being called anti-Hindu.

He made his feelings about the same known in the state legislative assembly. He said that his and his colleagues' conduct was better than those who called themselves the sole agents of Hindutva. He added that he was not opposing the construction of the Ram temple, but Ram Janmabhoomi–Babri Masjid was a disputed spot, and the issue pending in the court could be resolved only by dialogue.[26]

As CM of Uttar Pradesh, Mulayam Singh Yadav had access to the papers of a meeting that the VHP leaders had attended on 27 September 1989 in Lucknow. N.D. Tiwari had convened the meeting as the then Uttar Pradesh CM, and senior VHP leaders who attended this meeting included Dau Dayal Khanna, Shirish Chandra Dikshit,

---

[24]Ibid.
[25]Ibid.
[26]Ibid.

Onkar Bhave, Mahesh Narayan Singh, Suresh Gupta, Ashok Singhal, Mahant Avaidyanath and Mahant Nritya Gopal Das. Union Home Minister Buta Singh had also attended this meeting. An agreement was signed indicating that the VHP would abide by the directives of the Lucknow bench of Allahabad High Court on 14 August 1989, 'to the effect that the Parties to the Suits shall maintain the status quo and shall not change the nature of the property in question and ensure that the peace and communal harmony are maintained'.[27] With this, the state government had given a nod to allow the shila processions, with the VHP also agreeing to the following: (1) the VHP would give prior intimation to respective authorities about the shila procession routes, (2) no provocative slogans would be raised, (3) efforts would be made to carry 'sanctified' bricks in trucks, (4) the VHP would guide the processions, and (5) the collection of bricks would be done in Ayodhya at a spot to be decided in consultation with the authorities.[28]

Yadav said they (VHP leaders) were not waiting for the court's orders, and added that Lord Rama was being linked to politics of votes. 'Why was this agreement violated?' he asked. He added that the Madhya Pradesh government freed criminals, gave them arms, and sent them to Etawah. He gave the example of a former dreaded dacoit who had challenged his family, and the latter went from village to village in the name of Ram Jyoti and arranged for provocative slogans being written on the walls there.[29]

Mulayam Sees Conspiracy

Mulayam Singh Yadav left no opportunity to target the PM, and accused him of not being in favour of arrests linked to the Ram temple movement on 4 and 5 October 1990, ahead of the VHP's kar seva in

---

[27]'The Agreement', *Frontline*, 16 February 2002, https://tinyurl.com/mvw4pjbt. Accessed on 11 August 2024.
[28]Ibid.
[29]Uttar Pradesh Vidhan Sabha Proceedings, Tenth Legislative Assembly, Fourth Session, 20 November 1990, p. 37, https://tinyurl.com/mr3hcbn2. Accessed on 12 August 2024.

Ayodhya on 30 October. He felt his chief ministership was at stake as the protection of Babri Masjid was his government's responsibility and posed the biggest challenge to it. He saw a conspiracy to instigate riots and destabilize his government when passions were high in the name of Ram Jyoti Yatra. He said that the VHP and the BJP did not want the Ram temple to be constructed. If they wanted to construct a temple, would they have climbed up the mosque, he asked. He stated that he had spoken to those dealing with the issue at the Centre, and Uttar Pradesh's chief secretary had written to the Centre about the need to stop violence. He affirmed that his government wanted to arrest those instigating violence and a list of 23 such persons was worked out who, according to him, were arrested on 4 and 5 October 1990.[30]

Senior Congress leader and Leader of Opposition N.D. Tiwari was Uttar Pradesh CM when the Rajiv Gandhi-led government allowed laying of the foundation stone of the Ram temple in Ayodhya on 9 November 1989. Tiwari claimed there was perfect coordination between his government and the central government (led by Rajiv Gandhi) when an agreement was reached with the VHP in September 1989. This was the same agreement that the Hindu leaders had signed, and Yadav obviously referred to the same to make his point that the agreement was not being followed.

Baseless Campaign

Tiwari said that as per the September 1989 pact, the VHP had agreed to honour the Allahabad High Court's order and maintain status quo. According to him, following this agreement, the Rajiv Gandhi-led government had allowed the VHP to lay the foundation stone for the Ram temple on the undisputed land, not on the disputed land. Tiwari insisted that the Babri Masjid remained safe. He stated that a baseless campaign, however, was launched during 1989 Lok Sabha elections that claimed that the Masjid had been demolished, or that

---

[30]Ibid.

the construction of the temple had not been allowed after laying of the foundation stone. He said that the VHP did not declare any programme for construction of the temple after the foundation stone was laid.[31]

He explained the reasons for his party's support to Chandra Shekhar as the PM and Mulayam Singh Yadav as the CM of Uttar Pradesh. He obliquely referred to the political pressures on the Yadav-led government and the excessive use of force against the kar sevaks. Tiwari defended Yadav to some extent. There was anger against the government because of the strict action taken in Ayodhya. Tiwari said that the Mulayam Singh Yadav government remained under a lot of pressure for political reasons that exceeded the CM's orders, and more than necessary force was used. He asked who the officers were who committed atrocities while following the CMs orders and requested clarification because the government was being blamed and the CM was being held responsible for these excesses.[32]

As the police swung into action, the administration in Uttar Pradesh's capital declared Lucknow University to be a temporary jail to lodge the kar sevaks. The vice chancellor of Lucknow University filed a petition in the Allahabad High Court challenging the administration's move. Tiwari expressed scepticism over how such a conspiracy, which would result in Lucknow University being declared a jail to lodge the kar sevaks and the vice chancellor filing a petition in the High Court, could be hatched. He didn't believe that the government could pass such orders.

Administrations in some other parts also committed excesses. In one of these districts, some people chanting 'Ram naam satya hai' (The name of Rama is the truth) in a funeral procession were arrested. Tiwari objected to this claim. He believed that chanting these words was an age-old practice and that it was not possible that such orders were passed by the government. Additionally, Tiwari, being senior to Mulayam Singh Yadav, advised him to exercise restraint in his speeches. 'I am not sure whether the CM said "Vahan parinda par nahin maar

---

[31]Ibid.
[32]Ibid.

sakta". I have no personal knowledge about this. But if these words have been uttered, this is a challenge… Political challenges are alright. But no challenge should be given on religious issues."[33]

As discussed earlier in this chapter, Chandra Shekhar replaced V.P. Singh as PM on 10 November 1990. The change of PM changed political equations as well. It eased the strained relations between the Centre and the Uttar Pradesh government. Advani, who was stopped on his way to Ayodhya, was allowed to perform puja there.

Prime Minister Chandra Shekhar made fresh moves to find a solution to the Ram temple issue, and he, along with CM Mulayam Singh Yadav, met L.K. Advani. It was decided that Advani would be allowed to go to Ayodhya on 19 November. He went there with a large crowd. Tiwari believed that when Advani had wanted to go to Ayodhya on 30 October, there could have been talks with him.[34]

Kalyan Singh Is CM in Uttar Pradesh

P.V. Narasimha Rao became PM of the Congress-led government following the 1991 Lok Sabha elections that witnessed assassination of former PM Rajiv Gandhi in Sriperumbudur, Tamil Nadu, where he had gone for a poll campaign on 21 May 1991. The BJP came to power in Uttar Pradesh following the 1991 state legislative assembly elections. The BJP government led by Kalyan Singh acquired 2.77 acres of land vide notification dated 7 October 1991 and 10 October 1991 for expeditious implementation of projects for conserving cultural heritage and pride, and for providing facilities to pilgrims in Ayodhya. Some changes, including removal of small temples in the name of clearing hindrances and levelling the ground, were made there. The BJP government contended that the acquisition of land was made for the construction of the Ram temple through Ram Janmabhoomi Nyas. In June 1992, the Kalyan Singh-led state government was requested to allow Chaturmas programmes. According to Hindu calendar,

---

[33]Ibid.
[34]Ibid.

Chaturmas is the four-month period of penance, self-discipline and religious observances, beginning in June–July and ending in October–November. Ayodhya saw large crowds for Chaturmas programmes. Some construction work, like raising a platform on the spot of shilanyas, was started on 9 July 1992. This was to be the spot of the *singhdwar* (main gate) of the Ram temple. The Allahabad High Court, however, did not allow construction work. Prime Minister Rao asked the RSS and the VHP to stop the construction. The VHP leaders spoke about the delay in getting justice. Some religious leaders were flown to New Delhi on 23 July 1992 to meet the PM. After the meeting, they agreed to defer the construction. The PM wanted three months, but that period also passed without finding a solution.

Intelligence Bureau's Warning

The VHP convened a meeting of the Dharam Sansad on 29–30 October 1992 to seek guidance. A decision was taken to resume kar seva on 6 December 1992. Any activity in Ayodhya was having a nationwide impact, giving rise to communal tension. On 10 July 1992, the Intelligence Bureau sent out a warning to all chief secretaries, home secretaries and DGPs about a possible communal flare-up. The *Frontline* gave details about this warning: 'In the wake of developments in Ayodhya by certain organizations for construction of a temple, there is a possibility of a communal flare up.' If this in itself was not a remarkable deduction, the subsequent instructions in the letter were explicit. 'All developments directly or indirectly contributing to communal violence should be nipped in the bud,' the message read. 'Intelligence machinery in the entire states may be geared up and all precautionary measures undertaken. State governments/UTs (Union Territories) may also consider rounding up of communal agitators.'[35]

The VHP gave a call for kar seva in Ayodhya on 6 December 1992. A meeting of the National Integration Council (NIC) was convened

---

[35]Katakam, Praveen Swamianupama, 'The Tale Documents Tell', *Frontline*, 21 July 2001, https://tinyurl.com/49c437ky. Accessed on 11 July 2024.

on 23 November to discuss the communal situation. Uttar Pradesh CM Kalyan Singh had earlier attended a meeting of the NIC held in New Delhi on 2 November 1991. The NIC noted at this meeting that one of the factors adding immensely to the building up of communal tension was the Ram Janmabhoomi–Babri Masjid dispute. The Council expressed its concern over the recent happenings in Ayodhya and hoped that such a situation would not occur. It further noted that the Ram Janmabhoomi–Babri Masjid issue had evaded a satisfactory solution. It appealed to all parties concerned and organizations to work towards an amicable and negotiated solution.

Kalyan Singh Assures Protection

Kalyan Singh, on 2 November 1991, had assured the NIC that: (1) all efforts will be made to find an amicable solution to the issue; (2) in case of a pending final solution, the government of Uttar Pradesh will hold itself fully responsible for the protection of the Ram Janmabhoomi–Babri Masjid structure; (3) orders of the court in regard to the land acquisition proceedings will be fully implemented; and (4) judgement of the Allahabad High Court in the cases pending before it will not be violated. The council appealed to the people to maintain peace and tranquillity and create an atmosphere conducive to the satisfactory settlement of the dispute.[36]

Kalyan Singh decided to stay away from the 23 November 1992 meeting of the NIC amid rising tension between his government and the Centre. Former PMs V.P. Singh and Chandra Shekhar attended the meeting. Harkishan Singh Surjeet, CPM leader, moved a four-line resolution that the NIC adopted. The NIC resolution read:

> After considering all aspects of the Babri Masjid–Ram Janmabhoomi dispute and the report of the Government, the Council extends its wholehearted support and cooperation in

---

[36]'Written Answers', *Parliament Digital Library, Lok Sabha*, 25 November 1991, https://tinyurl.com/ypwtvx7y. Accessed on 22 August 2024.

whatever steps the PM considers essential in upholding the Constitution and the rule of law, and in implementing the Court's orders.[37]

Why Kalyan Singh Stayed Away from the NIC Meet

Kalyan Singh's absence from the NIC meeting was a big issue. The Opposition raised it in the state legislative assembly on 24 November. Speaking there, Singh explained the circumstances and reasons that had compelled him to stay away from the NIC meet. He said:

> I did not go to attend the meeting of the NIC. Now it is being said that this violated the Constitution of India, broke the law and violated the dignity of the house. I want to say that there was a meeting of the criminal justice administration on 13 November. The PM inaugurated the meeting. I asked (the PM) if there was any proposal to convene a meeting of the NIC as I have read in the newspapers. I understand this will not solve the issue if thinking is going on about convening the meeting. Instead, this will complicate the issue. The PM told me categorically that there was no such proposal. He said that that he would consult me if such a proposal came up for consideration. Sir, I met him on 18 November between 6 (and) 7 in the evening. The PM was there. The Defence Minister was there. Then I met him on 19 November. The PM asked me to stay back for a day. I stayed back. At the next day's meeting, the PM was there along with Union home minister and defence minister and I was the fourth person present there. (Sharad Pawar was defence minister of India.) I told him categorically that there was no point in convening a meeting on the issue as anything said at the meeting would only complicate instead of solving the issue. The PM told me at that

---

[37]'Statement by Minister of Home Affairs SB Chavan, General Situation at Ayodhya in the Context of the Proposed Kar Seva', *Parliament Digital Library, Lok Sabha*, 3 December 1992, p. 539, https://tinyurl.com/ms9zh3nz. Accessed on 11 August 2024.

point too that there was no such proposal under consideration. Then he (PM) had discussions with my party's leader honourable Advaniji. He said he felt there was no propriety to convene the meeting and the meeting will not be convened.[38]

Despite this, the NIC meeting was called. I got a letter from the Union home minister a day before the meeting and I sent a reply. I want to emphasize today that the NIC has had two meetings on Ayodhya. Time is witness to it, there has been no forward moment to find a solution at these meetings. The NIC is not being used to find a solution, instead it has been given the shape of anti-BJP political forum. I am sorry to say the NIC is being used for politics.[39]

Kalyan Singh said he was in favour of finding a solution. He had already attended two meetings of the NIC up till then. He felt that the NIC was complicating the issues instead of finding a solution to them. Singh stated the NIC had turned into an Ayodhya council: the leaders speaking there delivered similar speeches, and there was no difference in their approach to the issue. He felt that the Union government appeared to be in the mood to take the course of confrontation instead of finding a solution. He questioned the Union government's move of sending the CRPF to Ayodhya without the consent of the state government. Singh used the occasion to target the Rao-led Congress government for not meeting the state government's demand for more CRPF companies to counter terrorism, and said that the Union government provided only 43 CRPF companies against the demand for 80. He, however, also asserted that there was no threat to law and order in the state, and his government would not allow peace to be disturbed. 'There is no disturbance. If there is any disturbance it is among the leaders of the Opposition, at the NIC, in Lok Sabha. There is no disturbance in Ayodhya,' he stated firmly.[40]

---

[38]'Uttar Pradesh Vidhan Sabha Proceedings', Eleventh Legislative Assembly, Second Session, 24 November 1992, https://tinyurl.com/ck8bz8n7. Accessed on 19 August 2024.
[39]Ibid.
[40]Ibid.

Kalyan Singh's Prediction

Kalyan Singh repeatedly said he would not violate the Constitution of India and would not resign or recommend dissolution of the house. He said his government would last a full five-year term and get the Ram temple constructed in Ayodhya. He said two-thirds of those in Opposition would not be re-elected if any election is held, while the BJP's tally would go up from 222 to 300.[41]

Next day, on 25 November 1992, the Opposition raised the issue again in the house through a question of propriety.

The P.V. Narasimha Rao government contemplated a move to make a presidential reference to the Supreme Court of India on the Ram Janmabhoomi–Babri Masjid dispute. So, when CM Kalyan Singh met the PM on 18 and 19 November, the issue was raised before him. Kalyan Singh said that the Union government wanted to make a one-point one point reference (on the Ram temple dispute) to the Supreme Court and sought his consent. Singh instead asked the PM about his opinion on the documents that were exchanged between the VHP and the AIBMAC. Chief Minister Singh said that the PM's office (PMO) did not work as a post office, so he must have arrived at some conclusion after studying documents his office got from both sides.

Kalyan Singh said that the defence minister (Sharad Pawar) had been present at the meeting and told him that the issue would go in the BJP's favour if he accepted their point. Singh had asked the defence minister how that would be. The latter responded that he had seen all the evidence thoroughly, and it could be proved that a Hindu structure existed at the disputed spot.[42] Pawar then asked him to give his consent for the reference to the Supreme Court. Singh in turn asked the defence minister what would happen after that, and the latter said that the Supreme Court would say there was a Hindu structure there, and that they would make a law to take the disputed

---
[41]Ibid.
[42]Uttar Pradesh Vidhan Sabha Proceedings, Eleventh Legislative Assembly, Second Session, 25 November 1992, https://tinyurl.com/ck8bz8n7. Accessed on 19 August 2024.

structure and hand it over to the trust, which was when construction of the temple would begin.[43] It occurred to Singh that if the Union government was convinced and the evidence proved that a Hindu structure existed there, why it lacked the political courage to tell the people. He also said that there appeared no need for a reference. 'Have you thought about the complications of making a reference?' asked Kalyan Singh, adding, 'I am not an advocate. But I can understand with my humble mind that this will open Pandora's Box.'[44]

Kalyan Singh used the forum of the Uttar Pradesh legislative assembly to request the PM to rise above political considerations, show political will, and 'come out of clutches of the Left' to resolve the issue. He said that the PM had sought three months; a period of more than four months had passed. 'My government has violated neither any law nor any court order. I have said this in the meeting of NIC and saying again that the arrangements for the security of the disputed structure are complete... Ten days are still left. This period of 10 days is not a short time. A solution may be found in 10 days,' Kalyan Singh said. [45]

Kalyan Singh was either too optimistic or made shrewd political moves. The Ram Janmabhoomi–Babri Masjid issue had remained entangled in a legal battle for decades. It was an issue of faith connected to the identity of Hindus. A series of events took place in the next 10 days. These included meetings, court hearings, orders, assurances, missives, visits of court observers to the disputed site, exchanges of communication between the Centre and the state government, and statements from leaders of various political parties. The Uttar Pradesh legislative assembly was adjourned on 25 November after discussing the Ayodhya issue. This proved to be the last day of the Eleventh Legislative Assembly, which was dissolved following the demolition of the disputed structure and subsequent imposition of President's rule on 6 December 1992. Parliament, too, was in session. In the demolition

---

[43]Ibid.
[44]Ibid.
[45]Ibid.

week, it discussed the issue nearly every day till the weekend break on 4 December 1992.

Uncertainty over Kar Seva

The Kalyan Singh-led state government assured that adequate security arrangements had been made to protect the disputed structure and maintain the status quo. This assurance was given to the Supreme Court, too. In its affidavit of 27 November 1992, filed before the Supreme Court, the Kalyan Singh government reiterated that it was fully committed to safeguard and protect the disputed Ram Janmabhoomi structure in Ayodhya. The affidavit further stated that the state government was frequently reviewing security arrangements of the disputed structure and was taking all necessary steps to ensure its safety. It added that entry to the disputed structure was being carefully controlled: every person was being checked; metal detectors and closed-circuit television cameras were in operation; and road-barriers were being used for controlling the crowd.

On 28 November 1992, the state government filed an undertaking ensuring that no construction machinery or construction material would move into the acquired land, and that no construction activity would take place or be carried out. It also expressed its readiness and willingness to ensure that no constructional activity, either temporary or permanent, would take place or be allowed to take place on the acquired land in the name of kar seva. It further submitted that kar seva would be a symbolic occasion for carrying out certain religious activities and would not be allowed to be exploited for any constructional activities, symbolic or otherwise.

On the same day, the Supreme Court took note of the emphatic assurance and undertaking given by the state government and refrained from appointing a receiver. An application had requested the apex court to appoint the Centre as the receiver. The Supreme Court decided to appoint a judicial officer as an observer for a period of two weeks in the first instance to observe and monitor the situation, and submit a report to it whenever developments tending to be detrimental to the effectuation of the court's order would take place. The issue came up again before the Supreme Court on 30 November and 1 December 1992.

The Supreme Court, in its order on 1 December 1992, directed the state government and the Union government to give due publicity to the fact that the proposed kar seva would not involve any construction activity or moving of any building material into the acquired land, with a view to informing all those concerned about the limitations of the purpose of the gatherings. The court also took note of certain deficiencies regarding the security arrangements for the Ram Janmabhoomi–Babri Masjid structure. It felt that these should be brought to the notice of the state government, and this was done. S.B. Chavan, Union minister for home affairs, also wrote to Uttar Pradesh CM Kalyan Singh on this subject on 1 December 1992. On 2 December, nearly 40,000 kar sevaks reached Ayodhya. The Supreme Court was informed that the BJP leaders were fanning out to different places in order to inform kar sevaks that there would be no constructional activity during the kar seva and that it would be confined to religious functions. The reports, however, indicated that some leaders associated with the proposed kar seva were asserting their intention to undertake constructional activities.[46]

The Kalyan Singh government's assurance to the Supreme Court clearly indicated that there would be no construction activity and kar seva would only be symbolic. Anger was growing among the kar sevaks who were reaching Ayodhya from different parts of the country in large numbers. They were not willing to let their journey to Ayodhya go to waste. Uncertainty over the kar seva had made them restive. The VHP's Kendriya Margdarshak Mandal was scheduled to take a call on how and to what extent kar seva would be performed on 6 December 1992.

---

[46]'Statement by Minister of Home Affairs SB Chavan, General Situation at Ayodhya in the Context of the Proposed Kar Seva', *Parliament Digital Library*, 3 December 1992, Lok Sabha, pp. 541–3, https://tinyurl.com/ms9zh3nz. Accessed on 11 August 2024.

The Kendriya Margdarshak Mandal finally met on 5 December 1992. It decided on a symbolic kar seva, keeping in view the Kalyan Singh government's assurance to the Supreme Court and orders of the apex court. The kar sevaks were from all walks of life. They were ready to sacrifice their lives for the cause of the Ram temple. Several of them wanted the Babri Masjid, a symbol of oppression by the Mughals, to be gone. The kar sevaks were asking the VHP leaders to resolve the uncertainty. They were starting to get aggressive and began questioning the VHP leaders over what had been planned for 6 December. Several senior VHP leaders avoided facing the wrath of the kar sevaks by not visiting the Kar Sevak Puram, where a large number of them were camping.

Frankenstein's Monster Is Born

Recounting the events from its archives, *India Today* observed that the mood had started to change by December 5.

> Hundreds of Kar Sevaks stormed the Maniram Chavani where two of the religious leaders—Mahant Ramchandra Paramhans and Mahant Nritya Gopal Das—were subjected to a volley of angry questions. In the narrow, serpentine lanes of Ayodhya, the slogans were becoming more menacing. '*Jis Hindu ka khoon na khaula, khoon nahin woh paani hai* (If a Hindu's blood doesn't boil, then it's water, not blood)'. In the Karsevakpuram area, thousands converged to express their wrath against the leadership. The Frankenstein's monster had been born. And its creators were now its immediate victims.... Ashok Singhal, general secretary of the VHP, pleaded with the mahants to bridge the ominous chasm that had suddenly opened up between the Janki Mahal Trust—the camp headquarters of the leaders—and Karsevakpuram, where angry kar sevaks were clustered in open defiance. The mahants, sensing the ugly mood, stayed put. Only Vinay Katiyar, Bajrang Dal chief and Faizabad MP, dared to cross over to Karsevakpuram, where the hostile mob immediately surrounded him demanding

that the leaders reconsider their decision of a symbolic kar seva. Katiyar's message about the militant mood was passed on to L.K. Advani and company. But by now, the movement had been clearly hijacked by the hotheads. As a worried Paramhans said: 'Who except Ram Lalla can know about the kind of kar seva which will be undertaken tomorrow.'[47]

Amid simmering anger in Ayodhya, the fate of the disputed Ram Janmabhoomi–Babri Masjid structure hung in the balance. Those watching the developments from outside kept their fingers crossed. The stage was thus set for D-Day, 6 December 1992.

---

[47]Ibid.

8

The Demolition

A large number of kar sevaks thronged the narrow streets of Ayodhya as the sun rose on the temple town on 6 December 1992. The VHP announced its kar seva plan on 6 December 1992, but the kar sevaks had started assembling in Ayodhya much before D-Day.

They had boarded buses and trains, taken boat rides, and walked miles to reach Ayodhya at any cost, crossing all the hurdles on the way. While some came from nearby districts and states, others came from the remote corners of the country.

The kar sevaks belonged to different castes, classes, and geographical and linguistic regions. They hailed from different social and economic strata but shared a common aim. They camped together in village schools, local temples and open spaces. Locals had thrown their houses open for them. They were there for a common cause—they were on a mission to Ayodhya.

However, as stated earlier, uncertainty over the VHP's call for kar seva had made them restive. The Supreme Court had allowed only a symbolic kar seva. It was, however, only in the afternoon the previous day that the Kendriya Margdarshak Mandal had held its meeting and announced a symbolic kar seva in Ayodhya, with no violation of the court's order. The state's BJP government led by Kalyan Singh had given an assurance to the apex court that no harm would be caused to the disputed Ram Janmabhoomi–Babri Masjid structure. Additional companies of security forces were deployed at some distance from the disputed structure.

All eyes were on Ayodhya. A close watch was being kept on the movement of all kar sevaks. The situation in the area was peaceful thus far. The police had put up barricades on all the roads leading to the town and the disputed structure. A large number of journalists from national and international media organizations had assembled in the town ahead of D-Day.

Amid apprehensions about the danger that the large assembly of kar sevaks in Ayodhya might pose to the disputed structure, the announcement for a symbolic kar seva had come as a relief to the authorities. They were under the impression that kar sevaks would disperse after the symbolic kar seva in the same manner as they did after the Chaturmas gathering in July 1992. No one had any inkling about the volcano that was about to erupt there on Sunday.

At a distance of about 250 m from the disputed structure was the Ram Katha Kunj. Its rooftop was being used as the dais for the proposed kar seva programme. The three domes of the disputed structure were clearly visible from the dais. Senior leaders of the BJP and the VHP as well as the saints associated with the temple movement had begun assembling there. Several of them had reached and were about to begin addressing the crowd of kar sevaks that continued to swell consistently. At a nearby platform, about 150 m away from the disputed spot, the puja for the symbolic kar seva was to be performed. The spot for the puja was purified with water from the Saryu River. Kar sevaks were to shower water and flower petals there to mark the beginning of the symbolic kar seva as allowed by the Supreme Court.

Kalyan Singh Felt No Harm Would Be Done

Chief Minister Kalyan Singh felt no harm would be caused to the disputed structure. He enquired about the developments in Ayodhya.[1] Everybody kept their fingers crossed. No one knew what was going to happen next. Vinay Sitapati, who scrutinized the day's developments

---

[1]Interview with senior journalist Brajesh Shukla.

The Demolition

in *Half Lion: How P.V. Narasimha Rao Transformed India,* observed that Rao was an early riser.

> On 6 December 1992, he woke up at 7 a.m., later than usual since it was a Sunday. He read the day's newspapers... The PM then spent thirty minutes walking on a specially installed treadmill. His personal physician, K. Srinath Reddy, arrived soon after. They chatted in Telugu and English, while Reddy took samples of Rao's blood and urine. Since it was a Sunday, Reddy, a cardiologist at AIIMS hospital, spent the rest of the day at home with his family.[2]

At about 10.00 a.m., the large crowd of kar sevaks was surging towards the Ram Janmabhoomi–Babri Masjid area from all sides. A number of them were seen waiting for their turn to get frisked and cross the police barriers at the main entrance gate near Manas Bhawan that was serving as the media centre. Those who had entered the area moved towards the dais. Senior BJP leaders, including L.K. Advani, Murli Manohar Joshi, Sadhvi Uma Bharati, Sadhvi Ritambhara, (late) Pramod Mahajan and Kalraj Mishra; VHP leader Ashok Singhal; Bajrang Dal leader Vinay Katiyar; prominent Hindu saints and others had reached the dais by then.

Advani, whose yatra from Somnath in Gujarat to Ayodhya was stopped by then CM of Bihar Lalu Prasad Yadav in Samastipur, Bihar, on 23 October 1990, had arrived in Ayodhya from Lucknow late on the evening of 5 December 1992. Two police officers provided security cover to Advani from Lucknow, where he had addressed a public meeting along with senior party leader Atal Bihari Vajpayee, who later became the PM of India. In the temple town of Ayodhya, a young IPS officer of 1990 batch, Anju Gupta, who was then posted as additional superintendent of police (ASP), Faizabad, escorted Advani, who, along with other leaders, including the VHP's Ashok Singhal and the BJP's Murli Manohar Joshi, had just reached the spot.

---

[2]Sitapati, Vinay, *Half Lion: How P.V. Narasimha Rao Transformed India*, Penguin Random House, New Delhi, 2016, p. 225.

Some Commotion in the Crowd

As Advani and other leaders reached the dais, there was some commotion in the crowd. They visited the area where the symbolic kar seva was to be performed. Everything appeared fine till this time. Priests and saints were ready to perform the puja at the designated spot. Some kar sevaks wanted to catch a glimpse of the veteran leaders. They had been waiting for this day for years. Many of them were happy knowing that the BJP and VHP leaders, including L.K. Advani, had agreed to a symbolic kar seva. When Advani arrived at the dais on the top of the Ram Katha Kunj, where senior BJP and VHP leaders were addressing the crowd, there was a hubbub in the crowd at the venue. Senior journalist Hemant Sharma in his book *Ayodhya: A Battleground* has observed that 'Kar Sevaks got aggressive after seeing Advani. They thought he had come there to suspend the Kar Seva once again, so they got violent, broke barricading and tried to get to the platform where rituals were to be performed.'[3] Prime Minister Rao was monitoring the developments in Ayodhya. He was getting updates about the movements of kar sevaks in Ayodhya and the assembly at the Ram Katha Kunj. Rao, in his book *Ayodhya: 6 December 1992*, stated that a large crowd of kar sevaks estimated to be around 50,000–100,000 had already assembled at the Ram Katha Kunj. He noted that everything was going as per plan for a symbolic kar seva there. About 150 kar sevaks, in a sudden move, broke the police cordon and indulged in stone pelting at the police when the leaders at the dais were addressing the crowd.

> Many of those who were not in Ayodhya tuned in to radio or television sets to get news updates. Rao's personal physician Srinath Reddy, who was a cardiologist at AIIMS, tuned in his television and saw three domes of the Babri Masjid intact.[4]

---

[3] Sharma, Hemant, *Ayodhya: A Battleground*, Rupa Publications, India, 2000, p. 2.
[4] Sitapati, Vinay, *Half Lion: How P.V. Narasimha Rao Transformed India*, Penguin Random House, New Delhi, 2016, p. 225.

Kar Sevaks Reach the Top

Some of the kar sevaks were making attempts to enter the frisking gate near Manas Bhawan from the side of the Ram Chabutra. The police tried to stop the group at the barrier and eventually resorted to lathi charge. This action infuriated the kar sevaks, and some of them started pelting stones towards the police personnel. By that time, they had started moving towards the disputed structure from all the sides. Within minutes, some of them were seen reaching the top. The tear gas shells lobbed on them did not have any deterrent impact. Soon they were seen with steel pipes used for setting up barricades. The police later claimed that some kar sevaks were seen carrying shovels, pickaxes, spades and ropes.

Rao Stares at the Television

Recalling the events of the day, Sitapati stated:

> At 12.20 p.m., Reddy (Rao's personal physician) saw live on television, the assault on the first dome by thousands of Hindu activists. By 1.55 p.m., the first dome had collapsed. Reddy watched, numb... Almost immediately after, Reddy thought to himself, 'The PM is a heart patient. How will he be feeling?' A bypass surgery in 1990 had nearly caused Rao to retire from politics.
>
> Reddy rushed to the PM's office. Rao was standing when he entered, a gaggle of officials and politicians around him. They were all staring at the television. The third dome of the mosque had just fallen. 'Why have you come now?' Rao angrily asked Reddy. But the doctor insisted that his patient be examined. Rao moved to a small anteroom. 'His mind was elsewhere,' Reddy remembers, 'but he was an obedient patient.'
>
> Srinath Reddy checked the PM's pulse and blood pressure. 'As I expected, his heart was racing away...pulse was very fast...BP had risen. His face was glowing red, he was agitated.' Dr Reddy

gave Rao an extra dose of beta blocker, and left only when the PM had visibly calmed.[5]

Advani in his autobiography also took note of this development. He, however, observed that a group of kar sevaks had reached the top of the disputed structure much before any leader could begin addressing the crowd from the dais.[6]

The Crowd Raised Slogans

Recalling the sequence of events, Anju Gupta, IPS, in her statement before the Central Bureau of Investigation (CBI) court, said:

> I received L.K. Advani on Barabanki-Faizabad borders and took him to Janki Mahal Trust (where he had to stay for night) at 11.30 p.m. On 6 December 1992, I piloted him to the residence of Vinay Katiyar and took him to the disputed complex at 10.15 a.m. When he (Advani) reached the disputed complex, a crowd surrounded him. The crowd began raising 'Advaniji zindabad' and 'Murli Manohar Joshi zindabad' slogans. Advani went to the spot where puja (for symbolic kar seva) was scheduled to be performed and reached the dais on the Ram Katha Kunj. When he reached, there was a crowd of thousands. I saw from the dais that the crowd was increasing…. The Ram Katha Kunj was a single-storeyed building and its upper roof was being used as dais situated at a distance of about 150–175 m from the disputed structure.[7]

Temple Will Be Constructed Here

Additional Superintendent of Police Anju Gupta added:

---

[5]Ibid. 225–6.
[6]Advani, L.K., *My Country My Life*, Rupa and Co., New Delhi, 2008, p. 400.
[7]From Anju Gupta's statement in the Raebareli court (as mentioned by Special Court Ayodhya Affairs, Lucknow, in judgement, 30 September 2020). Author's translation.

When I reached there with L.K. Advani and Murli Manohar Joshi, Vinay Katiyar was pointing to the crowd in obvious sarcasm—see this is the place 'jahan parinda bhi par nahin maar sakta'. I remember the speech Murli Manohar Joshi delivered that day. He said, 'Narasimha Rao says... (could not be heard). We say, *'Mandir yahin banega. Masjid kahin banao* (The temple will be constructed here. A mosque may be constructed anywhere).' Advani also addressed the crowd. His speech was full of vigour. He spoke about 2.77 acres of land and repeated 'mandir yahin banega' again and again ... I could not hear his full speech as I took his car fleet from the road in front of police control room to the Ram Katha Kunj.[8]

Control Room Informed

Gupta said that while coming back with the fleet, she saw the people climbing to the top of domes for the first time from a road behind the disputed structure, especially from the southwest side.

> When I saw the destruction, I tried to inform the Ayodhya control room. After many attempts, my first contact with the police control room was at about 12.10 p.m. I gave my location and asked for force too. But I did not get any positive response... I was taking the VVIP fleet, and when I reached the Ram Katha Kunj, I informed the police control room and asked for force again at about 12.30 p.m. When I reached the dais, I saw the people on the top of the disputed structure, and they were indulging in destruction.[9]

It had all been near normal in the morning. Everything went out of control by noon. Within a short span of time, about 100 kar sevaks reached the top of the domes that were inaccessible to the crowd. Those listening to the speeches of the BJP and the VHP leaders also

---
[8]Ibid.
[9]Ibid.

began moving towards the disputed structure. The kar sevaks were raising slogans of 'Jai Sri Ram' and *'Ek dhakka aur do, Babri Masjid tod do* (Give one more push, demolish Babri Masjid)' as the disputed structure was being demolished. Soon, the media became the target of the kar sevaks. Senior officers were seen moving towards the disputed structure, but they were clueless about the next course of action. Those deployed inside the disputed structure also came out. There was a frenzy of destruction all around.

Kar Sevaks Fall from Domes

Giving further details of what was happening on the dais and on the administrative front, Anju Gupta recalled:

> When I reached the dais, Advaniji asked me what was happening inside the dispute structure. I told him, on the basis of information from wireless messages, that the people were inside the disputed structure and were indulging in destruction. I also told him that many of them were falling from the domes and getting badly injured. Advani appeared concerned to know this and he told me that he wanted to go there to take down these people from the domes. I consulted two superintendent of police-level officers who had accompanied Advani's yatra from Lucknow and advised him not to go as the situation could worsen if he was injured in any way. Later he consulted others on the dais and told me that I would have to take Uma Bharati there. Then I took her to the site in my jeep. My jeep was stopped by the crowd on the way, and Uma Bharati walked down towards the disputed structure from there. I came back to the Ram Katha Kunj. When I reached the dais again, I heard the people on the dais saying, 'Don't do kar seva from the top. Do it from the ground.' This was repeated again and again. After some time, the people came down from the dome. But soon they climbed to the top again and the demolition continued…All the three domes came down one by one, and the last one fell at 4.30 p.m. The first dome fell

at about 2.30 p.m. and the second one at about 3.30 p.m. When the domes were falling down, those on the dais were happy; they were hugging each other. Sweets were being distributed and there was a mood of celebration. Kar sevaks were being prompted to demolish the mosque. Uma Bharati and Ritambhara were very happy, and they were hugging each other and others on the dais including Advani and Murli Manohar Joshi... Soon after the demolition began, Advani asked me whether I would be able to arrange his (telephonic) conversation with CM Kalyan Singh. I expressed my inability to connect him to the CM but sent a message to the DM and the SSP. After some time, Advani came down from the dais to the office at the Ram Katha Kunj. I was told he spoke to the CM from there. [10]

Advani Speaks to Kalyan Singh

Did Advani ask Kalyan Singh to stop the kar sevaks? Those aware of the developments said that the two had a telephonic discussion when the disputed structure was being demolished. What transpired between them? Advani, later in his autobiography, referred to his request while speaking with Anju Gupta (without naming her), and made a mention of his conversation with Kalyan Singh on phone; he also talked about the kar sevaks manhandling Ashok Singhal. He said that the mood of elation in the crowd began having influence on some of the leaders on the dais by the time the third dome fell. He also said that he refused to have sweets when distribution of sweets began following the demolition of the three domes. About his conversation with Kalyan Singh, Advani noted:

> The essence of my conversation with him was that, in view of his government's failure to abide by the assurance he had given to the Supreme Court, he ought to tender his resignation. He agreed.[11]

---

[10]Ibid.
[11]Advani, L.K., *My Country My Life*, Rupa and Co., New Delhi, 2008, pp. 401–2.

Kalyan Singh Takes Responsibility

Kalyan Singh, who had assured complete protection to the disputed structure, took moral responsibility for the incident and said that he had asked the officers not to open fire. He even called the demolition a matter of national pride, with no regret, repentance or grief.[12] P.V. Narasimha Rao, who had spoken to Vinay Katiyar early in the morning and got an assurance that everything was under control, noted that at 2.00 p.m., Union Home Minister S.B. Chavan spoke to CM Kalyan Singh to enquire about the action taken for protection of the disputed structure. Rao had a different take on the happenings on the spot. He said the Uttar Pradesh police moved away when the kar sevaks crossed the barriers and climbed to the top of the domes. He said the officers remained mute spectators, and this inaction was because of orders from CM Kalyan Singh, who refused to allow use of force.

Senior British journalist William Mark Tully, *BBC*'s former India correspondent, was in Ayodhya on 6 December 1992. After 25 years of the demolition, he recounted his experience with the *BBC* saying:

> As I watched the last cordon collapse and the police walk away with their wicker shields held above their heads for protection from the stones raining down on them, with an officer pushing his men aside to get out first, I realized I was witnessing a historic event—the most significant triumph for Hindu nationalism since independence and the gravest setback to secularism.[13]

Officers Find Shelter under a Tree

J.B. Singh (now retired IAS officer), who was then deployed at the sanctum sanctorum under the central dome of the disputed structure,

---

[12] 'Kalyan Singh in an Interview Called December 6, 1992, a Matter of National Pride with No Regret, Repentance or Grief', *Organiser*, 6 December 2023, https://tinyurl.com/429juucf. Accessed on 12 July 2024.

[13] 'How the Babri Mosque Destruction Shaped India', *BBC*, 6 December 2017, https://tinyurl.com/4sfzxe6y. Accessed on 13 August 2024.

admitted that the police force present there withdrew, and most of the officers present on the spot moved out and assembled under a nearby tree. 'Initially brickbats were thrown towards the disputed structure. At this other magistrates and police officers standing there came inside the sanctum sanctorum,' said Singh.[14]

Another retired officer who was deployed there as a young magistrate said:

> A group of 10 to 15 kar sevaks soon came running inside the disputed structure. A police officer of the CRPF opened fire in the air when the first batch of kar sevaks entered the sanctum sanctorum. He was, however, hit by a fellow CRPF officer. Others also realized that there were no orders to open fire and firing could have led to an ugly situation. Within minutes we, along with others, came out of the sanctum sanctorum and the CRPF deployed there assembled in the nearby area and continued to watch the unfolding developments from a distance.[15]

Priest Picks up the Idol

J.B. Singh also said that the kar sevaks indulged in the demolition soon after they entered the disputed structure. He said he safely took out a family member of a priest of Ram Lalla. He stated:

> A female member of the family of the Ram temple priest, seeing the CRPF personnel leaving the spot to be at a safe distance from the mob, came asking me for help. She wanted to leave the spot for a safer place. I held the hand of the woman and took her out of the disputed structure. We saw some kar sevaks on the top of the structure. They began hitting the disputed structure with whatever they had in their hand. I am not sure who else was inside the sanctum sanctorum under the central

---

[14]Telephonic interview with J.B. Singh.
[15]Telephonic interview with a now-retired magistrate on condition of anonymity.

dome of the disputed structure when the they were hitting the walls to bring it down.[16]

Acharya Satyendra Das, the main priest of Ram Lalla in Ayodhya, was also in the central dome of the disputed structure at that point of time. His mentor Guru Abhiram Das had got the idol of Ram Lalla installed under the central dome on the intervening night of 22 and 23 December 1949. Acharya Satyendra Das, in his statement before the court, recollected:

> When they began demolishing the second dome I along with my co-priests (assistant priests) picked up the idol of Ram Lala and held the same in our hands. The idol was held in hands and was not handed over to anybody. The idol was not taken out of the (then disputed) complex.[17]

Kalyan Singh Orders Not to Open Fire

The Ministry of Home Affairs (MHA) was informed about the damage being caused to the disputed structure. The MHA was also informed about the Uttar Pradesh police's failure to take any action to stop the kar sevaks who indulged in the demolition of the disputed structure. P.V. Narasimha Rao, later speaking in Lok Sabha on 21 December 1992, gave a detailed account about the efforts to move the Central Paramilitary Forces in Ayodhya and how the central forces were asked to return when Kalyan Singh ordered not to open fire.

> At 2.20 p.m. DG (director general), ITBP, informed MHA that three battalions which had moved from DRC (camp) had met resistance and obstructions enroute, there were a lot of road blocks and people stopped vehicles. After talking to the people enroute, the convoy reached with great difficulty at Saket Degree

---

[16]Telephonic interview with J.B. Singh.
[17]Acharya Satyendra Das's statement in Raebareli court (as mentioned by Special Court Ayodhya Affairs, Lucknow, in judgement, 30 September 2020).

college where the forces were again stopped and the road was blocked. Minor pelting of stones also took place. The Magistrate asked them in writing to return. DG, ITBP, further informed that three battalions had returned accordingly. The Commissioner had been contacted, who informed, the CM, Uttar Pradesh had ordered that there will be no firing under any circumstances.[18]

Central Forces Unable to Move

The Uttar Pradesh government's move to ask the central forces to return became a cause of concern to the Union government. Senior officers of the MHA got in touch with the state government's officers and requested them to ask the officials in Ayodhya for use of force. Rao said the state government officials assured the MHA that they would requisition the central forces after consulting the CM. He felt there were some difficulties in imposing President's rule in Uttar Pradesh.

> The Home Secretary (Madhav Godbole) spoke to Principal Secretary, Home, Government of Uttar Pradesh (Prabhat Kumar) at the CM's residence asking him to persuade the CM to accept the assistance of the Central Forces. The Principal Secretary, Home, Government of Uttar Pradesh said that he would requisition Central Forces after consulting the CM. At no point of time was it refused? This is what I am trying to impress. When does that moment arise when we come to the conclusion that the governance of the State cannot be carried on according to the provisions of the Constitution? So, these are some of the difficulties. If only one word had been there, in Article 356 which says, 'a situation has arisen if after that it could have been added—is likely to arise.' Then the Governor gets, the President gets a greater leeway. But, then, one has to go into greater detail.

---

[18]'Motion of No Confidence in Council of Ministers', *Parliament of India: Lok Sabha—Digital* Library, 21 December 1992, pp. 635–6, https://tinyurl.com/2s3dc5kt. Accessed on 13 August 2024.

> This is the first time in the history of the Constitution, in the history of Article 356 when it has been put to a time-based test, it was never put to before and it has not been able to stand the test. Never mind who used it, never mind who did not use it, howsoever you look at it you will find that there is lacuna and that would have to be made good.[19]

P.V. Narasimha Rao, in his book, has noted that the Union home secretary then spoke to the defence secretary and asked him to keep helicopters ready if any force was to be moved immediately by air. Rao observed that the defence secretary was also requested to keep two transport planes ready for movement of additional troops if necessary.

> Between 3.30 p.m. and 4.30 p.m., the Home Secretary was informed that communal incidents had started occurring in Ayodhya, and spoke to the DGP, Uttar Pradesh, and told him that the situation was fast deteriorating; not only were the Central Forces unable to move but there was serious apprehension of communal riots. The DGP, Uttar Pradesh, informed that the situation could not be controlled without firing and orders of the CM were being obtained.[20]

The Rao government failed to act to stop the demolition. Had it worked out any plans of action to handle such an eventuality? Did the Union home ministry have any contingency plans? *The Print* has reported that the perception that the Union home ministry under S.B. Chavan couldn't do enough to prevent the demolition of the Babri Masjid is false. It quoted then Union Home Secretary Madhav Godbole saying that the MHA had made plans to take over the disputed structure long before the incident, but PM P.V. Narasimha Rao failed to give the go-ahead to implement it. 'The plan was prepared soon after Hindu organizations and BJP leaders started kar seva on 9 July 1992. The plan

---
[19]Ibid. 636.
[20]Rao, P.V. Narasimha, *Ayodhya: 6 December 1992*, Penguin Random House, India, 2006, p. 156.

was to first take control of the disputed site at midnight, a time when no one was around, followed by the dismissal of the state government and the imposition of President's rule,' stated *The Print*.[21]

Makeshift Temple Comes Up

By 4–4.30 p.m., the entire structure was demolished. It was time to level the area and return Ram Lalla's idol to the same spot in the makeshift temple that came up there. Acharya Satyendra Das, now chief priest of the Ram Janmabhoomi Temple, has been quoted as saying that he stood holding the idol of Ram Lalla when the disputed structure was being demolished. He further observed:

> We took the idol of Ram Lalla along with the *singhasan* (ornate chair) to the same spot, where the idol was placed before the demolition, at about 7.00 p.m. The levelling work continued till the time the CRPF stationed outside Ayodhya reached there on 8 December 1992. When I was installing the idol, the VHP's Shambhu Singh was giving instructions to the kar sevaks for levelling the field. The forces present there did not take any action to stop the kar sevaks. Instead, they (personnel from central paramilitary forces) moved away from there.[22]

Officers Perform Kar Seva

This is a recollection of the first-hand account of how the makeshift Ram temple came up at the disputed site soon after the demolition (as relayed to the court by the main priest responsible for performing puja of Ram Lalla). When the disputed structure was being demolished,

---

[21] Kumar, Anshuman, 'Home Ministry Had a Plan to Prevent Babri Demolition, but PM Rao Didn't Allow It', *The Print*, 6 December 2017, https://tinyurl.com/2mzh7dzd. Accessed on 19 August 2024.
[22] Acharya Satyendra Das's statement in the Raebareli court (as mentioned by Special Court Ayodhya Affairs, Lucknow, in judgement, 30 September 2020).

a section of kar sevaks sitting on the ground were singing the praise of Lord Rama. Once the demolition was complete, the officers who had moved away from the scene during the day, including magistrates and police, returned to the spot to watch the unfolding developments. This was the time when the idol of Ram Lalla was being reinstalled at the disputed spot, and a makeshift temple was coming up at the spot where the disputed structure had stood. This group of visiting officers also did some kar seva, with some contributing symbolically and carrying the construction material to the spot for construction of the makeshift Ram temple.

Rao Couldn't Talk

As the reports of kar sevaks climbing atop the disputed structure and damaging it started coming in, there was shock and dismay all around. Many Congress leaders tried to get in touch with PM P.V. Narasimha Rao. None of them were able to reach him.

Vinay Sitapati has dealt with this issue in his book. He has quoted a friend, who was then present with Rao, to make his point that the PM could not talk for some time after seeing the demolition on television. The PM apparently had trusted the Kalyan Singh government. He said that the PM was not asleep and later spoke to the director of the Intelligence Bureau and Union Home Minister S.B. Chavan as well.[23]

Kalyan Singh Was Inaccessible

Kalyan Singh was inaccessible for some time. He was apparently upset at the unfolding developments. He felt he had been let down. He kept an eye on the day's developments in Ayodhya. When the situation demanded use of force, he ensured there was no firing on the kar sevaks. He owned the responsibility for giving such instructions. When he became sure that a makeshift temple had come up at the disputed

---

[23]Sitapati, Vinay, *Half Lion: How P.V. Narasimha Rao Transformed India*, Penguin Random House, New Delhi, 2016, p. 247.

site, he reached the Raj Bhawan in Lucknow by evening and handed over his resignation to then Uttar Pradesh Governor B. Satya Narayan Reddy. On the other hand, the Union cabinet was called the same day at 6.00 p.m. in New Delhi. The cabinet decided to recommend dismissal of the Kalyan Singh-led government, and dissolution of the Uttar Pradesh legislative assembly. By about 7.30 p.m., S.B. Chavan took the papers to the President of India, and around 9.10 p.m. the President signed the papers, imposing President's rule in Uttar Pradesh under Article 356 of the Constitution of India.[24] The Centre appointed two advisors to assist the governor of Uttar Pradesh.

Soon after the demolition, riots broke out in the streets, close to the demolished structure in Ayodhya. Some houses of members belonging to a particular community were targeted and set on fire. The administration decided to impose curfew in Ayodhya. Faizabad DM R.N. Srivastava and the district police chief D.B. Rai were suspended. Senior IAS officer Arvind Verma was sent as the Faizabad divisional commissioner.

Magistrates Refused to Accompany Forces

Those aware of the developments said that new divisional commissioner Arvind Verma convened a meeting of all magistrates at the divisional commissioner's residence in Faizabad. Was a plan to send an army to evacuate the disputed area discussed? A former IAS officer who was deployed as magistrate on 6 December 1992 said that he was not sure whether the district administration or the state government held any consultations with the defence ministry for deployment of the army. He said that some officers of the Indian Army, who might have been posted in Faizabad, were apparently consulted. This gave an impression to the officers present there that the Indian Army might

---

[24]'Motion of No Confidence in Council of Ministers', *Parliament of India: Lok Sabha—Digital* Library, 21 December 1992, p. 640, https://tinyurl.com/2s3dc5kt. Accessed on 13 August 2024.

be called to carry out the operation.[25] The divisional commissioner told the magistrates that they would have to accompany the forces in the operation to evacuate the disputed spot.

When the group of magistrates was about to leave, one senior officer, Khem Singh Khadak, said that there was no point in sending the magistrates as this was going to be an army operation. According to the story narrated by the retired IAS officer present there as a magistrate, Khadak asked the divisional commissioner: 'What is the need to send magistrates for an operation that the Indian Army is supposed to carry out?' Khadak obviously wanted to distance himself from any operation that involved use of force on the kar sevaks at the disputed spot. 'We don't want to go for the operation,' said Khadak, according to the retired IAS officer.

At this, the divisional commissioner Arvind Verma got upset and apparently lost his cool. He took out a piece of paper and showed the same to the officers present there. The divisional commissioner announced that those who did not want to go for the operation should sign the paper. 'Khem Singh Khadak signed the paper immediately,' said the retired IAS officer.

'Anybody else?' asked the divisional commissioner, and about 10 to 12 magistrates signed the paper. The officer said that the magistrates were apparently apprehensive about the unfolding events and felt that there could be bloodshed if any force was sent to evacuate the disputed spot. Soon enough, the divisional commissioner also calmed down and said that he took charge of the division in Ayodhya knowing all the officers deployed in the temple town would back him. 'How can I work when the officers are refusing to go with the force for an operation,' said the divisional commissioner.

At this, Umesh Chandra Tiwari, an officer known as Ram Lalla Tiwari among his colleagues and well-wishers because of his association with Ayodhya, said, 'I am ready to sacrifice my life for my younger brothers (officers). I will go alone.' The retired IAS officer

---

[25]Telephonic interview with the retired magistrate who was deployed in Ayodhya on 6 December 1992.

recollected, 'Shri Prakash Singh, another officer who later held various senior posts in the state government, also agreed to go.'[26]

No Crowd on Spot

He said that finally the Central Reserve Police Force (CRPF) was sent to vacate the disputed spot. 'But when the CRPF reached there, there were hardly any kar sevaks left there. A group of 40 to 50 women volunteers was present, but they too were getting ready to leave the next morning,' he said. He added that nothing much happened there as there was nobody present to be forcibly removed from the area.[27]

The Ram Janmabhoomi station house officer (SHO) Priyamvada Nath Shukla lodged the FIR numbered 197/92 at 5.15 p.m. on 6 December 1992, saying that the kar sevaks got agitated when efforts were made to stop them. On being lathi charged, they began raising slogans of 'Jai Shri Ram' and many of them attacked the disputed structure from all sides. They soon started to demolish the disputed structure. All the tear gas squads available there were asked to lob tear gas shells on the kar sevaks. But the latter had a layer of protective material on their faces, and so the gas did not have any impact on them. Instead, the kar sevaks pelted stones at the police and began demolishing the disputed structure. A large number of kar sevaks were injured after being lathi charged. The disputed structure was completely demolished by them.

Ganga Ram Tiwari, who was the in-charge of the police outpost at the Ram Janmabhoomi complex, lodged another FIR numbered 198/92 at 5.25 p.m. on the same day against Ashok Singhal, Giriraj Kishore, L.K. Advani, Murli Manohar Joshi, Vishnu Dalmia, Vinay Kumar, Uma Bharati and Sadhvi Ritambhara, saying that these speakers were present on the dais and instigating the kar sevaks.

It was stated that repeated instructions were issued from the dais to do kar seva from the ground, and slogans like 'Ek dhakka aur do' to

---

[26]Ibid.
[27]Ibid.

demolish the mosque were raised. It was also said that slogans using derogatory words for a community were raised. L.K. Advani, who was one of the accused named in the FIR, however, has said that the leaders on the dais requested the kar sevaks to come down from the top of the domes. Advani noted in his autobiography:

'The leaders on the dais immediately started pleading through the public announcement system with the Kar Sevaks on the top of the domes to come down. This was, however, to no avail. In fact, more and more people appeared to be climbing the dome. Soon, I could see them carrying some implements and hammering away at the domes. I was upset, and so were other leaders on the dais.'[28]

Supreme Court Reviews the Situation

Besides the FIRs filed by the police against L.K. Advani and others in Ayodhya, 47 more FIRs were lodged by media persons who had been beaten up by the mob. The Supreme Court was monitoring the developments. The apex court was upset at the turn of events in Ayodhya. It took a serious note of the incident and summoned the senior Counsel of Uttar Pradesh government. P.V. Narasimha Rao noted in his autobiography:

> Until late in the evening on 6 December, the Supreme Court was reviewing the happenings in Ayodhya. When the final news of the demolition reached the Court, they expressed annoyance and distress at the unfortunate turn of events. The state government had deliberately misled the Supreme Court over the past few days and when the ultimate vandalism took place, the senior Counsel of the state government was called for an explanation. To this, the counsel replied, 'I was misled by the party and my head hangs in shame.'[29]

---

[28] Advani, L.K., *My Country My Life*, Rupa and Co., New Delhi, 2008, pp. 400–1.
[29] Rao, P.V. Narasimha, *Ayodhya: 6 December 1992*, Penguin Random House, India, 2006, p. 159.

About why Kalyan Singh didn't allow the central forces that were stationed nearby to handle the situation, Anil Swarup, a retired bureaucrat who worked with Singh as director, Information Department, and as secretary to the CM, said that it was well known that the central forces were not allowed to reach Ayodhya. Swarup added that this did not automatically mean that the central forces were held back to allow demolition, stating, 'Kalyan Singh believed that, as in July, the kar sevaks would go back after performing puja and that no harm would come to the Masjid. However, on this occasion, he turned out to be wrong.'[30]

Swarup, who is also the author of *Encounters with Politicians*, said that Kalyan Singh wanted a grand temple to come up at Ayodhya, and he was diligently working towards finding a peaceful and amicable solution to the vexed issue. He said that a few such options had been emerging. 'One such solution involved the construction of a new Masjid close to the disputed spot. He even cited the example of the shifting of mosques when Aswan Dam was being constructed in Egypt. The idea was gaining currency. He was engaging intensively with all stakeholders in the controversy. However, he was totally against the aggressive posturing of right-wing religious outfits.'[31]

Meanwhile, communal tension rose in different parts of the country as the situation turned from bad to worse. Curfew was enforced in many cities in Uttar Pradesh. The BJP claimed moral responsibility for the developments that took place in Ayodhya on 6 December 1992. Kalyan Singh was angry when the reports about demolition of the disputed structure reached him. His government had assured the Supreme Court that the structure would be protected. Though his government was the one that had allowed the assembly of such a large number of kar sevaks in Ayodhya on 6 December 1992, he was not the one who formulated any plans to carry out the demolition.

---

[30]Swarup, Anil, *Encounters with Politicians*, Unique Publishers, 2024, p. 73.
[31]Ibid. 71–2.

Kalyan Singh Was Not Aware

Anil Swarup expressed his view that Kalyan Singh was not aware of the demolition moves, if they were pre-planned. He said:

> Those who believe that Kalyan Singh was the man behind this demolition overlook the fact that he had absolute majority in the assembly. Why would he want to bring his own government down in case the Masjid got demolished? He would have surely known the consequences of the demolition. In his repeated interactions with the central leadership, he was arguing against the congregation of kar sevaks at the site. This became evident on the 6th of December in his telephonic conversation with Bhairon Singh Shekhawat, then CM of Rajasthan. I was present when this conversation took place. Kalyan Singh was livid. He reiterated that he was against such a congregation, but he was overruled and no one listened to him.[32]

Kalyan Singh was a good administrator and a good orator. At various public platforms, he never shied away from reiterating that his government would protect the disputed structure and implement the court's order for the symbolic kar seva in letter and spirit. At the same time, he consistently asserted that his government was committed to the construction of the Ram temple in Ayodhya, and the BJP came to power in Uttar Pradesh in the 1991 assembly elections with this mandate.

Advani Leaves Ayodhya

A sense of victory prevailed among the BJP and the VHP cadres following the demolition on 6 December 1992. The Muslims felt betrayed. Advani felt disturbed by the events that unfolded over the day, and senior party leader Pramod Mahajan advised him to leave Ayodhya to change his mood. So he left with Mahajan at about

---

[32] Swarup, Anil, *Ethical Dilemma of a Civil Servant*, Unique Publishers, 2021, pp. 78–9.

6.00 p.m. He recalled that the police, however, stopped his car on way to Lucknow:

> On seeing that the car carried Pramod Mahajan and me, a senior officer of the Uttar Pradesh government walked up to us and said, 'Advaniji kuchh bacha to nahin hai na? Bilkul saaf kar diya na? (I hope nothing of the structure is surviving and that it has been totally razed to the ground.)'[33]

Advani noted that the incident reflected the people's mood after demolition of the disputed structure. It led to a spread of riots not only in Ayodhya but in many other places too. The district administrations resorted to imposition of curfew at many places that had witnessed violence. At a number of places, the army was put on alert. Several died in the violence that followed the demolition.

Former President of India Pranab Mukherjee, who was then deputy chairman of the Planning Commission of India, was in Mumbai on the day of demolition of Babri Masjid. Senior Congress leader Jairam Ramesh was the officer on special duty in the Planning Commission. He informed Mukherjee about the demolition on telephone. The former President of India has recalled the day's developments in his book *The Turbulent Years* and said that he could not believe what he heard, and so he repeatedly asked Ramesh about the demolition. He stated that a pilot car and an escort were organized for him on his way to the airport as he was to pass through certain sensitive areas. Mukherjee wrote further:

> I could see people in small groups standing at street corners. There were stones and bricks strewn on the roads, indicating that there had been a violent exchange just before we had passed through. The next day's newspapers confirmed in graphic detail the rampage that had occurred in those areas.[34]

---

[33] Advani, L.K., *My Country My Life*, Rupa and Co., New Delhi, 2008, p. 402.
[34] Mukherjee, Pranab, *The Turbulent Years 1980–1996*, Rupa Publications, India, 2016, p. 153.

Kalyan Singh Was in a Relaxed Mood

Those who followed the developments in Lucknow also feel that Kalyan Singh was sure that no harm would be done to the disputed structure. The Union government had informed him about the aggressive stance of the kar sevaks on 5 December 1992. He must have received the same information from the state government's own agencies. Yet, he continued to believe that the disputed structure would remain protected. He was in a relaxed mood in the forenoon of 6 December 1992. It was when the reports about the kar sevaks climbing atop the disputed structure first reached him that he lost his cool. Singh spoke to senior BJP leaders, including Advani, who advised the CM to tender his resignation. When senior administrative and police officers informed him that the situation was going from bad to worse, he gave clear instructions to them against opening fire on the kar sevaks.

Kalyan Singh took the responsibility for having given instructions to the officers against using any force. He went to the Raj Bhawan only when the makeshift temple came up at the spot of the demolished disputed structure. When asked about who was to be held accountable for the demolition, Kalyan Singh said that history would decide.[35]

---

[35]Interview with senior journalist Brijesh Shukla.

9

The Dispute Continues: Who Demolished the Mosque?

Ablaze of communal frenzy gripped the country following the demolition of the disputed Ram Janmabhoomi–Babri Masjid structure on 6 December 1992. It shocked the nation. It was a criminal act. It questioned the myth of Hindu tolerance.

It changed India forever.

The communal violence that followed the demolition led to the killing of hundreds of people and this further strained the country's already fragile social fabric. The VHP referred to the day as *shaurya divas* (bravery day). The BMAC called the day a black day. This was seen as an assault on democracy and marked a new era of aggressive Hindutva.

The communal riots that followed the demolition, according to initial reports, killed more than 200 persons and injured 100 more.[1] The violence spilled over into neighbouring countries as angry Muslims in Pakistan and Bangladesh attacked Hindu temples and Indian embassies in retaliation for what they perceived as a vicious attack on Islam.[2]

This was the worst-ever communal violence to have been reported since Partition. There are estimates showing that over a thousand people died in the religious hatred that engulfed the nation in the

---

[1] Anderson, John Ward, and Molly Moore, '200 Killed In Riots Following Mosque Destruction', *The Washington Post*, 7 December 1992, https://tinyurl.com/36uhxhcb. Accessed on 15 July 2024.
[2] Ibid.

subsequent months.[3] Another estimate shows 2,000 deaths in the rioting throughout India.[4]

Rao's Resignation Demanded

As Parliament was in session, both Houses witnessed stormy scenes over the issue the next day. A ban on the VHP, action against the BJP senior leader L.K. Advani, and resignation of PM P.V. Narasimha Rao were some of the demands raised by the members. The Lok Sabha assembled at 11.00 a.m. on 7 December 1992. Agitated members from both sides, the treasury benches and Opposition rose to make their points. There was pandemonium in the House, as the members trooped into the well of the House to draw attention towards what had happened in Ayodhya on 6 December 1992.

'Mr Speaker, Sir, we want a ban on the VHP…interruptions… Mr Advani has no right to sit in this House,' said Congress's Digvijaya Singh, MP from Rajgarh, Madhya Pradesh. P.C. Thomas, a Kerala Congress (M) member from Muvattupuzha, said that the BJP should be banned. Ram Vilas Paswan, a Janata Dal member from Rosera, Bihar, said, 'Mr Advani should be arrested.' Ram Prasad Singh, Janata Dal MP from Bikramganj, Bihar (abolished later), said, 'Home minister should resign. The Congress is involved in it. The government has completely failed. The PM should resign.' Suraj Mandal of the Jharkhand Mukti Morcha from Godda, Bihar (now Jharkhand), said, 'The BJP should be banned.' Another member, Rajnath Sonkar Shastri of the Janata Dal from Saidpur, Uttar Pradesh, said, 'Advaniji should resign.' At 11.01 a.m., Ebrahim Sulaiman Sait, a Muslim League member from Ponnani, Kerala, and some other members came to the floor near the table and the Speaker adjourned the house till 2.00 p.m.[5]

---

[3] 'Bloody Aftermath of Babri Masjid Demolition across India', *India Today*, 5 December 2011, https://tinyurl.com/35jer2wc. Accessed on 15 July 2024.
[4] 'Mob Rips Apart Mosque in Ayodhya', *BBC*, https://tinyurl.com/bdept34a. Accessed on 15 July 2024.
[5] Lok Sabha Debates (English Version), Fifth Session (Tenth Lok Sabha), *Parliament Digital Library*, 7 December 1992, https://tinyurl.com/4ephb6w6. Accessed on 20 June 2024.

Demand to Ban the VHP

When the House reassembled at 2.00 p.m., there was again a demand for the resignation of PM P.V. Narasimha Rao, with members saying that his government had no right to continue in office following its failure to protect the disputed structure. 'Mr Speaker, this government has no right to continue. They have failed to protect the disputed structure,' said Sobhanadreeswara Rao Vadde, a Telugu Desam MP from Vijayawada, Andhra Pradesh. Nirmal Kanti Chatterjee of the CPI (M) from Dum Dum, West Bengal, said, 'The PM should resign and go.'[6]

Digvijaya Singh said:

> The BJP has gone against the Constitution. They cannot sit here. The BJP has no right to sit in this House. They have violated the Constitution. The BJP has finally proved that they are communal organization. They have betrayed this country. Mr L.K. Advani has no right to be in Parliament... They have no right to be a political party in this country. They have been misleading the highest judicial authority in the country. They have misled the Supreme Court and they have misled the PM and they have misled this country. Ban the VHP.[7]

A makeshift temple came up on the spot where the disputed structure stood till 6 December 1992. President's rule was imposed in Uttar Pradesh within hours of demolition of the disputed structure. Senior BJP leader L.K. Advani, who called the demolition very unfortunate, resigned as the Leader of Opposition owning moral responsibility for the incident/violence.[8] The BJP governments in Himachal Pradesh, Rajasthan and Madhya Pradesh were also subsequently dismissed on 15 December 1992. The VHP was banned on 9 December 1992. The

---

[6]Ibid.
[7]Ibid.
[8]'Mob Rips Apart Mosque in Ayodhya', *BBC*, https://tinyurl.com/bdept34a. Accessed on 15 July 2024.

RSS, Bajrang Dal, Islamic Sevak Sangh (ISS) and Jamat-e-Islami Hind were also banned in an apparent balancing act. The Unlawful Activities (Prevention) Tribunal lifted the ban on the RSS and the Bajrang Dal after six months.[9]

Kalyan Singh Wins Again

President's rule continued in Uttar Pradesh till 4 December 1993, when a new government led by SP leader Mulayam Singh Yadav (after a coalition between the SP and the BSP) was installed following elections to the state legislative assembly. Kalyan Singh, who emerged as the hero of the demolition, contested from Atrauli and Kasganj seats of the Uttar Pradesh legislative assembly. He won both the seats. On 17 December 1993, Congress MLAs Naresh Agarwal and Jagdambika Pal (both of them are now in the BJP) targeted Kalyan Singh in the legislative assembly. Agarwal's son Nitin Agarwal is a minister in the Yogi Adityanath-led BJP government, while Jagdambika Pal is a BJP MP from Domariyaganj Lok Sabha seat of Uttar Pradesh. Naresh Agarwal and Jagdambika Pal said a letter be sent to the ECI seeking disqualification of Kalyan Singh for not following the conditions mentioned in the affidavit filed in the Supreme Court on 27 November 1992.

The Congress leader Pramod Tiwari accused Kalyan Singh of betraying the people and the court.[10] Senior BJP leader Rajendra Kumar Gupta raised the issue of his arrest in the state legislative assembly on 20 December 1993. The former said that following the demolition of the disputed structure on 6 December, top BJP leaders and the BJP president were arrested and kept at Matatila Jail for 34 days (a makeshift jail had been set up at Matatila, Lalitpur). The BJP's Brahm Dutt Dwivedi, who later came into focus for saving the BSP

---

[9]Singh, N.K., 'Defeating the Ban: Even after Imposing Ban, Govt Fails to Neutralise VHP', *India Today*, 15 July 1995, https://tinyurl.com/y2vd7yz7. Accessed on 15 July 2024.
[10]'Uttar Pradesh Vidhan Sabha Proceedings, Twelfth Legislative Assembly, First Session, 17 December 1993, pp. 29, 30, 34, https://tinyurl.com/mr3hcbn2. Accessed on 14 August 2024.

president Mayawati in the state guest house incident of Lucknow, Uttar Pradesh, on 2 June 1995,[11] said that Kalyan Singh was detained on false charges in violation of rules to ensure that he was not able to attend the House proceedings.[12]

As it turned out, the BJP did not get the results the party had expected in the 1993 Uttar Pradesh legislative assembly elections. This was the state's first assembly election after the demolition of the disputed structure on 6 December 1992. The BJP, though it emerged as the single largest party winning 177 out of 422 seats[13] contested in the assembly of undivided Uttar Pradesh, could not muster sufficient numbers to form the next government. The poll outcome was a big setback for the BJP, and the SP–BSP combine formed the government in Uttar Pradesh. The demolition, however, inculcated a renewed sense of confidence and power in the leaders of the saffron brigade. The RSS and its affiliated organizations like the VHP—called the Sangh Parivar—did not give up and continued to push for the Ram temple agenda. The BJP remained defensive for some time after the demolition. Kalyan Singh was undertaking tours to different parts of the country and receiving a heroic welcome everywhere.

Kalyan Singh Becomes Hero of Demolition

During a discussion in the Lok Sabha on 23 February 1993, Union Home Minister S.B. Chavan observed:

> Now Mr Kalyan Singh, the former CM of Uttar Pradesh, is being paraded throughout the country as if he has done something very

---

[11]'Guest House "Assault": The 1995 Infamous Incident That Had Turned SP-BSP Bitter Foes', *The Indian Express*, 14 January 2019, https://tinyurl.com/2ryc82hd. Accessed on 15 July 2024.
[12]Uttar Pradesh Vidhan Sabha Proceedings, Twelfth Legislative Assembly, First Session, 20 December 1993, pp. 4, 16, https://tinyurl.com/mr3hcbn2. Accessed on 14 August 2024.
[13]Election Commission of India, *Statistical Report on Elections*, 1993, https://tinyurl.com/84f4ppc5. Accessed on 14 August 2024.

heroic. He (Kalyan Singh) has become a great hero for them, he goes everywhere and takes (addresses) big rallies. There he announces there was nothing wrong and we (BJP leaders) take pride that this structure was demolished. He got some kind of a divine inspiration and out of that divine inspiration he says that he could not do anything (to stop demolition) and now he feels proud for that. Then, there is a competition going on between the Shiv Sena and the VHP in claiming the responsibility for the demolition of the structure. Now both are claiming the responsibility for the demolition. One was claiming in the beginning and thereafter, even the VHP also is now claiming the responsibility saying that only Shiv Sena cannot take the credit and they are also equally responsible for demolishing the same.[14]

Advani, Joshi and Others Named in FIRs

As mentioned earlier, the police registered two FIRs with regard to the demolition. The first FIR, registered at 5.15 p.m. by Priyamvada Nath Shukla, SHO, Ram Janmabhoomi, Ayodhya (case crime number 197/92), named unknown kar sevaks for committing the crime under sections 395, 397, 332, 337, 338, 295, 297 and 153 of the IPC and indulging in dacoity, robbery, causing hurt to deter public servant from duty, causing hurt to any person by acting rashly, injuring/ defiling places of public worship with intent to insult religion of any class, promoting enmity on grounds of religion, and provocation with an intent to cause riots. After a gap of 10 minutes (5.25 p.m.), Ganga Ram Tiwari, the sub-inspector in charge of the police outpost at Ram Janmabhoomi (under the Ram Janmabhoomi police station), filed a second FIR with case crime number 198/92 under sections 153A, 153B and 505 of the IPC, against eight senior leaders associated with the Sangh Parivar for giving hate speeches from the dais erected

---

[14]Lok Sabha Debates (English Version), Sixth Session (Tenth Lok Sabha), *Parliament Digital Library*, 23 February 1993, p. 759, https://tinyurl.com/mrx57v4h. Accessed on 15 July 2024.

at the Ram Katha Kunj, Ayodhya. They included the VHP chief Ashok Singhal; BJP leaders L.K. Advani, Murli Manohar Joshi and Uma Bharati; Bajrang Dal leader Vinay Katiyar; Hindu nationalist ideologue Sadhvi Ritambara; and Hari Dalmia and Giriraj Kishore of the VHP.

Time of Demolition

Incidentally, the FIR in the case crime number 197/98 mentioned 12.00 p.m. as the time of the demolition. The second FIR of the case crime number 198/92, however, stated 10.00 a.m. as the time for the same crime. It was noted in the latter that the leaders present on the dais at the Ram Katha Kunj, to organize the symbolic kar seva on 6 December 1992, were instigating the kar sevaks with 'Ek dhakka aur do, Babri Masjid tod do'.

Liberhan Commission

The P.V. Narasimha Rao-led government, nearly 10 days after the demolition incident, set up a commission of inquiry known as the Liberhan Ayodhya Commission of Inquiry headed by Justice Manmohan Singh Liberhan, on 16 December 1992. The commission, which submitted its report after nearly 17 years, concluded that the demolition of the Ram Janmabhoomi–Babri Masjid structure was carried out in a duplicitous and under-planned manner. It said that such an act was 'not worthy of a democratically elected government of a constituent state of this great nation'. It also claimed that the CM, ministers and mandarins of the state of Uttar Pradesh supported the destruction with tacit, open, active and material support at every step, but did not make it part of the officially stated agenda. The report stated that they were conscious of their acts and conduct, ensuring the achievement of their concealed intent to demolish the disputed structure.

Kalyan Singh, his ministers and his handpicked bureaucrats created man-made cataclysmic circumstances which could result in no consequences other than demolition of the disputed structure and broadened the cleavage between the two religious communities resulting in massacres all over the country. They denuded the state of every legal, moral and statutory restraint and wilfully enabled and facilitated the wanton destruction and the ensuing anarchy... There is no doubt admissible in the culpability and responsibility of the CM, his ministers and cohorts who were handpicked to occupy selected posts. Ramchandra Das Paramhans, Ashok Singhal, Vinay Katiyar, Vishnu Hari Dalmia, Vamdev, K.S. Sudarshan, H.V. Sheshadari, Lalji Tandon, Kalraj Mishra, Govindacharya and others named in my report formed this complete cartel led by Kalyan Singh and supported by the icons of the movement like L.K. Advani, M.M. Joshi, A.B. Vajpayee.... Chief Minister Kalyan Singh stood on guard against the possibility of any pre-emptive or preventive action by the central government or the Supreme Court of India or the other courts or any other institution.[15]

The commission's report has remained only a subject of academic discussions, and no leader from the BJP, the VHP or other parties was brought to justice on the basis of the report. M. Narayanan, former joint director at the CBI, in his book titled *Voice of CBI*, has noted:

When the Justice Liberhan Commission submitted its report, the Ministry of Home Affairs and the home minister wanted to know whether on the information mentioned in the report anymore person could be charge-sheeted by the CBI out of those listed out in the Report. The possibility of making one person from the list as accused was explored. Examination of the report indicated that there is no material to bring in anymore persons as accused in the case already pending in the Court. Symbolic

---

[15] *Report of the Liberhan Ayodhya Commission of Inquiry*, pp. 921–3, https://tinyurl.com/mvvt4ncd. Accessed on 14 August 2024.

kar seva was allowed by the Hon'ble Supreme Court vide order dated 28.11.1992 and therefore making arrangement for the same was not an offence.[16]

Herculean Task

After registration of the FIRs, the investigating agencies faced a mammoth task of going through the sequence of events that led to the build-up of the demolition on 6 December 1992. The scrutiny, which continued in the courts for nearly 28 years, began with the investigations first handed over to Ram Prakash Tandon, the circle officer, Reserve Police Lines, Faizabad. He began with recording statements of the constable clerk Prathvinath Mishra. On 8 December, he got the statement of Priyamvada Nath Shukla. He also got the statements of some eyewitnesses. The names and addresses of the injured kar sevaks were collected as well. On 12 December, the investigations in the case were transferred to the Crime Branch, Crime Investigation Department (CB–CID). It got possession of all documents from the local police, had the spot and adjoining areas videographed, and visited the demolition spot. The investigation of case crime number 197/92 was handed over to Deputy Superintendent of Police (DSP) Tara Dutt Baila, while the investigation of case crime number 198/92 was given to Inspector Akhilanand Mishra, who was named chief investigating officer (CIO) of the case.

CBI Probe

On 12 December, the Uttar Pradesh government issued a notification requesting the Union government to transfer the investigation of case crime number 197/92 to the CBI. The Union government accepted the request, and orders to transfer the case to the CBI were issued on 13 December. A special cell to probe the Ayodhya case was subsequently

---

[16]Narayanan, M., *Voice of CBI*, Manas Publications, New Delhi, 2014, p. 41.

set up with two CBI units. One of the two units functioned in New Delhi while the other was set up in Lucknow. The CBI team visited the spot on 16 December and spoke to the state police officers, including SHO, Ram Janmabhoomi, who briefed the CBI team about the whole incident. The CBI team captured videos of the disputed spot and gathered other details of police deployment. It procured the pre-demolition map of the disputed structure and began collecting pictures of the incident and a list of those injured.

M. Narayanan, who was the joint director at the CBI, became the CIO of the case. He was the DSP in 1992 and was promoted to the post of superintendent of police in 1993. He was assisted by DSPs N.S. Wirk, T.P. Jha and S.C. Yadav, and inspectors J. Nayak, Hari Singh, Malkiat Singh, S.R. Singh and others. In his book, Narayanan noted:

> The main case of demolition Crime No. 197/92 was entrusted to the CBI on 13.12.1992 whereas the Case Crime No. 198/192 was investigated by the Crime Branch, Uttar Pradesh, which filed a charge sheet/report under Section 173 of Code of Criminal Procedure on 27.2.1993, against the same 8 accused persons for offences under Sections 153 A, 153 B, 505, 147, 149 IPC, in the Special Court so created for that case at Lalitpur.[17]

When this case was pending in Lalitpur, the Special Court was shifted from Lalitpur to Raebareli in July 1993. The CBI investigated the theory of conspiracy to demolish the disputed structure and its logistics—planning the demolition, training selected kar sevaks, provocative sloganeering by the leaders before and on 6 December, from the dais or otherwise, and attacks on media persons. M. Narayanan added: 'The video cassettes so collected contained extra-judicial confessions of some accused about the conspiracy to demolish the structure and therefore CBI added offence under section 120-B IPC to the FIR of Crime No. 197/92 (CBI Case No. 8(S)/1992) and continued investigation.'[18]

---

[17]Ibid. 38–9.
[18]Ibid. 39.

Kalyan Singh Draws Large Crowds

Kalyan Singh was drawing large crowds at his public meetings across the country. A huge crowd gathered on the Lucknow–Ayodhya route when he went for darshan of Ram Lalla a few weeks after the demolition of the disputed structure. His road journey that should have taken not more than three hours took nearly 13 hours. His cavalcade struggled for long to push its way through the large and excited crowd to reach Ayodhya.

People on the entire route showered flower petals on him and performed his aarti. Senior BJP leader Brahm Dutt Dwivedi accompanied him on the way to Ayodhya. Kalyan Singh was overwhelmed to see the people's response. For the first time, on this journey to Ayodhya, he told the journalists that the demolition would not be known as a day of *sharm* (shame) in history. This was instead to be seen as a day of pride for the country. He had developed his own style to connect with the people. At almost every public meeting, he hinted that he had established an invisible line of communication with Ram Lalla, and that he had spoken to the lord on the hotline. At many places, when it rained during the public meetings, Kalyan Singh told the people not to leave. He said the rain would stop as soon as he would speak with Ram Lalla. It was a coincidence that the rain stopped at many places as and when Kalyan Singh made an announcement in this regard at his public meetings.[19]

BJP Rallies Banned

At many places, the government banned BJP rallies after the demolition of Babri Masjid. The Delhi unit of the BJP had proposed a rally at the Talkatora Stadium in December 1992. Atal Bihari Vajpayee was scheduled to address the rally. However, it was banned. In order to protest, Vajpayee sat on a fast. Advani raised the issue in Lok Sabha on 23 February 1993. He said the BJP had proposed a rally at the Boat

---

[19] Interview with senior journalist Rakesh Pandey.

Club in New Delhi on 25 February 1993 too, and that the government did not use the word 'ban' but instead decided not to give permission for the rally.[20] He assured the government that the BJP would not indulge in any violence there. Advani stated that the government's move to dismiss four BJP governments, ban the RSS, the VHP and the rally could not be considered a mature step.

Union Minister of State for Home Affairs Rajesh Pilot said that he had pointed out to Atal Bihari Vajpayee and L.K. Advani that the crowd, which may assemble in Ayodhya, might not be controllable and the mosque might be demolished. Pilot said, 'On that day (November 27, 1992) I pointed out that they (the BJP and VHP leaders) would not be able to control the mob and the mosque would be demolished. But both of you (Atal and Advani) kept mum. Advaniji, on that day, it was your advantage to keep mum, so you speak only for your benefit.'[21]

Somnath Chatterjee, the CPI (M) leader, said he had watched a video recording of Kalyan Singh's speech in Calcutta.

> He said because of divine inspiration the mosque could be demolished in five-six hours, otherwise it would have taken a month and a half. This is the way they are creating frenzy. Mr Kalyan Singh said, 'Even where the debris go, I could not know. It is all divine blessings.' Is this the way, the country is being run?[22]

Contempt of Court

As the Kalyan Singh-led government failed to protect the disputed structure on 6 December 1992, contempt proceedings were launched against Kalyan Singh in the Supreme Court. He had submitted an affidavit in the apex court assuring that adequate security arrangements were made to protect the disputed structure, and that his government

---

[20] Lok Sabha Debates (English Version), Sixth Session (Tenth Lok Sabha), *Parliament Digital Library*, 23 February 1993, p. 650, https://tinyurl.com/mrx57v4h. Accessed on 15 July 2024.
[21] Ibid. 662.
[22] Ibid. 666.

would not allow any damage to the same. His government, however, failed to keep the promise, and the disputed structure was demolished. On 16 December 1992, the Supreme Court *suo motu* issued contempt notices. Kalyan Singh and six others who were issued notices took three months to file a reply. But this contempt case could not come up for hearing and was closed on 30 August 2022 following the death of Kalyan Singh on 21 August 2021. Justices Sanjay Kishan Kaul and Abhay S. Oka referred to the Supreme Court's judgement of 9 November 2019 in favour of the construction of the Ram temple.

> You can't keep flogging a dead horse. We are only making an attempt to take up old matters. Some may survive, some may go. The large issue has already been decided by a five-judge bench. The petitioner has died; the contempt petition against respondents is closed,' the court said, burying the petition. Besides Singh, who passed away on 21 August 2021, other BJP leaders who got relief include former Union Ministers Murli Manohar Joshi, Uma Bharti and Sadhvi Ritambhara.[23]

The Kalyan Singh-led government had also allowed construction of a platform in July 1992 (as discussed earlier), despite the Supreme Court's orders for maintaining status quo. On 24 October 1994, the Supreme Court delivered a judgement holding Kalyan Singh guilty of 'flagrant breach' of his undertaking to the apex court and sentenced him to one-day imprisonment. *The Indian Express* observed:

> This was for allowing a platform to be constructed despite the status quo order in July 1992. The same day, the SC, in a 3:2 verdict, upheld the constitutional validity of The Acquisition of Certain Areas of Ayodhya Act, 1993, under which the 67.703 acres of land adjoining Babri Masjid was acquired.[24]

---

[23]Kumar, Parmod, 'SC Drops Kalyan Singh Contempt Case', *Deccan Chronicle*, 31 August 2022, https://tinyurl.com/cb5xbbkr. Accessed on 16 July 2024.
[24]Vishwanath, Apurva, '30 Years Later, Curtains on a Babri Contempt Case', *The Indian Express*, 4 September 2022, https://tinyurl.com/y99k8752. Accessed on 16 July 2024.

Kalyan Singh Sent to Tihar Jail

All eyes were set on the Supreme Court on 24 October 1994 for its final verdict in this contempt case. H.P.S. Virk, deputy commissioner of police (DCP), Delhi Police, was posted as in-charge of security at the Supreme Court. There was concern about the possible fallout of the Supreme Court ordering Kalyan Singh to jail. This could have had an impact on the law-and-order situation. The authorities at the police headquarters were worried. A large number of media persons, waiting for the Supreme Court's order for a long time, reached the office of H.P.S. Virk to know about the unfolding developments. Virk, however, continued to beat around the bush and did not divulge anything to the media.

As the issue was drawing attention and considered politically sensitive, a heavy deployment of armed police was made in and out of the premises of the apex court. Those deployed within the campus of the Supreme Court of India were in civil clothes, while those outside the premises of the apex court—on Bhagwan Das Marg, Mathura Road and Tilak Marg—were in uniform.

No one was aware of the ongoing developments inside the court. All eyes were set on the Supreme Court's likely orders. The court had ordered a day's imprisonment for Kalyan Singh, but this was still not leaked to the media. It was about this time that Registrar (administration) L.C. Bhadoo called Virk to the former's office and asked him to deliver the Supreme Court's order incarcerating Kalyan Singh for a day at Tihar Jail in the capital. Virk said his jurisdiction was limited to the premises of the apex court, and delivering orders to Kalyan Singh was outside his jurisdiction.

Soon the SHO, Tilak Marg police station, was summoned and asked to serve the Supreme Court's order to Kalyan Singh, who was in Uttar Pradesh Bhawan, New Delhi. The SHO, Tilak Marg, rushed to Uttar Pradesh Bhawan and picked up Kalyan Singh from there to take him to Tihar Jail with police escort.

This news spread like wildfire and, within minutes, began making news headlines. The media persons waiting for the Supreme Court order at the apex court's premises were taken by surprise when they got calls from the newsrooms of their respective organizations. Some of them went to Virk's office and confronted the officer, accusing him of breach of trust.

As mentioned earlier, Kalyan Singh was taken to Tihar Jail with police escort. India's first female IPS officer, Kiran Bedi, who was instrumental in introducing prison reforms in the country, was posted as DG, Tihar Jail. Virk got a message to connect with her post haste. She wanted clarification on the one-day jail term awarded to Kalyan Singh, and requested Virk for the same from the Chief Justice of India.

Virk, in a post on social media, has observed, 'Picking up courage I approached the CJI for this simple clarification getting an expected reprimanding answer, "It is for your learned Kiran Bedi to consult an elaborate jail manual for this specific answer." Thus, such a consequential event passed off peacefully without escalating into any major law and order problem.'[25]

Other Cases Too Given to CBI

The Uttar Pradesh government had, in August 1993, transferred the investigation of case crime number 198/92 and other 47 assault cases of media persons also to the CBI. The latter registered FIRs again in these cases again, investigated them, and filed a consolidated charge sheet against 40 accused on 5 October 1993. These 40 accused included Advani, Joshi, Singhal and others named in case crime number 198/92.

Former Joint Director, CBI, M. Narayanan noted that a Special Court of magistrate and another of additional sessions judge were created in Lucknow to dispose of all the cases relating to demolition of the disputed structure, as investigated and chargesheeted by the CBI.[26] On this, the Raebareli Court (which was shifted from Lalitpur

---

[25]'Babri Demolition Case: A Day When Supreme Court Sent Kalyan Singh to Tihar Jail', *Rakshak News*, 25 November 2018, https://tinyurl.com/3ft7vpx8. Accessed on 16 July 2024.
[26]M. Narayanan, *Voice of CBI*, Manas Publications, New Delhi, 2014, p. 39.

to Raebareli) transferred all the records of case crime number 198/92 to the Lucknow Court on 25 January 1994. A supplementary charge sheet was filed by the CBI on 11 January 1996 against nine more accused following further investigations, taking the total number of accused to 49.

The Special Judge at Lucknow on 9 September 1997 ordered that there was a prima facie case for framing of charges against all the accused. The Special Judge also ordered that there was sufficient evidence to slap charges of criminal conspiracy under section 120 B of the IPC.[27] Thirty-three of the accused challenged this order in the High Court through four review petitions: Moreshwar Sabe versus Uttar Pradesh State; Miss Uma Bharti alias Gajra Singh and others versus Uttar Pradesh State; Ravindra Nath Srivastava and others versus Uttar Pradesh State; and Ashok Singhal and others versus Uttar Pradesh state.

Technical Defect

The High Court heard the four petitions and stated on 12 February 2001 that the transfer of case crime number 198/92 to the Special Court, Lucknow, from Raebareli was technically defective. It was observed that the High Court had not been consulted before doing so. The High Court, however, gave the state government the option of issuing a fresh

---

[27]Special Judge ordered that there was sufficient evidence against eight accused named in case number 198/92 and 18 others for slapping charges under sections 147 (rioting), 153-A (promoting enmity on grounds of religion, race, place of birth, residence, language, etc., and doing acts prejudicial to maintenance of harmony), 153 B (imputations, assertions prejudicial to national integration), 295 A (acts intended to outrage religious sentiments), and 505 (spreading false and mischievous information intended to upset the public tranquillity) read with 120 B (criminal conspiracy). For 22 other accused, the Special Judge ordered charges under sections 332 (voluntarily causing hurt to deter public servant from discharging his/her duty), 338 (causing grievous hurt to any person by doing any act so rashly or negligently as to endanger human life, or personal safety of others), 201 (causing disappearance of evidence of an offence or giving false information to protect the offender) read with 149 (member of unlawful assembly guilty of offence sharing a common objective), 395 (committing dacoity) and 120 B (criminal conspiracy).

notification to fix the technical defect. Special Judge, CBI (Ayodhya Matters), Lucknow, therefore ordered on 4 May 2001 that the Special Court in Raebareli would hear crime number 198/1992 against the eight accused. The case relating to the 13 other accused—Bala Saheb Thackeray, Kalyan Singh, Moreshwar Save, Satish Pradhan, Champat Rai Bansal, Mahant Avaidyanath, Ram Vilas Vedanti, Dharam Das, Mahant Nritya Gopal Das, Mahamandleshwar Jagdish Muni Maharaj, Baikunth Lal Sharma, Ramchandra Das Paramhans and Satish Kumar Nagar—against whom the CBI had filed charge sheets in the Special Court, Lucknow, was also to be tried in Special Court, Raebareli.

CBI Files Revision Petition

The CBI challenged the order of the Special Judge, CBI (Ayodhya Matters), Lucknow, filing a revision petition number 217/2001, CBI versus Bala Saheb Thackeray, in the division bench of the High Court, Lucknow. The High Court heard the revision petition and upheld the order of the Special Judge Lucknow, on 20 May 2010. The High Court ordered the Special Judge to begin hearing (as it had remained suspended from 4 May 2001 to 20 May 2010). A special leave petition (SLP) was filed in the Supreme Court by one Muhammad Aslam Bhure, challenging the Allahabad High Court's order dated 12 February 2001 on the four petitions on 19 June 2001. The Supreme Court, on 29 November 2002, dismissed the SLP, observing that the petitioner had no *locus standi* and that case crime number 198/92 be tried in the designated court in Raebareli.

According to M. Narayanan, the CBI meanwhile requested the Uttar Pradesh government to rectify the defect by issuing a fresh notification. But the state government turned down the CBI's request stating that it was a conscious decision to keep case crime number 198/92 separate. A presiding officer was appointed for the Special Court at Raebareli for case crime number 198/92. The CBI filed a supplementary charge sheet for the same in the Raebareli court against the eight named accused persons whom the CB-CID had already chargesheeted.

Court Takes Cognizance of Charges Against Seven Accused

On 19 September 2003, the Raebareli court took cognizance of the charges against only seven accused. It did not take notice of the charges against L.K. Advani and acquitted him. Advani was then the deputy PM of India. His acquittal raised many questions. Senior journalist Praful Bidwai wrote in *Frontline*:

> The waywardness of India's police and justice delivery systems has few parallels when it comes to punishing communal offences and hate crimes. What began as a devious process of manipulation of the FIRs in the Babri mosque demolition case, and the totally illegitimate dropping of conspiracy charges against the principal accused, turned into a grotesque parody of justice on September 19 when the Special Court of Magistrate Vinay Kumar Singh in Raebareli framed charges against seven persons, including Murli Manohar Joshi, Uma Bharati, Vinay Katiyar and other VHP leaders, but discharged Deputy PM L.K. Advani. Advani is the man who spearheaded, planned and ideologically inspired the raucous agitation that led to the razing of the mosque on 6 December 1992.[28]

Advani's acquittal remained a point of discussion in corridors of power. The seven accused challenged this order in the High Court. The CBI filed a review petition. The High Court heard the revision petitions and passed an order on 6 July 2005 that all the eight accused, including Advani, should appear before the court of the special judicial magistrate, Raebareli, to face further legal proceedings. On 28 July 2005, the accused—L.K. Advani, Murli Manohar Joshi, Ashok Singhal, Vinay Katiyar, Giriraj Kishore, Vishnu Hari Dalmia, Uma Bharati and Sadhvi Ritambhara—appeared before the court of special judicial magistrate, Raebareli, and were charged under sections 147, 149, 153-A, 153-B and 505 (1)(B) of the IPC. The accused pleaded not guilty.

---

[28] Bidwai, Praful, 'Between Despair and Hope', *Frontline*, 10 October 2003, https://tinyurl.com/yxtsett5. Accessed on 14 August 2024.

The CBI thereafter produced 57 witnesses to testify in court till 19 April 2017. The Special Court also summoned 27 accused in accordance with the High Court's order of 20 May 2010. Charges were framed on 17 August 2010 against the accused Pawan Kumar Pandey, Brij Bhushan Sharan Singh, Jai Bhagwan Goel, Om Prakash Pandey and Sakshi Maharaj.

CBI Files SLP

The CBI filed SLP number 2275/2011 on 9 February 2011 against the High Court's order on revision petition number 217/2001, CBI versus Bala Saheb Thackeray, given on 20 May 2010. The Supreme Court, on 19 April 2017, ordered that the proceedings vis-à-vis case crime number 198/92 would stand transferred from the court of special judicial magistrate at Raebareli to the court of additional sessions judge (Ayodhya Matters) in Lucknow. The Supreme Court ruled that the Court of Sessions would frame an additional charge under Section 120-B against L.K. Advani, Vinay Katiyar, Uma Bharti, Sadhvi Ritambhara, Murli Manohar Joshi and Vishnu Hari Dalmia. The apex court said the Court of Sessions would frame additional charge under Section 120-B and other provisions of the IPC, as mentioned in the joint charge sheet filed by the CBI against Champat Rai Bansal, Satish Pradhan, Dharam Das, Mahant Nritya Gopal Das, Mahamandleshwar Jagdish Muni, Ram Vilas Vedanti, Baikunth Lal Sharma and Satish Chandra Nagar.

Kalyan Singh's Immunity

Kalyan Singh was the governor of Rajasthan at this point of time. The Supreme Court observed that being a governor, he enjoyed immunity from any criminal liability under Article 361 of the Constitution as long as he remained the governor, and the Court of Sessions would frame the charge and move against him as soon as he ceased to be governor. The Supreme Court ordered that after transfer of the proceedings from Raebareli to Lucknow, and framing of additional charges within four weeks, the Court of Sessions would take up all the matters on a day-to-day basis until conclusion of the trial.

There would be no *de novo* trial. The Supreme Court said there would be no transfer of the judge conducting the trial until the entire trial concluded. The case, it ruled, would not be adjourned on any grounds except when the Sessions Court found it impossible to carry on trial for that particular date. The Supreme Court ordered that in case of grant of adjournment to the next date or a closely proximate date, the court would record the reasons for the same in writing. The Supreme Court asked the CBI to ensure presence of some prosecution witnesses on every date so that the matter was not adjourned for want of witnesses.

Kalyan Singh Loses Immunity

Kalyan Singh lost the constitutional immunity on relinquishing the gubernatorial office on 3 September 2019. He joined the BJP on 9 September 2019, and appeared at the Special Court in Lucknow on 21 September 2019 following the summons issued to him. In compliance with the Supreme Court's order, charges were framed against him on 27 September 2019. Charges were reframed against Advani, Murli Manohar Joshi, Vishnu Hari Dalmia, Vinay Katiyar, Uma Bharti and Sadhvi Ritambhara. Besides them, charges were also framed against Satish Pradhan, Dr Ram Vilas Vedanti, Baikunth Lal Sharma alias Prem, Champat Rai Bansal, Mahant Nritya Gopal Das and Dharam Das on 30 May 2017.[29]

---

[29]Charges were framed against Kalyan Singh under sections 120-B, 153-A read with 120-B; 153-B read with 120-B; 295 read with 120-B; 295-A read with 120-B; 505 read with 120-B of the IPC. Charges were reframed against Advani, Murli Manohar Joshi, Vishnu Hari Dalmia, Vinay Katiyar, Uma Bharti and Sadhvi Ritambhara under sections 120-B, 147, 153-A read with 149/120-B; 505 (1)(B) read with 149/120-B of the IPC on 30 May 2017, in accordance with the Supreme Court's order in SLP number 2275/2011. Charges were also framed against accused Satish Pradhan, Dr Ram Vilas Vedanti, Baikunth Lal Sharma alias Prem, Champat Rai Bansal, Mahant Nritya Gopal

All Accused Acquitted

The cases against all the accused, which had remained trapped in legal wrangling for nearly 28 years, came to the stage of final disposal following the Supreme Court's order. The presiding officer, Special Court, (Ayodhya Matters), Surendra Kumar Yadav, was given a service extension for a year. His extended term ended on 30 September 2020, the day when he pronounced the verdict in the case. He delivered the judgement in Lucknow, acquitting all the accused. Lack of conclusive evidence against the accused was stated to be the reason for the acquittal. The court ruled out the criminal conspiracy theory of the demolition. It observed that the demolition was a spontaneous act and not pre-planned. The prosecution could not establish the role of any of the 32 accused in the demolition. Seventeen of the total 49 accused in these cases had died. The judge pronounced the verdict in the presence of 26 of the remaining 32 accused at the court.

L.K. Advani, Murli Manohar Joshi, Kalyan Singh and Nritya Gopal Das were not present in the court when the judgement was pronounced. It was observed that the CBI's videos produced before the court had not been certified or tested in a forensic laboratory to ascertain their authenticity. The court thus did not consider such videos and other evidence as admissible. The CBI also was not able to produce original negatives of the pictures presented to support its case, and these pictures were, therefore, not treated as evidence.

No Clue about Demolition Plans

Many of the witnesses that the CBI produced before the court admitted that three-tier security arrangements were made at and around the disputed structure. Priyamvada Nath Shukla, Ram Janmabhoomi police station SHO who lodged one of the two the FIRs, observed in the

---

Das and Dharam Das on 30 May 2017, in accordance with the orders of the apex court under sections 120-B, 147, 153-A read with 149/120B; 153-B read with 149/120-B; 295 read with 149/120-B; 295-A read with 149/120-B; 505 read with 149/120-B of the IPC.

court that there were sufficient security arrangements at the spot. He admitted that lakhs of kar sevaks were checked by security persons before they went for darshan and puja. He said this arrangement had continued till about 12.00 p.m., and no untoward incident had taken place till the time the kar sevaks continued to have darshan in a disciplined manner. He admitted that he had no clue about any plans to demolish the disputed structure.

The CBI produced 351 prosecution witnesses. Of them, 57 witnesses were produced at the Special Court, Raebareli, while 294 witnesses were produced at the Special Court, Lucknow. Kalyan Singh, who was CM of Uttar Pradesh, was also charged. Kalyan Singh in his statement made in the court said:

> I and my government made foolproof arrangements for security of the disputed structure in Ayodhya and three-layer security arrangements had been made to give strong security to the (disputed) structure. Directives were given from time to time to respective administrative officers to make arrangements for security of the disputed structure. At the behest of then central government, I have been wrongly implicated by levelling false and baseless charges against me for political animosity. I am completely innocent.[30]

Kalyan Singh said the RSS and the VHP workers were controlling the kar sevaks and directives were given to push out the unruly ones. He said when Ashok Singhal asked the kar sevaks not to move towards the disputed structure, they became aggressive towards him, went atop the disputed structure and demolished it.

Advani Chants 'Jai Shri Ram'

Former Deputy PM L.K. Advani, former Union Minister Murli Manohar Joshi, and former Madhya Pradesh CM Uma Bharti were

---

[30] Special Court, (Ayodhya Prakaran) Lucknow, Judgement, 30 September 2020, p. 2286.

also among those acquitted. Advani called the verdict very important and greeted the same with 'Jai Shri Ram'. 'It is a very important decision and a matter of happiness for us. When we heard the news of the court's order, we welcomed it by chanting "Jai Shri Ram"', Advani said. Joshi said the court verdict proved that there was no conspiracy or planning with regard to the 6 December 1992 incidents in Ayodhya, and the events had unfolded rather suddenly.[31]

Who Demolished the Mosque?

Who demolished the mosque and who conspired are questions that remain unanswered. Most accused may have made their point to prove their innocence in the court. However, a large number of them had bragged and claimed credit for demolition of the disputed structure. Ahead of Uddhav Thackeray's visit to Ayodhya in 2018, Shiv Sena leader Sanjay Raut claimed that the Shiv Sainiks demolished the mosque within 17 minutes. 'It took only around 17 minutes for us—the Ram bhakts—to bring down the Babri Masjid... So, how long should it take to bring an ordinance?' he told a news agency.[32] Raut questioned the delay in bringing the ordinance for construction of the Ram temple, as the BJP was in power both at the Centre and in Uttar Pradesh. It was Raut who was among the first leaders (on behalf of the Shiv Sena) to welcome the verdict acquitting the 32 accused in the Babri demolition case.

Pawan Pandey, an ex-MLA and former Uttar Pradesh Shiv Sena leader, is another person who boasted of having a role in the demolition. Pandey was also acquitted, as were others. Pandey, at the twenty-fifth anniversary of the demolition, in 2017, asserted that the demolition of the Babri Masjid was well-planned. Pandey, speaking

---

[31] Hindustan Times, "'Welcomed Babri Verdict with Jai Shri Ram Chant': LK Advani on Acquittal', *YouTube*, 30 September 2020, https://tinyurl.com/3jm89234. Accessed on 16 July 2024.
[32] 'Took 17 Min to Pull Down Babri Masjid: Shiv Sena's Raut Pitches for Temple Law', *Hindustan Times*, 23 November 2018, https://tinyurl.com/39wt6uaa. Accessed on 16 July 2024.

to media persons in various interviews, proudly claimed that he was among those who climbed up the disputed structure and revealed that the demolition was planned. He said trained kar sevaks had attacked the Babri Masjid from the backside while others climbed up from the front. He added that the kar sevaks had taken away parts from the mosque as a memento following the demolition. 'We take pride in removal of the disputed structure which was a black spot,' he said.[33]

What Leaders Did

True, Shiv Sainiks turned up in large numbers for the kar seva in Ayodhya on 6 December 1992, when the Babri Masjid was demolished. But the leaders who led the Ram temple movement and those who consistently delivered inflammatory speeches, too, need to take the blame. It was L.K. Advani's Rath Yatra that built up an atmosphere in favour of the Ram temple in 1990. The build-up of emotions culminated in a sequence of events that resulted in demolition of the disputed structure. Mulayam Singh Yadav took over as Uttar Pradesh's CM following the 1989 state legislative assembly elections. It was he who used challenging tones in his speeches at a number of public meetings, declaring 'Parinda bhi par nahin maar payega' when Advani was leading his Rath Yatra. It was on his orders that fire was opened on the kar sevaks on 30 October and 2 November 1990, which resulted in violence at a number of places. After becoming CM of Uttar Pradesh, Kalyan Singh had promised protection of the disputed structure in Ayodhya on 6 December 1992. When kar sevaks climbed atop the disputed structure, it was he who had directed his team of officers not to open fire.

Acquittal of all the accused reflects the botched-up investigations and failure of the prosecution to bring those responsible to justice.

---

[33] ABP News, 'Huge Revelation on Demolition of Babri Masjid: It was Pre-Planned, Says Pawan Pandey', *YouTube*, 24 April 2017, https://tinyurl.com/5n7waz5k. Accessed on 14 August 2024.

The CBI's failure to prove the charges of demolition against the 32 accused attracted sharp criticism following their acquittal. The premier investigating agency's failure to establish its theory to prosecute the leaders in the case has been identical to what unfolded in many other high-profile cases, like the Bofors scandal or the 2G spectrum scam.

A Well-Concealed Plan?

The Liberhan Commission, in its report, under the section 'The Joint Common Enterprises', observed:

> The incidents of 6 December were neither spontaneous, nor unpreventable. They were the zenith of a concerted and well laid-out plan which encompasses an entire pantheon of religious, political and mob leadership. It was (a) successful and well-concealed plan of the authors of the movement who also managed to stay outside the public limelight until the actual events unfolded.
>
> It is an undisputed fact many leaders including the so-called Sadhus and sants, politicos and others including L.K. Advani, M.M. Joshi, K.S. Sudershan, Uma Bharti, H.V. Sheshadhari, Pramod Mahajan, Ashok Singhal, Param Hans Ramchander Das, Vamdev Maharaj, Acharya Giriraj Kishore, Vishnu Hari Dalmia, Vinay Katiyar, Professor Rajinder Singh, Champat Rai, R.S. Agnihotri shielded the name of many others whose names could not have therefore be ascertained despite a prolonged enquiry. Witnesses repeated well-rehearsed stories and evaded cross examination by pleading a sudden loss of memory or lack of knowledge. They denied or failed to admit even those details mentioned in the BJP's own white paper. The witnesses consistently made efforts to protect the principal leaders like L.K. Advani, M.M. Joshi and A.B. Vajpayee who in their assessment were likely to come to power. They were also over protective of the principal RSS leaders like K.S. Sudarshan and Vamdev Maharaj for obvious reasons. All these people were incontrovertibly

present in Ayodhya or even in the Ram Janmabhoomi complex on the 6th of December with the exception of A.B. Vajpayee who was travelling from Lucknow to Delhi.[34]

Atal Bihari Vajpayee was one of the co-founders of the BJP. A poet at heart, Vajpayee was a modest leader of the BJP who navigated his way in politics with finesse even under most adverse circumstances. He was not in Ayodhya that day, and this is a known fact. Vajpayee, addressing a public meeting in Lucknow on 5 December 1992, had said that he wanted to be in Ayodhya but was asked to be in New Delhi the next day. The Liberhan Commission apparently questioned his absence: 'In totality, it becomes obvious that some leaders were consciously kept out of the operational area or planning in order to protect them and preserve their secular credentials for later political use.'[35] Was the Babri Masjid demolition part of a well-conceived plan or an outcome of a sudden outburst of angry kar sevaks? This question shall always remain a riddle.

---

[34] *Report of the Liberhan Ayodhya Commission of Inquiry*, pp. 722–3, https://tinyurl.com/mvvt4ncd. Accessed on 14 August 2024.
[35] Ibid. 725.

10

A Grand Ram Temple

At last, Ram Lalla is now seated in a majestic and imposing temple, a marvel of tradition and culture, at his birthplace in Ayodhya. The grand Ram Temple is a reality today. It is a confluence of ancient tradition and modernity. It is built in traditional Nagar style. The temple has a length (east–west) of 380 feet, width of 250 feet and height (up to pinnacle from ground at sanctum sanctorum) of 161 feet.[1] The Ram Temple is designed three-storeyed with each floor being 20 feet tall. It has a total of 392 pillars and 44 doors.[2]

A nearly 51-inch-tall idol of Ram Lalla's avatar (of not more than four to five years) has been installed in the sanctum sanctorum on the ground floor of the Ram temple. The lotus platform, on which the idol has been installed in a standing posture, elevates Ram Lalla's idol to a height of 96 inches (8 feet). Prime Minister Narendra Modi presided over the Pran Pratishtha or consecration ceremony of Ram Lalla's idol at the newly constructed temple; it was held in the presence of Uttar Pradesh Governor Anandiben Patel, CM Yogi Adityanath, RSS chief Mohan Bhagwat, various politicians, industrialists and celebrities at around 12.30 p.m. on 22 January 2024. Pandit Ganeshwar Shastri Dravid of Kashi worked out the *abhijit muhurta* (auspicious time) for the consecration ceremony.

The Ram temple was thrown open for pilgrims a day after the consecration ceremony. Entry to the temple is allowed through the

---

[1] @ShriRamTeerth, X (formerly Twitter), 4 January 2024, 9.29 a.m., https://tinyurl.com/49y2hk83. Accessed on 16 July 2024.
[2] Ibid.

Singh Dwar, the main entrance, which has statues of elephants, lions, Hanuman and Garud sculpted from pink sandstone sourced from Rajasthan's Bansi Paharpur village. There are 32 ascending stairs (height 16.5 feet) leading to the main temple, though provisions have been made for ramps and lifts to facilitate the differently abled and elderly in reaching there.

The Ram temple is well designed and equipped with advanced technology, with leading national institutes, including Council of Scientific & Industrial Research (CSIR), Department of Science and Technology, Indian Institutes of Technology (IITs), and Indian Space Research Organisation (ISRO), playing important roles at various stages from construction to inauguration. Some other institutes that provided assistance include Central Building Research Institute (CBRI), Roorkee; National Geophysical Research Institute (NGRI), Hyderabad; Indian Institute of Astrophysics (IIA), Bengaluru; and Institute of Himalayan Bioresource Technology, (IHBT) Palampur, Himachal Pradesh.

Surya Tilak

Central Building Research Institute, Roorkee, which was involved in the construction of the Ram temple from the early stages, contributed towards the structural design of the main temple, designed the *surya tilak* mechanism, vetted the design of the foundation, and monitored the structural health of the main temple. A team of experts worked on the design and architecture of the temple and developed an apparatus round the clock to evolve a mechanism for surya tilak, ensuring that the sunlight falls on the forehead of the idol of Ram Lalla at 12.00 p.m. every Ram Navami, the Hindu festival marking the deity's birthday. The IIA provided technical support on the sun's path and Optica, Bengaluru, was involved in manufacturing of the lenses and brass tubes.[3]

---

[3]PIB Delhi, 'Ministry of Science & Technology', 21 January 2024, https://tinyurl.com/mrstcjky. Accessed on 15 August 2024.

The sun rays illuminated the forehead of Ram Lalla's idol with surya tilak on the occasion of the first Ram Navami celebrated at the new temple on 17 April 2024. The festival generally falls in the month of March or April every year, according to the Gregorian calendar, which is now in use in most parts of the world. Ram Navami is considered an auspicious day. Lord Rama, it is believed, was born at 12.00 p.m. The devotees of Lord Rama observe a day-long fast and worship him on this day.

The whole system is based on an optomechanical system which is specially designed to converge and focus sun rays on the idol's forehead.

The scientists from the Central Building Research Institute (CBRI) in Roorkee involved in the project were aware about the intense heat that is generated when sun rays are concentrated through a system of lenses and mirrors onto a single point...To address this, the system incorporates an infrared filter which is constructed from a heat-absorbing material. It blocks or deflects high-energy photons that would otherwise transfer heat to the idol. This filter is placed at the aperture itself.

The aperture is an opening on the first floor through which sunlight enters the '*garbhagriha*' or the sanctum sanctorum. When the Sun is 'at the right place', the rays enter from the top of garbhagriha through the infrared filter in the aperture. A combination of four lenses and an equal number of mirrors placed at a specific angle inside the brass pipes converge the rays into a single beam that falls on Ram Lalla's forehead. In order to avoid scattering of light, black powder has been coated on the inner surface of the pipes, elbows and joints.[4]

---

[4]'Explained: How Technology Helped Ram Lalla's Surya Tilak at Ayodhya Ram Mandir', *The Times of India*, 20 April 2024, https://tinyurl.com/332kn24t. Accessed on 16 July 2024.

Three Idols

Lord Vishnu, also known as Narayana or Hari, is one of the principal deities in Hinduism. As discussed earlier, Lord Rama is the seventh of ten avatars of Vishnu who, along with Brahma and Shiva, completed the Holy Trinity in Hinduism.

The Ram Janmabhoomi Teerth Kshetra Trust got three idols of Ram Lalla prepared for installation. The Trust roped in the country's three best sculptors who carved Ram Lalla's idol. The idol sculpted by Mysuru-based Arun Yogiraj in *krishna shila* (black stone) was selected and installed in the sanctum sanctorum. The inspiration behind the sculpture was a sketch made by the internationally acclaimed artist Vasudeo Kamath, who is known for his paintings on mythology and history. Arun Yogiraj also carved a 12-foot statue of Adi Shankaracharya in Kedarnath, which was unveiled by PM Narendra Modi last year.[5]

While Ganesh Bhatt of Karnataka used krishna shila, Satya Narayan Pandey of Rajasthan chiselled out Ram Lalla's idol from Makrana white marble. Both of these idols have been given appropriate place in the Ram temple.[6]

Devshila from Nepal

The Trust had earlier decided to get two rare and sacred rocks from Nepal for the temple in Ayodhya. Two *devshila*s (rocks) were taken from the Himalayas in Nepal to Ayodhya on 2 January 2023. It was decided that the rocks would be preserved at the Ram Mandir complex but would not be used in the making of Ram Lalla's idol. The latter was a tough decision to make. The *Hindustan Times* observed:

---

[5]Dixit, Pawan, 'Three Sculptors to Carve out Ram Lalla Idol, Trust to Select Best for Installation', *Hindustan Times*, 31 May 2023, https://tinyurl.com/mwzsnmdh. Accessed on 16 July 2024.
[6]Ibid.

These (two devshilas) were 14-tonne calcite and 26-tonne quartzite rocks procured from Nepal's Gandaki river in the Muktinath area of the Himalayan nation.... According to a member of the Trust, during trial rocks from Nepal had developed cracks so it was decided not to use them for the deity's idol.[7]

Another article by the newspaper stated: 'However, the trust has decided to retain these rocks at the Ram Mandir complex itself so that devotees can worship them. They are devshilas and will be given full respect.'[8]

Strong Foundation

The Ram Janmabhoomi Teerth Kshetra Trust finalized various other parameters for the Ram temple. A strong foundation has been laid for the temple to withstand the pressure of the superstructure for more than a thousand years. The decision regarding the design of the temple foundation makes for an interesting story. A pile foundation was initially considered to be a good idea for the three-storeyed Ram temple. A pile foundation is a long cylindrical column made of materials such as concrete or steel to support a heavy superstructure and transfer the load at the desired depth. However, when this was put to test, three out of five piles fixed there tilted. So, a decision to explore alternative ways of laying the foundation was taken. The chairman of the Ram temple construction committee, Nripendra Mishra, a former IAS officer who earlier worked as principal secretary to PM Narendra Modi, besides having held various other important positions at the Centre and in Uttar Pradesh, held consultations with experts. A committee was also set up to get opinions on the matter. The experts, however, did not reach any conclusion on the issue.

---

[7] Ibid.
[8] 'Sacred Nepal Rocks to be Worshipped at Ram Mandir Complex', *Hindustan Times*, 5 June 2023, https://tinyurl.com/33fesmsx. Accessed on 16 July 2024.

The Seismic Tests

The NGRI, Hyderabad, was requested to conduct a seismic study of the Ram temple site and submit a report that could help decide the design of the foundation. The NGRI teams conducted a study involving various experiments at the Ram temple site from November to December 2020, amid the peak of spread of Covid-19.

> Weeks-long tests conducted by NGRI scientists on the soil under the site of the Ram Mandir used radars and crane-mounted giant generators for a range of experiments using geology, geomorphology and remote sensing.
>
> One of them was the Ground Penetration Radar study in which electro-magnetic pulse was applied on the earth at the site to learn about the broad soil layers and their moisture content and if there is any discontinuity in the natural fabric of the soil layer.
>
> In another experiment, called Multichannel Analysis of Surface Waves, artificial shear waves were generated using big 20-pound hammers to know how strong the rock underneath was.... Among other experiments were Deep Resistivity Sounding and Electrical Resistivity and IP Tomography to understand general moisture content and properties of soil and rock up to a depth of more than 100 metres, and Acceleration and Displacement Response Spectra to learn how the soil would behave in the event of an earthquake...one model was created based on the site's response to the studies. The construction companies, too, had their own models for seismic risks. The seismic hazard analysis by NGRI scientists, to determine the engineering properties, resistance, load bearing, moisture bearing capacity and liquefaction of the underground soil, considered resistance to a possible earthquake of magnitude 8 on the Richter scale.[9]

---

[9]Khan, Faizal, 'Ayodhya: Earthquake Hazard Tests for Ram Mandir Matched Those for Big Dams & Nuclear Power Plants', *Moneycontrol*, 17 January 2024, https://tinyurl.com/4vdeh99k. Accessed on 15 August 2024.

The NGRI submitted its report in January 2021 suggesting removal of top soil at the temple site by 15–20 m.[10] Ultimately, the roller-compacted concrete (RCC) technique was used for the foundation. This method involved open excavation of the area. After this, about 1.85 lakh cubic metres of stratified culture, civilizational debris and old loose soil was removed from nearly 6 acres of land that included the site where the makeshift temple existed after demolition of the disputed structure on 6 December 1992. The IHBT, on the other hand, made its contribution when the Ram temple was being inaugurated. It had sent tulip blooms for the inauguration ceremony of the Ram temple held on 22 January 2024.[11] Ahead of the Ram temple inauguration, ISRO shared satellite images of Ayodhya's Ram Mandir. The images, captured by the Indian Remote Sensing Satellite, showed the Dashrath Mahal, the Saryu River and the Ayodhya railway station as well.[12]

Ram Lalla's idol was shifted to a makeshift temple in a fibre structure at a new location within the same premises to pave way for construction the new Ram temple. Uttar Pradesh CM Yogi Adityanath was present when Ram Lalla's idol was shifted at 4.00 a.m. to Manas Bhawan, Ayodhya. Yogi had reached Ayodhya a night before to attend the special ceremony for shifting the idol to the bulletproof structure early next day. The ceremony was organized on the first day of Ram Navami, on 25 March 2020. The shifting of the idol paved the way for laying of foundation stone for the construction of the Ram temple.

Excavation of Site

After the excavation work, the site for construction of the Ram temple was converted into a large pit with a depth of about 14 m at the sanctum sanctorum and 12 feet around it. A team of experts

---

[10]Ibid.
[11]'Tulips from Palampur Adorn Ram Temple in Ayodhya', *The Tribune*, 23 January 2024, https://tinyurl.com/y4rbrjrc. Accessed on 15 August 2024.
[12]'Ram Mandir Inauguration: ISRO Remote Sensing Satellite Captures Images Of Ayodhya's Ram Mandir', *ABP Live*, 21 January 2024, https://tinyurl.com/3kpmmxa7. Accessed on 16 August 2024.

worked on structural evaluation. According to Dr Manu Santahanam, Professor at the Department of Civil Engineering in IIT Madras, his team worked on selection of material for the Ram temple foundation. He said the top soil at the site was loose and so excavation had to be carried out up to 12 m, and the pit created was filled with RCC in layers to create engineered rock. Roller-compacted concrete is a mix of cement, flyash, sand, stone with water—the use of cement was minimum.[13] About 45 to 60 concrete layers were put there. One raw layer of 12 inches was compacted by a heavy-duty roller down to 10 inches. The compaction density was critically measured along 58 layers at the sanctum sanctorum site. It was also measured along 48 layers in the remaining area. It took nearly five months to complete the work that lasted from April 2021 to September 2021. A man-made mammoth bedrock was thus created to ensure longevity and stability of the underpinning for at least a thousand years. On the top of the underground RCC, another thick, self-compacted concrete raft[14] (about 9,000 cubic metres in volume) with higher load-bearing capacity was poured in segments using multi-batching plants, boom placer machines, and mixers, over four months. A professor from IIT Kanpur and one senior engineer associated with a nuclear reactor also contributed at this stage of raft construction. Both the RCC and the raft act as the foundation bedrock and supporting foundation of the temple superstructure. The raft construction started in October 2021 and was completed by January 2022.[15]

The Three-Storeyed Structure

The Ram Temple's three-storeyed superstructure is on a 6.5-m (21 feet) plinth that is to take the direct load of the structure. The Ram Temple

---

[13]SipSci, 'Scientific Series on Ayodhya Ram Temple—Contribution of IIT Madras', *YouTube*, 20 January 2024, https://tinyurl.com/tazdrd9u. Accessed on 15 August 2024.
[14]A raft in construction terminology is used for a compacted concrete slab under a building, 'floating' on ground like a raft floats on water.
[15]@ShriRamTeerth, X (formerly Twitter), 23 May 2022, 8.36 p.m., https://tinyurl.com/mr23fzfb. Accessed on 15 August 2024.

Trust selected granite stone to carry out the plinth work. About 17,000 granite stone blocks (measuring 5 ft x 2.5 ft x 3 ft) have been used for the plinth construction using the interlocking technique. The weight and size of the stones was a challenge to handle. The Container Corporation of India and Indian Railways were engaged for transportation of the granite stones. The Indian Railways created a green corridor for transporting the granite stone blocks that brought down the schedule for completion of the plinth work by two months. The National Institute of Rock Mechanics, Bengaluru, was engaged for expert opinion on monitoring the quality of granite stones at mining sites and at the Ram temple construction site.

There are five *mandap*s (halls) on the ground floor: Nritya Mandap, Rang Mandap, Sabha Mandap, Prarthana and Kirtan Mandap. The iconography work on the pillars continued even after the consecration of Ram Lalla's idol, and statues of deities, gods and goddesses adorn the pillars and the walls.

A *parkota* (a rectangular compound wall) with a length of 732 m and a width of 14 feet is erected around the temple. There are to be four temples, of Surya Dev (Sun God), Goddess Bhagwati, Lord Ganesha and Lord Shiva, on the four corners of the temple compound. One temple each of Maa Annapurna and Lord Hanuman on the northern and southern arm of the temple, respectively, are part of the design. Sita Koop (a historic well), which dates back to ancient period, can also be found near the temple.[16] The temples dedicated to Maharshi Valmiki, Maharshi Vashishtha, Maharshi Vishwamitra, Maharshi Agastya, Nishad Raj, Mata Sabri and others have also been proposed there.

The VHP Workshops

The VHP had entrusted a large number of artisans with the work of carving stones procured from Rajasthan at the workshops running in Ayodhya since the 1990s. It had also engaged artisans for the workshops

---

[16]@ShriRamTeerth, X (formerly Twitter) 4 January 2024, 9.29 a.m., https://tinyurl.com/49y2hk83. Accessed on 17 July 2024.

running in Rajasthan. Besides a workshop in Ayodhya, three more were being run in Sirohi district of Rajasthan. Over 1,200 artisans worked at these workshops from time to time.

The Ayodhya Development Authority unanimously cleared the map for the Ram temple during its board meeting held on 2 September 2020.

L&T Expressed Interest a Decade Ago

Larsen & Toubro (L&T) had put up a proposal to be given the project for the construction of the Ram temple, to the then VHP chief Ashok Singhal sometime in early 2000s. The company showed its interest in the construction of the temple again after the Supreme Court verdict on 9 November 2019. Singhal also contacted Chandrakant Sompura, the man who designed the Ram temple 30 years ago. Sompura said he designed the Ram temple when he was not allowed to carry tape for measurement inside the disputed complex and so he used his footsteps as a measuring unit. Sompura narrated this to NDTV:

> Mr Ashok Singhal decided in 1988 that the temple should be constructed here and he reached out to G.D. Birla. Our family had been working with Mr Birla for decades. So I got a call from Mr Birla and he asked me to come to Delhi, visit Ayodhya with him and prepare the design for the temple... At that time, we were not allowed to take measuring tapes. I was told just have a look around alone. It was very difficult for me to envision a temple without proper measurement. So, I used my feet and counted the steps. I remembered all the steps—from left to right, across, and replicated the design inside a big hall where I could take proper measurement.[17]

The then Ram Temple Trust had signed an agreement with M/s Sompura in 1992, and this was revalidated with supplementary

---

[17] 'Meet Chandrakant Sompura, Man Who Designed the Ayodhya Ram Temple', *NDTV*, 20 January 2024, https://tinyurl.com/3h32hz5j. Accessed on 2 October 2024.

additional provisions after the Supreme Court's verdict on 9 November 2019 paving the way for construction of the Ram temple. M/s Tata Consulting Engineers Limited was also roped in as the design and build contractor and project manager consultant. M/s Design Associates Inc. was appointed for master planning and specified architecture design services for developing the complex.

Appropriate arrangements have been made for security of the temple complex, keeping in view the arrival of a large number of domestic and international tourists for darshan of Ram Lalla at the temple. The security of the temple has remained a cause of concern over the years since the terror attack on the makeshift Ram temple complex on 5 July 2005, in which five terrorists were killed in the ensuing gunfight with security personnel. The state government made tight security arrangements with a *kavach* (shield) of high-tech equipment installed to guard the temple round the clock.[18]

History Revisited

The Ram Temple in Ayodhya has become a reality after years of agitations and a seven-decade-long legal battle fought in courts. History appeared to be revisiting Ayodhya after a gap of 30 years when the Supreme Court of India delivered its historic and much-awaited verdict on 9 November 2019. As a matter of coincidence, the foundation stone of the Ram temple had been laid exactly 30 years ago on 9 November 1989. The Supreme Court's verdict, the full text of which runs into 1,045 pages, came after marathon rounds of hearing for 40 days on a daily basis, starting 6 August 2019, to facilitate a lawful resolution to the dispute that spanned the period of the Mughal Empire, the British rule and independent India. The Supreme Court's five-judge Constitution bench that delivered its verdict in a special sitting on a Saturday included then Chief Justice of India Ranjan Gogoi, Justice S.A. Bobde, Justice Dhananjaya Y. Chandrachud, Justice Ashok Bhushan

---

[18]Singh, Rohit Kumar, 'Ram Temple to Have Hi-Tech 24x7 "Kavach"', *Hindustan Times*, 5 January 2024, https://tinyurl.com/5n8kzjmr. Accessed on 15 August 2024.

and Justice S.A. Nazeer. Justice Chandrachud later became the Chief Justice of India.

India Today, following the Supreme Court's landmark verdict, observed: 'After decades of mandir-masjid politics in the country, the Supreme Court of India gave the land to God on Saturday (November 9). Lord Ram—the deity Ram Lalla, was recognized as a legitimate legal personality and given the title to the entire 2.77-acre disputed property in Ayodhya.'[19]

A *BBC* report observed that Hinduism is the religion of the majority community while the first Islamic dynasty was established in India in early thirteenth century. The report said:

> The Ayodhya dispute, which stretches back more than a century, is one of India's thorniest court cases and goes to the heart of its identity politics. Hindus believe that Ayodhya, a city in the northern state of Uttar Pradesh, is the birthplace of one of their most revered deities, Lord Ram.
>
> Muslims say they have worshipped there for generations.
>
> The Supreme Court has now ruled that the site should be given to Hindus to build a temple there.[20]

The SC Observation and Land Allotment for Mosque

In its verdict, the Supreme Court observed:

> The history and culture of this country have been home to quests for truth, through the material, the political, and the spiritual. This Court is called upon to fulfil its adjudicatory function where it is claimed that two quests for the truth impinge on the freedoms of the other or violate the rule of law. This Court is tasked with

---

[19] 'Ayodhya Verdict: Ram Temple to be Built on Disputed Land, Muslims Get 5-Acre Land for Mosque—Key Takeaways', *India Today*, 10 November 2019, https://tinyurl.com/a5kysxck. Accessed on 17 July 2024.
[20] 'Ayodhya Dispute: The Complex Legal History of India's Holy Site', *BBC*, 9 November 2019, https://tinyurl.com/5n755ubc. Accessed on 17 July 2024.

the resolution of a dispute whose origins are as old as the idea of India itself.

The apex court ordered allotment of a prominent and suitable 5-acre plot to Muslims for construction of a mosque.

The Uttar Pradesh government has allotted 5 acres of land to Sunni Central Waqf Board in Dhannipur village of Ayodhya.[21] It is situated close to the highway and about 18 km away from the district headquarters of Ayodhya, and about 25 km away from Ayodhya town where the Ram temple has come up now.[22] The Ayodhya Development Authority has given all the necessary clearances for construction of the mosque. The Indo-Islamic Cultural Foundation has worked out the design for the new mosque which will be different from the disputed Babri Masjid structure. The foundation also proposes to construct a research institute, a library, a hospital and a community kitchen at the site.

Addendum

The Supreme Court's five-judge bench further observed: 'One of us, while being in agreement with the above reasons and directions, has recorded separate reasons on:—Whether the disputed structure is the birth-place of Lord Ram according to the faith and belief of the Hindu devotees. The reasons of the learned judge are set out in an addendum.'[23] The Addenda, containing 116 pages, have been given on page numbers 930 to 1045 of the apex court's judgement. Its concluding paragraph observes: 'It is thus concluded on the conclusion that faith and belief of Hindus since prior to construction of Mosque and subsequent thereto has always been that Janmasthan of Lord Ram is the place where

---

[21]Singh, Rajesh Kumar, 'UP Govt Allots 5-Acre Plot for Mosque to Sunni Waqf Board near Ayodhya', *Hindustan Times*, 9 September 2020, https://tinyurl.com/3ef25hy2. Accessed on 15 August 2024.
[22]Ibid.
[23]*M Siddiq (D) Thr Lrs vs Mahant Suresh Das & Ors*, (2019), CA 10866-10867/2010, p. 929, https://tinyurl.com/bdfjzf3k. Accessed on 25 August 2024.

Babri Mosque has been constructed which faith and belief is proved by documentary and oral evidence discussed above.'[24]

The Allahabad High Court's Lucknow bench had earlier given its verdict on the dispute on 30 September 2010. The verdict ran into 4,304 pages. The High Court division bench comprising Justice S.U. Khan, Justice Sudhir Agarwal and Justice D.V. Sharma ordered division of the disputed-structure land into three parts: for Ram Lalla and his birthplace, the Nirmohi Akhara, and the Muslim parties. The NDTV quoted the High Court's three-judge bench order observing:

> (The High Court) ruled in a majority judgement 2:1, that there be a three-way division of the disputed land—one-third for the Sunni Waqf Board, one-third for the Nirmohi Akhara and one-third to the party for 'Ram Lalla'... the High Court has said that the portion below the central dome under which the idols of Lord Rama and other Gods are placed in a makeshift temple, belongs to Hindus. All three judges agreed that the portion under the central dome should be allotted to Hindus.[25]

All three parties went to the Supreme Court to file an appeal against the Allahabad High Court verdict in 2011. The Supreme Court dismissed the remedy of dividing the disputed area. Justice Sudhir Agarwal (retd) said he was under 'pressure' not to give the ruling (on Ram Janmabhoomi–Babri Masjid issue) and added that had they (the High Court bench) not done so, there would not have been any verdict in the matter for the next 200 years.

'After delivering the judgment... I felt blessed... There was pressure on me to postpone the judgment in the case. There was pressure from within home and also from outside. Family members and relatives used to suggest to somehow pass time and not deliver the judgment,' he added.[26]

---

[24]Ibid. 1045.
[25]'Ayodhya Verdict: Allahabad High Court Says Divide Land in Three Ways', *NDTV*, 1 October 2010, https://tinyurl.com/dmbv5pmp. Accessed on 17 July 2024.
[26]PTI, 'There Was Pressure on Me to Postpone the Verdict: Former Allahabad High

When the Supreme Court pronounced its verdict on 9 November 2019, paving the way for construction of the Ram temple, the mood in the temple town was that of optimism. The verdict ended one of the longest-running legal disputes in the country's history that saw a number of twists and turns.

Here is an excerpt from the Supreme Court's final verdict:

805. We accordingly order and direct as follows:

1. (i) Suit 3 instituted by Nirmohi Akhara is held to be barred by limitation and shall accordingly stand dismissed;
(ii) Suit 4 instituted by the Sunni Central Waqf Board and other plaintiffs is held to be within limitation. The judgement of the High Court holding Suit 4 to be barred by limitation is reversed; and
(iii) Suit 5 is held to be within limitation.

2. Suit 5 is held to be maintainable at the behest of the first plaintiff who is represented by the third plaintiff. There shall be a decree in terms of prayer clauses (A) and (B) of the suit, subject to the following directions:

(i) The Central Government shall, within a period of three months from the date of this judgement, formulate a scheme pursuant to the powers vested in it under Sections 6 and 7 of the Acquisition of Certain area at Ayodhya Act 1993. The scheme shall envisage the setting up of a trust with a Board of Trustees or any other appropriate body under Section 6. The Scheme to be framed by the Central Government shall make necessary provisions in regard to the functioning of the trust or body including on matters relating to the management of the trust, the powers of trustees including the construction of a temple and all necessary, incidental and supplemental matters.

(ii) Possession of the inner and outer courtyards shall be handed over to the Board of Trustees of the Trust or to the body so

---

Court Judge on Ram Janmabhoomi-Babri Masjid Case', *The Telegraph online*, 3 June 2023, https://tinyurl.com/49ckmcer. Accessed on 17 July 2024.

constituted. The Central Government will be at liberty to make suitable provisions in respect of the rest of the acquired land by handing it over to the Trust or body for management and development in terms of the scheme framed in accordance with the above directions; and

(iii) Possession of the disputed property shall continue to vest in the statutory receiver under the Central Government, until in exercise of its jurisdiction under Section 6 of the Ayodhya Act of 1993, a notification is issued vesting the property in the trust or other body.

3. (i) Simultaneously, with the handing over of the disputed property to the Trust or body under clause 2 above, a suitable plot of land admeasuring 5 acres shall be handed over to the Sunni Central Waqf Board, the plaintiff in Suit 4.

(ii) The land shall be allotted either by

The Central Government out of the land acquired under the Ayodhya Act 1993; or

The State Government at a suitable prominent place in Ayodhya. The Central Government and the State Government shall act in consultation with each other to effectuate the above allotment in the period stipulated.

(iii) The Sunni Central Waqf Board would be at liberty, on the allotment of the land to take all necessary steps for the construction of a mosque on the land so allotted together with other associated facilities;

(iv) Suit 4 shall stand decreed to this extent in terms of above directions; and

(v) The directions for the allotment of land to the Sunni Central Waqf Board in Suit 4 are issued in pursuance of the powers vested in this court under Article 142 of the Constitution.

4. In exercise of the powers vested in this court under Article 142 of the Constitution, we direct that in the scheme to be framed by the Central Government, appropriate representation may be given in the Trust or body, to the Nirmohi Akhara in such manner as the Central Government deems fit.

5. The right of the plaintiff in Suit 1 to worship at the disputed property is affirmed to any restriction imposed by the relevant authorities with respect to the maintenance of peace and order and the performance of orderly worship.
806. All the appeals shall stand disposed of in the above terms. Parties are left to bear their own costs.[27]

Dispute Ends

Prime Minister Narendra Modi, who inaugurated the Ram temple on 22 January 2024, had remained closely associated with the movement. He had accompanied Advani in the Rath Yatra from Somnath to Ayodhya, performed Bhoomi Pujan and kept an eye on the progress of work following the inauguration of the commencement of construction work on 5 August 2020.

A Ram temple in Ayodhya was a lifetime dream of most of the religious leaders associated with the movement and the devotees of Lord Rama. Most of India's PMs have dealt with the issue one way or the other. After the placement of the idol under the central dome during the tenure of India's first PM Jawaharlal Nehru, Ayodhya came into focus again during the tenure of Indira Gandhi in 1983 with the Muzaffarnagar meeting, where a demand for liberation of Ram Janmabhoomi in Ayodhya, Krishna Janmabhoomi in Mathura, and Kashi Vishwanath temples was made. Indira Gandhi began making efforts to give a facelift to Ayodhya town soon after the VHP brought the issue into focus. She was aware of the political importance of the issue; so were other PMs who assumed office after her. Her son Rajiv Gandhi too wanted an early solution to the issue. He is held responsible for opening of the locks of the disputed structure. His government also allowed laying of foundation stone of the Ram temple in an area close to the disputed spot. Rajiv Gandhi launched his poll campaign from Faizabad in 1989, promising Ram Rajya.

---

[27] *M Siddiq (D) Thr Lrs vs Mahant Suresh Das & Ors*, (2019), CA 10866-10867/2010, pp. 925–8, https://tinyurl.com/bdfjzf3k. Accessed on 25 August 2024.

As PMs, P.V. Narasimha Rao, Vishwanath Pratap Singh, Chandra Shekhar and others too realized the political importance of Ayodhya and took deep interest in finding a solution to the issue. Though the Rao government decided to dismiss the Kalyan Singh-led BJP government in Uttar Pradesh, along with the BJP governments in other states, he faced accusations of being responsible for demolition of the Babri Masjid. Rao's cabinet colleague opposed him and wanted to blame him for the demolition in the White Paper on Ayodhya that the Rao government placed in Parliament on 24 February 1993.

Vajpayee's Rail Journey

Prime Minister Atal Bihari Vajpayee always wanted to visit Ayodhya, but he decided to get a glimpse and feel of the temple town from the rail coach window of a running train. He undertook the rail journey on 7 February 2004 from Katra, situated on the outskirts of Ayodhya in Ambedkar Nagar district, to Faizabad, the headquarters of Ayodhya (earlier Faizabad) district. He was concerned about finding a solution to the entangled Ram Janmabhoomi issue. Those who travelled with Vajpayee in the special train saw the train slowing down when passing through the centre of Ayodhya, during the nearly 16-km stretch from Katra to Faizabad. A railway functionary who travelled on the PM special train said that Vajpayee probably took a nap as the train passed through Ayodhya.[28] Vajpayee did not share anything about the journey with the journalists who travelled with him. This gave more credence to the 'nap theory'. Vajpayee set up the Ayodhya cell in the PMO in January 2002 and Shatrughan Singh, a senior IAS officer, was made the officer in charge.

Various reasons, including differences within the saffron brigade over issues concerning the Ram temple, may have been behind Vajpayee's move to have a glimpse of Ayodhya distantly from his special train instead of making a stop at the town. He was a part of

---

[28]Interview with a railway official who travelled on the same train.

the BJP trio that also included L.K. Advani and Murli Manohar Joshi. However, Vajpayee was not in Ayodhya on 6 December 1992 when the Babri Masjid was demolished in the presence of Advani and Joshi.

Vajpayee's Speech before Demolition

On 5 December 1992, the day before the demolition, Vajpayee had made an important speech at Jhandewala Park (Aminabad), Lucknow. He said he was not aware of what would happen in Ayodhya the next day. He said he wanted to be in Ayodhya on the day but had been asked to go to New Delhi, and hence he was following the orders. He, however, did not clarify who had asked him not to go to Ayodhya. He said that the kar seva scheduled for 6 December in Ayodhya was not in violation of the Supreme Court's order. On the eve of the demolition, he said during a public meeting at Lucknow:

> The SC (Supreme Court) order does not stop us from performing the kar seva. In fact, the SC has given us the right to perform the kar seva. No question of stopping us. The kar seva in Ayodhya tomorrow will in no way be in violation of the SC order. By performing the kar seva the SC's order will be respected...[29]

Vajpayee Was Not on Speaking Terms with Singhal

Vajpayee's support to the kar seva assumed significance as he also spoke about levelling the ground at Ayodhya at the same meeting in Lucknow.

> There are sharp boulders at the disputed site. No one can sit on them. The ground will have to be therefore levelled. The ground will have to be levelled (made fit for sitting) there. I am not

---

[29]NMF News, 'Babri Masjid Demolition Ke Pehle Suniye Atal Bihari Vajpayee ka Unseen Speech', *YouTube*, 20 April 2017, https://tinyurl.com/2bznza74. Accessed on 17 July 2024.

sure what will happen there (in Ayodhya). I wanted to go to Ayodhya. But I have been asked not to go and I obey orders… The issue is in the Supreme Court and the SC has appointed an observer there.[30]

Vajpayee was not on speaking terms with VHP leader Ashok Singhal when he decided to undertake a train journey to Ayodhya to get a feel of the temple town. Was this his reason for refraining from visiting Ayodhya, even though his government continued to work to find a solution to the Ram temple issue?

The Art of Living founder Sri Sri Ravi Shankar, whom Vajpayee deputed to initiate a dialogue to find a solution to the issue in 2001, made a mention of the same in a blog post that was also published in *The Times of India*. He felt that some of the VHP's demands might have been impractical because the government of the time depended on support of coalition partners that were not on the same page on the issue, and made this point to the VHP chief. Singhal, however, was focused on his Ram temple agenda. He did not care much about the BJP's challenges or that accepting the VHP's demands may lead to collapse of the government. He remained unconvinced.[31]

VHP Was Not Happy with the BJP's Ways

This was the time when the VHP was pushing the BJP government to take the Ram temple issue to the forefront. The VHP was not happy with the BJP's ways of handling the issue. 'Some of the VHP's demands seemed impractical given that the government at the time depended on support of other coalition partners and not everyone was on the same page on the issue. "I don't care even if it leads to the collapse of the government," he (Singhal) said. I replied saying, "Pray for it. With your commitment, all is possible." Ashok ji left unconvinced. At

---

[30]Ibid.
[31]Shankar, Sri Sri Ravi, 'The Play of Gods', *The Times of India*, 2 April 2022, https://tinyurl.com/ya4da385. Accessed on 17 July 2024.

that point, I intuitively felt it would take more like 14 years to build but I didn't share my thoughts with anyone.'[32]

The 'Shiladan'

The BJP had ruled out committing itself to the construction of the Ram temple in the party's manifesto for the 2002 Uttar Pradesh legislative assembly elections.[33]

The VHP gave a call for *shiladan* (donating a stone for temple construction). The first shila for the temple construction was to be donated on 15 March 2002. A large number of volunteers reached Ayodhya following the VHP's call. The party leaders and the district administration had long consultations on the issue. At last, the PMO's emissary Shatrughan Singh reached Ayodhya to receive the donation of the shila.

Anil Kumar Gupta, who then served as divisional commissioner Faizabad, recollected that he was present at the shiladan held in Ayodhya. As divisional commissioner, Gupta was the receiver for the Ram Janmabhoomi site, where the Ram temple has come up in Ayodhya. He said the shila was kept in double-lock at the district treasury. He said,

> This shila was donated in two parts for construction of Ram Mandir in Ayodhya. This is one of the shilas that have been carved out at the VHP's *karyashala* (workshop) set up in Ayodhya. Now when other shilas are going to be shifted from the karyashala to the construction site, this shila, kept in double lock of the district treasury should also be taken out and given for construction of temple.[34]

---

[32] Ibid.
[33] 'Timeline: Ayodhya Holy Site Crisis', *BBC*, 6 December 2012, https://tinyurl.com/24a3t735. Accessed on 17 July 2024.
[34] Raghuvanshi, Umesh, 'Donated 18 Years Ago, Shila for Ram Temple Lying in Ayodhya Treasury', *Hindustan Times*, 6 August 2020, https://tinyurl.com/3fdwr4j4. Accessed on 17 July 2024.

As the then chairman of Ram Janmabhoomi Nyas (Ram Temple Trust), Mahant Ramchandra Das Paramhans had donated the shila to the then PM Atal Bihari Vajpayee's emissary Shatrughan Singh at Bada Sthan, Ayodhya, on 15 March 2002. After taking the donation of the shila, Singh handed over the same to the district administration, asking the officers to place the same with respect under double lock of the district treasury. Gupta recollected:

> As the shila was to be donated to an emissary, the Centre decided to depute Shatrughan Singh from the Centre's Ayodhya cell to receive the donation. Singh was flown in by a special plane to Ayodhya to receive the shila.... Although the then VHP president Ashok Singhal was present on the occasion, the late Mahant Ramchandra Das Paramhans was the main donor of the shila.[35]

The Forgotten Shila

The shila has apparently been forgotten after the much-hyped shiladan held in Ayodhya on 15 March 2002. A decision about shifting the shila to the temple construction site may now be taken. 'This is the time when donations are pouring into the Ram temple trust. The state government should now transfer the donated "shila" from the district treasury to the trust for construction of Ram temple,' said VHP spokesman Sharad Sharma.[36]

Sri Sri Ravi Shankar made fresh attempts to get the Ayodhya issue resolved in 2017. He undertook the mission to Ayodhya in a bid to find an amicable solution to the dispute. Prominent stakeholders, however, stayed away from the Art of Living founder's mediation mission to Ayodhya on 16 November 2017. Sri Sri Ravi Shankar met CM Yogi Adityanath in Lucknow a day before departing for Ayodhya for his mediation mission. He had a nearly 40-minute meeting with the CM at the latter's official residence in Lucknow. He reached Ayodhya in

---
[35]Ibid.
[36]Telephonic interview with Sharad Sharma.

the morning, went for darshan of Ram Lalla at the makeshift temple, and held meetings in Ayodhya. However, nothing came out of these meetings there.

Failed Mediation

The Supreme Court made attempts to resolve the issue through mediation. It appointed a three-member panel for mediation in the Ayodhya case. The panel was headed by Justice F.M. Khalifulla, a retired judge of the Supreme Court. Sri Sri Ravi Shankar and senior advocate Sriram Panchu, who was also a trained mediator, were the two other members of the panel. The Supreme Court stressed upon the need of maintaining confidentiality in the mediation process. The panel submitted its report to the apex court in a sealed envelope and made last-ditch attempts to find an amicable solution but failed to do so.

A number of other attempts were made from time to time to find a solution to the complex Ram Janmabhoomi–Babri Masjid dispute. The VHP and the BMAC exchanged documents and held discussions on a number of occasions to find a solution. Both sides continued to stick to their guns, and thus finding an amicable solution to the dispute through dialogue remained a distant dream. Ayodhya appeared caught in a time warp over the years.

At last, a solution was found to the nearly 500-year-old dispute, following the top court's verdict. Today, large crowds turn up for darshan of Ram Lalla in the newly constructed Ram temple symbolizing faith and tradition. A new journey has begun in Ayodhya.

11

A New Beginning

As the sun rises over the holy town of Ayodhya, it raises new hopes for the people of the city that was once the seat of power of the valiant kings of the solar race, the Ikshvakus or the Suryavanshis, in ancient India.

Situated on the banks of the Saryu River, also known as the lower Ghagra or Ghaghara in the region, Ayodhya has seen many changes over the years. As part of its development as a city of faith and a major destination for tourists, a project for dredging the Saryu was undertaken over a 10-km stretch from Guptar Ghat to Ram ki Paidi to bring about the stream of the Saryu closer to various ghats in the city of Ayodhya.[1]

The Saryu River has changed its course, and so have the ways politics is done in India. Ayodhya, too, reverberates the politics of contemporary India. So, on 4 June 2024, when all eyes were glued to television sets in India for the 2024 Lok Sabha election results, Ayodhya came into focus again. Though the NDA led by the BJP has formed the government with PM Narendra Modi assuming office for the third consecutive term following the 2024 polls, the BJP's tally has come down considerably in the 2024 polls, and the party lost its Ayodhya seat too. The BJP, with 240 seats, fell short of the majority mark of 272 of the 543 Lok Sabha seats.

---

[1] Pushkar Pathak, 'Irrigation Department Documentary: Dredging Sarayu Pariyojana', *YouTube*, 1 July 2019, https://tinyurl.com/3z63nt2j. Accessed on 18 July 2024; 'Ram Ki Pairi Ke Paas Tak Pahunchegi Sarayu Nadi Ki Dhara', *Hindustan*, 16 October 2020, https://tinyurl.com/y5whys3d. Accessed on 18 July 2024.

The party, which attempted to ride the Rama wave to win the 2024 polls following inauguration of the Ram temple, is concerned about its defeat in Ayodhya. Various reasons, including the caste factors dominating the poll, are being attributed for the BJP's defeat there. *Frontline* observed:

> Despite playing the Ram Mandir card in a big way, the BJP suffered a major shock in Uttar Pradesh's Faizabad constituency, which includes Ayodhya. The SP's Awadhesh Prasad, a nine-time MLA and former Minister from the Pasi (Scheduled Caste) community, defeated two-time BJP MP Lallu Singh by over 55,000 votes. The SP, which won 37 of the 80 Lok Sabha seats in the State, based its campaign on the slogan: *'Na Mathura, na Kashi, abki baar Awadhesh Pasi'* (Neither Mathura nor Kashi, this time Awadhesh Pasi). The slogan was aimed to counter the BJP's attempt at communalizing the Mathura and Kashi disputes as well.[2]

With the Ram Janmabhoomi–Babri Masjid issue being resolved, Ayodhya embarks on a new journey after a fight of nearly 500 years. Besides contemporary politics, Ayodhya is brimming with commercial activities now. Several development projects, with estimated expenditure over ₹30,000 crore, are at various stages of implementation. Ayodhya is building bridges to connect tradition with contemporary India via the implementation of these projects.

Mirroring the Glory

Ayodhya's grandeur reached its pinnacle during the rule of Suryavanshi kings, the descendants of Manu Vaivasvata, the son of Vivasvant (the sun).[3] It was the capital city of Lord Rama who ruled Ayodhya in Treta Yuga. Hinduism preaches about four yugas: Satya Yuga, Treta Yuga,

---

[2]Sharma, Ashutosh, 'Why the BJP Suffered a Shocking Defeat in Faizabad, the Home of the Ram Mandir', *Frontline*, 7 June 2024, https://tinyurl.com/yc6u3rak. Accessed on 18 July 2024.
[3]Pargiter, F.E., *Ancient Indian Historical Tradition*, Motilal Banarsidass Publishers, Delhi, 1997, p. 253.

Dwapara Yuga and Kali Yuga. It is accepted by many that the present age is Kali Yuga. These four yugas are also described as Golden Age, Silver Age, Copper Age and Iron Age, respectively.

Rama's rule in Ayodhya earned him virtues and gave him the title of Maryada Purushottam. He is known for establishing a lawful state that evolved the concept of the proverbial Ram Rajya (a system where a society is run by the principles practised by Lord Rama), as visualized in the Ramayana and *Ramcharitmanas*.

Ayodhya is also called Ajodhya, Awadh or Oudh. The name is said to have derived its origin in *yudha* (Sanskrit), meaning 'war'. 'A' is prefixed to the word to refer to the quality of being invincible or signify one that cannot be won.

Ayodhya is one of the Sapta Puris, the seven centres of pilgrimage that bless the pilgrims and grant moksha. The Sapta Puris are Ayodhya, Mathura, Haridwar, Varanasi (Banaras or Kashi), Kanchipuram, Ujjain (Avanti) and Dwarka.

The city has remained important since time immemorial. Valmiki's Ramayana in Sanskrit and Tulsidas's *Ramcharitmanas* in Awadhi speak volumes about the importance of Ayodhya.

Referring to Ayodhya, the Encyclopaedia Britannica reads:

> An ancient town, Ayodhya is regarded as one of the seven sacred cities of the Hindus, revered because of its association in the great Indian epic poem Ramayana with the birth of Rama and with the rule of his father, Dashratha. According to this source, the town was prosperous and well-fortified and had a large population. In traditional history, Ayodhya was the early capital of the kingdom of Kosala, though in Buddhist times (6th–5th century BCE) Shravasti became the kingdom's chief city. Scholars generally agree that Ayodhya is identical with the town of Saketa, where the Buddha is said to have resided for a time. Its later importance as a Buddhist centre can be gauged from the statement of the Chinese Buddhist monk Faxian in CE 5th century that there were 100 monasteries there (although he cited 100, Faxian probably did not mean that exact number, just

that there were many monasteries). There were also a number of other monuments, including a stupa reputed to have been founded by the Mauryan emperor Ashoka (3rd century BCE).[4]

Both the Ramayana and the *Ramcharitmanas* have made stories about Rama popular among the masses. Rama, hero of the Ramayana, and Krishna, hero of the Mahabharata, are believed to be the seventh and eighth incarnations of Lord Vishnu, respectively. Both are worshipped as gods in India and have been part of divine myths. Some Western writers who worked on epics and other ancient scriptures noted that no serious attempts have been made in India to separate myth from history. Many of them do not recognize the accounts of Rama and Krishna as part of divine myths. Historical characters like King Janaka and stories wrapped in myth may indicate towards past events. There are also stories about heroes or other characters of the Ramayana and the Mahabharata that connect them with the gods or portray them as heavenly beings; many scholars may not agree with this.

The Ramayana's hero, Lord Rama, derives his lineage from the Sun, as discussed earlier in this book, is believed to be the seventh incarnation of Vishnu, and is worshipped as God. The Mahabharata's heart and soul, Krishna, believed to be the eighth incarnation of Vishnu, is also considered the Supreme Soul, and the epic has described him as the radiant sun of the lights.

Adityanam aham visnur
Jyotisham ravir amsuman
Maricir marutam asmi
Naksatranam aham sasi.

(Of the Adityas, I am Visnu, of lights I am the radiant, I am Marici of the Maruts, and among the stars, I am the moon.)[5]

---

[4]'Ayodhya', *Britannica*, 16 July 2024, https://tinyurl.com/4fky4vd3. Accessed on 18 July 2024.
[5]Bhaktivedanta Swami Prabhupada, 'Text 21, Chapter 10', *Bhagvad-gita As It Is*, Collier Books, New York, 2004, pp. 319–20.

This is also interpreted by others as Krishna saying, 'Among lights, I am Ravi (Sun).' Krishna is stated to be representing the sun.[6] Western writers have, however, questioned this. The *Cambridge History of India* has observed, 'It is doubtful whether Krishna was ever a form of the sun.' It has also noted that no attempts have been made to separate myths from the history of India.[7]

This may also be taken as an indication towards the existence of Ram in Treta Yug. Besides King Janaka, there are other kings too who find a mention in the tradition and can be connected to history. Prasenjit is one such king in the post-Mahabharata period who ruled Kosala or Ayodhya. The Buddhist sources indicate that Prasenjit, son of Mahakosala, was a contemporary of the Buddha. This indicates that the kings mentioned in the epics may have actually lived, though the existence of all of them may not be proved. The *Cambridge History of India* has also observed that some of the characters of the Mahabharata may have been real. It states that many of the characters of the Mahabharata appear to be real, historical figures. According to it, others, however, may be mythical representing a personality evolved from a divine name or a local hero-god.

> Thus the name of Arjuna is first a title of Indra, whose son the epic Arjuna is; but his cousin Krishna is local demi-god hero, and there is no reason to doubt the historical character of the king of Magadha who was a foe of this pair and a Civaite, though what is said about him in the epic may be merely the exaggeration of legend.'[8]

Several foreign travellers have given their account of the importance attached to the city of Ayodhya. The Supreme Court, while delivering its verdict on the Ram Janmabhoomi–Babri Masjid dispute, perused

---

[6]'The Sun Represents Lord Krishna', *Vedic Time Period*, https://tinyurl.com/mwe2zckv. Accessed on 3 October 2024.
[7]Hopkins, E. Washburn, *The Cambridge History of India, Volume 1: Ancient India*, Edward James Rapson (ed.), Cambridge University Press, 1922, pp. 257–8.
[8]Ibid. 257.

533 documentary exhibits, including books on subjects as diverse as history, culture, archaeology and religion in languages as varied as Sanskrit, Hindi, Urdu, Persian, Turkish, French and English. It, however, exercised caution in making deductions out of historical context, saying interpreting history is an 'exercise fraught with pitfalls'.[9]

The Supreme Court referred to travelogues of authors and geographers such as Joseph Joseph Tiefenthaler, Robert Montgomery Martin, P. Carnegy, Edward Thornton and William Finch, among others who visited India between seventeenth and nineteenth centuries, and observed that the oral and documentary evidence showed that devotees of Lord Rama hold a genuine, long-standing and profound belief in the religious merit attained by offering prayer at the site they believe to be the birthplace of the deity.[10]

The Supreme Court observed that it has to make a balanced analysis of 'loose fragments of forgotten history' related to the site. 'We are looking into historical events knit around legends, stories, traditions and accounts written in a social and cultural context different from our own. There are dangers in interpreting history without the aid of historiography,' it said.[11]

The apex court produced the account of the Ayodhya visit of Joseph Tiefenthaler, a Jesuit missionary and geographer who wrote his travel account in Latin in his book *Description Historique et Geographique De L'inde*. Tiefenthaler was reportedly proficient in Arabic, Persian and Sanskrit. He visited India in 1740.[12] A description of his visit to Ayodhya was made available in French. An English translation was furnished by the Government of India in pursuance of an order

---

[9]Press Trust of India, 'SC Referred to Books in Sanskrit, Urdu, Persian, French in Ayodhya Verdict', *India Today*, 4 April 2022, https://tinyurl.com/4fnx99ta. Accessed on 18 August 2024.
[10]Press Trust of India, 'Ayodhya Verdict: Travelogues, "Loose Fragments of History" Considered by SC', *Mint*, 10 November 2019, https://tinyurl.com/mrxfbxh5. Accessed on 18 August 2024.
[11]Ibid.
[12]*M Siddiq (D) Thr Lrs vs Mahant Suresh Das & Ors*, (2019), CA 10866-10867/2010, p. 664, https://tinyurl.com/bdfjzf3k. Accessed on 25 August 2024.

of the Allahabad High Court during hearing of the Ayodhya case. Tiefenthaler's account reads thus:

> Avad called Adjudea, by the educated Hindus, is a city of very olden times. Its houses are (mostly) made up of mud only, covered with straw or tiles. Many however are made up of bricks. The main street goes from South to North and it has a length of about a mile. The width (of the city) is a little lesser. Its western side and that of North as well, are situated on a mud hill. That of the north-east is situated on knolls. Towards Bangla it is united.
>
> Today, this city has been hardly populated, since the foundation of *Bangla* or *Fesabad* (1)—a new city where the Governor established his residence—and in which a great number (of inhabitants of Oude) settled in. On the South Bank (of Deva) are found various buildings constructed by the nobles in memory of Ram, extending from East to West.
>
> The most remarkable place is the one which is called *Sorgadaori* (Swarg Dwar or gateway to heaven), which means: the celestial temple. Because they say that *Rama* took away all the inhabitants of the city from there to heaven: This has some resemblance/similarity to the Ascent of Lord. The city, thus deserted, was repopulated and was brought back to its earlier status by Bikarmadjit—the famous king of Oude (OUDH) [OUDJEN].
>
> There was a temple in this place, constructed on the elevated bank of the river. But *Aurengzeb*, the sixth emperor of the Mughal Empire, who was always keen to propagate the creed of Mohammed and abhorred the noble people, got it demolished and replaced the same with a mosque and two obelisks, with a view to obliterating even the very memory of the Hindu superstition. Another mosque built by the Moors is adjacent to the one towards the East.
>
> Close to *Sorgadoari* is a building constructed lengthways by Nabairay—a Hindu, a former lieutenant of the Governor (proprietor) of this region (a). But a place especially famous

is the one that is called *Sitha Rassoi* i.e. the table of *Sita*, wife of *Rama*, adjoining the city in the South, and is situated on a mud hill.

Emperor *Aurengzeb* got the fortress called *Ramcot* demolished and got a Muslim temple, with triple domes, constructed at the same place. Others say it was constructed by *'Babor'*.[13]

Robert Montgomery Martin, an Anglo-Irish author, wrote *History, Antiquities, Topography and Statistics of Eastern India* in three volumes. Martin, born in Dublin in 1801, was a civil servant in British India. He spent 10 years practising medicine in Shillong, East Africa and New South Wales, besides working as a journalist in Calcutta where he established the *Bengal Herald*. About the ruins of the buildings he found in Ayodhya, Martin observed:

> Although they are built on what I have no doubt are the ruins of the palace that was occupied by the princes of the family of the sun, their being built on the spots, where the events which they are intended to celebrate, actually happened, would have been extremely doubtful, even had the elder Vikrama built temples on the various places which had been destroyed by Aurangzeb, so that the spots selected by Vikarma might be known by tradition; but the whole of that story being liable to strong suspicion, we may consider the present appropriation of names of different places as no better founded than the miracles, which several of them are said to commemorate.[14]

The Korean Links

Ayodhya has had historic cultural ties with international cities. It has a special connection with South Korea. The first lady of South Korea, Kim Jung-sook, reached Ayodhya on 6 November 2018, connecting her

---
[13]Ibid. 664–5.
[14]Ibid. 670.

ancestry with the city. There are Korean stories galore about an Indian princess, Suriratna, also known as Heo Hwang-ok, who went to South Korea and married a king there. The *BBC*, in a report, has observed that Ayodhya, which is best known as the birthplace of the Hindu god Rama, also holds special significance for some South Koreans, and many of them believe that they can trace their ancestry to the city. The report speaks about the story of Princess Suriratna who went to Korea in AD 48, some 2,000 years ago, and started the Karak dynasty by marrying a local king. It points out that some Chinese-language texts claim that the then king of Ayodhya had a dream where God ordered him to send his 16-year-old daughter to South Korea to marry King Kim Suro.

A popular South Korean book comprising fables and historical stories, *Samguk Yusa* (Memorabilia of the Three Kingdoms), mentions that Queen Hwang-ok was the princess of the 'Ayuta' kingdom.

> The royal couple prospered. They had 10 sons and both lived to be over 150 years old.
>
> An anthropologist named Kim Byung-mo Ayuta appeared to confirm the widely held belief that Ayuta was actually Ayodhya, as the two names are phonetically similar.[15]

About Queen Heo Hwang-ok, the *Indian Express* mentioned:

> She was a Korean queen who is believed to have been born Princess Suriratna of Ayodhya, daughter of King Padmasen and Indumati. Padmasen ruled the ancient kingdom of Kausala, a region that extended from present-day UP to Odisha. Her story is described in Samguk Yusa (Memorabilia of Three Kingdoms), a 13th-century collection of legends, folktales and history of Korea's three kingdoms—Goguryeo, Baekje and Silla—and some other regions.
>
> In 48 BC, the princess, then 16, travelled to Korea from the ancient land of 'Ayuta' and married Kim Suro, founder and King

---

[15]Mandhani, Nikita, 'The Indian Princess Who Became a South Korean Queen', *BBC*, 4 November 2018, https://tinyurl.com/5frxs4fa. Accessed on 18 July 2024.

of Geumgwan Gaya in south-eastern Korea. She travelled by boat along with an entourage, having been sent by her father, who is said to have had a dream about her marrying Suro. She became the first queen of Geumgwan Gaya, believed to be located around modern-day Gimhae city in Southern Gyeonsang province. The couple are said to have had 12 children.[16]

A large number of people from South Korea visit Ayodhya every year. Those from the Kim dynasty of South Korea believe that a princess of Ayodhya had gone to South Korea about 2,000 years ago and got married to King Kim Su-ro. The successors of the queen and the king are called Crock Clan members in South Korea. A sister-city agreement was signed between Ayodhya and Gimhae, South Korea, in 2000. Under the agreement signed between the two cities, the Crock Clan Society got a memorial of the legendary Korean queen Heo Hwang-ok built in Ayodhya.

A South Korean delegation, led by Gimhae Mayor Do Youn-soo (a descendant of Heo Hwang-ok—he called the queen his great grandmother), met Uttar Pradesh CM Yogi Adityanath on 23 December 2017.[17] Both sides signed memorandums of understanding (MoUs) on skill development, tourism, agriculture and culture. The MoUs gave new dimensions to the relationship between South Korea and Uttar Pradesh, and boosted opportunities for employment and development. Both sides have agreed to set up a South Korea cultural centre in Ayodhya, and strengthen cultural ties by holding cross-cultural festivals in Gimhae and Ayodhya.

Chief Minister Yogi Adityanath, speaking at a programme organized at Buddha Vihar Shanti Upvan, Lucknow, on 23 March 2023, said:

---

[16]Khurana, Suanshu, 'Explained: Queen Heo Hwang-ok of Korea, and Her Ayodhya Connection', *The Indian Express*, 26 October 2021, https://tinyurl.com/4abbfrxk. Accessed on 18 July 2024.

[17]'UP Government Signs MoU with South Korea', *The Pioneer*, 24 December 2017, https://tinyurl.com/nkpend9n. Accessed on 18 August 2024.

Korea's meditation cult Seon originated in Jetwan area of Shravasti district in Uttar Pradesh. The princess of Ayodhya travelled by waterway from Ayodhya to Korea about 2,000 years ago, where she married the local king, Kim Suro. The princess was named Heo-Hwang-ok. The Karak dynasty was established by Princess Heo-Hwang-ok and King Kim Suro. At present, a large population in Korea is associated with this lineage.[18]

The *Korea Times* reported:

> The solid emotional connection between the people of India and Korea has been attributed to the story of Queen Heo Hwang-ok (Princess Suriratna) who is believed to have travelled from Ayodhya in India at the age of 16 to marry the Korean King Kim Suro of Gimhae—the capital of Geumgwan Gaya. Also known as the Garak Kingdom, it was established by Kim Suro and Queen Heo and was based in Gimhae in present-day South Gyeongsang Province.
>
> The strong links and the common lineage between the people of the two countries is also visible in how the descendants of Queen Heo, having genealogical links with India, regularly visit Ayodhya to pay homage to the land of their queen. The historical tomb of King Kim Suro and Queen Heo in Gimhae is also an important historical site in Korea. [19]

A demand is being raised in South Korea to have a Ram temple on the lines of the one in Ayodhya. *Zee News* reported that Jena Chung, a Korean-Canadian female entrepreneur from Seoul, South Korea, camped in India for this very purpose. Chung has been in talks in India for several months; she has been working on garnering support

---

[18]Singh, Rajesh Kumar, 'Yogi Adityanath Says India Home to Korea's Spiritual Ancestors', *Hindustan Times*, 23 May 2023, https://tinyurl.com/2hj6d7e7. Accessed on 18 July 2024.
[19]Trivedi, Sonu, 'From Gimhae to Ayodhya: Symbolic Resurgence of Indian Heritage', *The Korea Times*, 18 January 2024, https://tinyurl.com/6m3hcxdd. Accessed on 18 August 2024.

for her proposal to build a Ram temple in the Korean city of Gimhae.[20] The Indo-Korean Business Culture Centre chief, Zena Chung, in a statement to *ANI*, reiterated the demand for a Ram temple in South Korea and said, 'We have a Ram temple in Ayodhya and a temple devoted to Lord Rama in South Korea will foster the 2,000-year-old historical and cultural connection between the two countries.'[21]

A Window to the Ramayana

As the construction of the Ram temple in Ayodhya has opened new vistas for the people of the temple town, the development projects being implemented are being consistently monitored. On 26 June 2021, PM Narendra Modi viewed the Yogi Adityanath-led government's virtual presentation on the development of the Ram temple city by 2047, when India celebrates 100 years of Independence. When developed, Ayodhya will find itself on the centre stage of the world as a modern city while maintaining its ancient cultural heritage and glory.[22]

Chief Minister Yogi Adityanath has spoken about the development of Ayodhya time and again. He has undertaken several visits to Ayodhya and continues to do so. His efforts to give greater dimensions to the development of Ayodhya and bestow on the temple town the identity of an international spiritual city keep the development work in Ayodhya in focus. On 22 February 2023, he announced that Ayodhya will be developed as a model solar city, and an international sports complex will also be built. An international airport has already come up in Ayodhya. It has been named Maharishi Valmiki International Airport Ayodhya Dham. At the same time, the revamped railway station of Ayodhya has been renamed Ayodhya Dham Junction.

---

[20] Bhaskar, Yashwant, 'After Ayodhya, Now Ram Temple to be Built in South Korea', *Zee News*, 27 May 2023, https://tinyurl.com/bu4fw3tx. Accessed on 18 July 2024.
[21] 'IKBCC Chief Reiterates Demand for Ram Temple in South Korea', *ANI*, 19 February 2024, https://tinyurl.com/yvwp4u5m. Accessed on 18 July 2024.
[22] Raghuvanshi, Umesh, 'Ayodhya Vision-2047 Gets Premier Focus as PM Modi Reviews Temple Town's Development Plan', *Hindustan Times*, 27 June 2021, https://tinyurl.com/3mzyktam. Accessed on 17 June 2024.

Ayodhya Vision 2047 provides for the putting up of road signs about shops/markets and public places in different languages, keeping in view international tourists who might be visiting the temple town in future.

Ayodhya is seeing development of public places in a manner that will transform the temple town to a modern one to give the visiting pilgrims and tourists a sublime religious and spiritual experience, with the depiction of the Ramayana's characters with technology-driven projects.

Ayodhya's Ram Katha Museum has a collection of paintings, photographs and artefacts related to the life of Lord Rama. The museum takes visitors on a fascinating journey through his life. It offers a unique window into the rich tapestry of the Ramayana, depicting various aspects of Lord Rama's life and legacy. The musuem's transformation, however, will now see a giant leap with forays into the field of cutting-edge technology. A high-tech gallery is also coming up there. These are part of the attempts to make the Ram Katha Museum the biggest centre of attraction for tourists in Ayodhya. When high-tech galleries come up there, the museum may turn out to be the biggest crowd-puller. Such transformations are set to catapult the temple town into a world-class city.

The Ayodhya administration has held competitions for designing of the city's logo, signage and welcome gates. Ayodhya Deepotsav has made history and finds a place in Guinness Book of World Records with the lighting up of over 22 lakh *diya*s (earthern lamps) at Ram ki Paidi in November 2023, on the occasion of the festival of Diwali. Asia News International reported: 'Ayodhya "Deepotsav" sets new Guinness World record with over 22.23 lakh diyas lit up.'[23] Ayodhya Deepotsav is a grand festival, and artistes dressed as Rama, Sita and Lakshmana descend via a helicopter (symbol of the Pushpak Viman) at the Ram Katha Park.

The VHP had clubbed together the issues concerning the three shrines of Ayodhya, Mathura and Kashi about four decades ago. It

---

[23]@ANI, X (formerly Twitter), 11 November 2023, 8.43 p.m., https://tinyurl.com/52te6s4w. Accessed on 18 August 2024.

has been raising the issue of Kashi and Mathura along with that of Ayodhya over the years. Slogans like '*Ayodhya to kewal jhanki hai, Kashi, Mathura baaki* hai (Ayodhya is only a trailer, Kashi and Mathura are yet to be achieved)' have been coined. Several petitions have been filed to remove the seventeenth-century Shahi Idgah Mosque from the Krishna Janmabhoomi in Mathura. These petitions are in various stages of hearing in the High Court and the Supreme Court. A demand to allow the petitioners to offer regular worship to 'Maa' Shringar Gauri in Gyanvapi Mosque complex has been made in the ongoing Kashi Vishwanath Temple–Gyanvapi Mosque dispute in Varanasi, and the issue is pending before the court.

The Ram Temple in Ayodhya is now open for the public, and it's already drawing large crowds. The VHP has begun working out ways to further expand its base in villages.[24] It is also working out outreach programmes for Scheduled Castes (SCs) and Scheduled Tribes (STs) amid reports that the BJP, in 2024 polls, won 54 of 131 Lok Sabha seats reserved for the SCs and the STs, compared to 77 in the previous elections.[25] The party's failure to get majority on its own in the 2024 Lok Sabha elections is a cause for concern for the Sangh Parivar. More programmes to reach out to different sections of society will obviously be worked out, besides ensuring better coordination between the RSS and its affiliate organizations. All eyes are now set on the possible next moves of the VHP in Mathura and Kashi, notwithstanding the message that the outcome of the 2024 Lok Sabha elections may have given.

---

[24]'VHP to Expand Footprint to One Lakh Villages', *Hindustan Times*, 26 February 2024, https://tinyurl.com/3rt9vnyb. Accessed on 18 August 2024.
[25]Pandey, Neelam, 'In SC/ST Outreach, VHP Plans Nationwide Dharm Sabhas, Padyatras to Take Up "Pressing" Issues of Hindus', *The Print*, 17 August 2024, https://tinyurl.com/nhaxrf8x. Accessed on 18 August 2024.

Acknowledgements

I extend my heartfelt appreciation to the supportive individuals who have been instrumental in the creation of this book, including family members, friends and colleagues who served as a source of inspiration throughout my journey as a journalist.

I am deeply thankful to all those who have provided guidance and assistance, both directly and indirectly, in the development of this work.

My special gratitude goes to the Rupa Publications team led by Dibakar Ghosh, for their unwavering support throughout the process.

I am grateful to my wife Renu Raghuvanshi and daughters Akshita and Ahana for their support and encouragement. I convey sincere thanks to my siblings—brother Akhilesh and sisters Bina, Abha and Neelam—for always being supportive.

I express my gratitude to the *Hindustan Times* team led by editor-in-chief Sukumar Ranganathan and editors Kunal Pradhan, Sunita Aron and Pranshu Mishra, among others.

Many thanks to Dev Chatterjee, a senior journalist based in Mumbai, whom I first met as a visiting scholar at the Graduate School of Journalism, University of California, Berkeley, USA. My colleague Brajendra Kumar Parashar's insightful suggestions have greatly enriched this work—I appreciate him deeply for this.

Additionally, I would like to acknowledge the valuable contribution of other senior journalists, friends and colleagues not named here, who have stood by me in my endeavours.

www.ingramcontent.com/pod-product-compliance
Lightning Source LLC
Chambersburg PA
CBHW030104170426
43198CB00009B/488